CATHERINE A. SANDERSON is the Man[...] Sciences at Amherst College. Her re[...] norms and their misperception influe[...] on campus, including safe sex and disordered eating. She gives talks on the science of happiness and the psychology of good and evil to groups and businesses. She has been chosen by Princeton Review as one of America's Best Professors and is the author of *The Positive Shift: Mastering Mindset to Improve Happiness, Health, and Longevity*.

'A fascinating look at why some of us will go to others' aid, while others do nothing ... [A] very readable drawing together of classic psychological studies – but parts are practical. Sanderson wants to shift us "from being silent bystanders to active helpers" when we witness bullying, sexual harassment or dodgy workplace activity ... An encouraging story from a surprisingly positive book'

Sunday Times

'Sanderson isn't interested in easy explanations about fearless heroes and callous bystanders ... A guide to how we can all change our behaviour and ensure we speak out, whether that be about discrimination on public transport, workplace fraud, sexual harassment or school bullies'

Guardian

'An examination of moral courage and its disappointing scarcity ... The book's chief virtue lies in its wealth of instructive examples'

Economist

'Fantastic ... It explains the misperception of stacked odds and personal powerlessness that stops individuals challenging bad behaviour. Stunning. Humbling. Thought-provoking'

KATHRYN MANNIX, author of *With the End in Mind*

'Makes a powerful argument for building, as early as possible, the ability to stand up for what's right in the face of peer pressure, corrupt authority, and even family apathy. Citing case after case revealing how easy it is for people's moral instincts to be muted, and detailing how that silence is visible on brain scans, Sanderson guides readers toward her inevitable conclusion: We can do better'

Psychology Today

'From bullying on the playground to sexual harassment in the workplace, perfectly nice people often do perfectly awful things. But why? In this thoughtful and beautifully written book, Sanderson shows how basic principles of social psychology explain such behavior – and how they can be used to change it. A smart and practical guide to becoming a better and braver version of ourselves'   DANIEL GILBERT, author of *Stumbling on Happiness*

'In an age of government misconduct, corporate malfeasance, and #MeToo, it's tempting to believe that bad things happen because of bad actors. But as Catherine Sanderson compellingly illustrates, these events aren't just due to a "few bad apples" – they are enabled and sustained by good people who are complicit in behavior they know to be wrong. This book is a must-read for anyone who wants to understand why we can become silent bystanders to unconscionable actions and what we can do to empower ourselves and others to speak out'   ASHA RANGAPPA, national security analyst for CNN and former FBI agent

'Bad things don't happen only because of bad actors. They happen because good people choose to look the other way. In lucid prose, Sanderson explores why many avert their eyes in the face of immoral behaviour, and offers strategies to help combat this pernicious tendency ... An essential read for building a kinder and more ethical society'   DAVID DESTENO, author of *Emotional Success*

THE BYSTANDER EFFECT

*The Psychology of Courage
and How to be Brave*

CATHERINE A. SANDERSON

WILLIAM
COLLINS

William Collins
An imprint of HarperCollins*Publishers*
1 London Bridge Street
London SE1 9GF

WilliamCollinsBooks.com

HarperCollinsPublishers
1st Floor, Watermarque Building, Ringsend Road
Dublin 4, Ireland

First published in Great Britain in 2020 by William Collins
First published in the United States as *Why We Act: Turning
Bystanders into Moral Rebels* by the Belknap Press of
Harvard University Press in 2020

This William Collins paperback edition published in 2021

1

Copyright © Catherine A. Sanderson in 2020

Catherine A. Sanderson asserts the moral right to be identified
as the author of this work in accordance with the
Copyright, Designs and Patents Act 1988

A catalogue record for this book is
available from the British Library

ISBN 978-0-0-0836166-2

Set in Sabon LT Std
Printed and bound in Great Britain by
CPI Group (UK) Ltd, Croydon

To Andrew, Robert, and Caroline,
with hope that you will never stay silent about things that matter

Contents

Preface

On August 25, 2017, my husband and I spent the day settling in our oldest child, Andrew, for the start of his first year at college. We went to Walmart to buy a minifridge and rug. We hung posters above his bed. We attended the obligatory goodbye family lunch before returning to our car to head home to a slightly quieter house.

Two weeks later Andrew called, which was unusual since, like most teenagers, he vastly prefers texting. His voice breaking, he told me that a student in his dorm had just died.

As he described it on the phone, the two of them seemed to have so much in common. They were both freshmen. They were both from Massachusetts and had attended rival prep schools. They both had younger brothers.

"What happened?" I asked.

He told me the student had been drinking alcohol with friends. He got drunk, and around 9 P.M. on Saturday, he fell and hit his head. His friends, roommate, and lacrosse teammates watched over him for many hours. They strapped a backpack around his shoulders to keep him from rolling onto his back, vomiting, and then choking to death. They periodically checked to make sure he was still breathing.

But what they didn't do—for nearly twenty hours after the fall—was call 911.

By the time they finally did seek help, at around 4 P.M. on Sunday, it was too late. The student was taken to a hospital and put on life support so that his family could fly in to say goodbye.

Now, it's impossible to know whether prompt medical attention could have saved his life. Perhaps it wouldn't have. But what is clear is that he didn't get that opportunity. And this story—of college students failing to do anything in the face of a serious emergency—is hardly unusual.

It's not just college students who choose not to act, even when the stakes are high. Why did most passengers sit silently when a man was forcibly dragged off a United Airlines flight, recorded on a video that then went viral? What leads people to stay silent when a colleague uses derogatory language or engages in harassing behavior? Why did so many church leaders fail to report sexual abuse by Catholic priests for so many years?

Throughout my career—as a graduate student at Princeton University in the 1990s and as a professor at Amherst College over the last twenty years—my research has focused on the influence of social norms, the unwritten rules that shape our behavior. Although people follow these norms to fit in with their social group, they can also make crucial errors in their perception of these norms. The more I thought about these seemingly disparate examples of people failing to act, the more I began to see the root causes as driven by the same factors: confusion about what was happening, a lack of a sense of personal responsibility, misperception of social norms, and fear of consequences.

I have discovered through my own work that educating people about the power of social norms, pointing out the errors we so often make in perceiving these norms and the consequences of our misperceptions, helps them engage in better behavior. I've done studies that show that freshman women who learn how campus social norms contribute to unhealthy body image ideals show lower rates of disordered eating later on, and that college students who learn that many of their peers struggle with mental health challenges have a more positive view of mental health services. Helping people understand the psychological processes that lead them to misperceive what those around them are actually thinking—to believe that all women want to be thin, that other college students never feel sad or lonely—reduces the mistakes and misunderstandings we make about other people and can improve our psychological and physical well-being. It can also push us to act.

In my very first introduction to psychology as an undergraduate at Stanford in 1987, I remember being fascinated when I learned how much being in a group influenced our own behavior. I was fortunate enough to have Phil Zimbardo—whose Stanford Prison Experiment remains one of the most famous and controversial studies in psychology—as my professor. It was quite an introduction to the field of social psychology!

Back then, researchers could design experiments and measure people's behavior, but we couldn't penetrate the mechanisms that explained them. We couldn't see what was happening in the brain. Recent breakthroughs in neuroscience have completely changed that. It is now possible to see in real time how certain scenarios, pressures, and experiences play out in the brain. As I'll describe throughout this book, these results have revealed that many of the processes that drive inaction occur not through a careful deliberative process, but at an automatic level in the brain.

My goal in writing this book is to help people understand the psychological factors that underlie the very natural human tendency to stay silent in the face of bad behavior, and to show how significant a role that silence plays in allowing the bad behavior to continue. In the first half of the book, I describe how situational and psychological factors can lead good people to engage in bad behavior (Chapter 1), or, more commonly, to stay silent in the face of bad behavior by others (Chapters 2 to 5). Next, I show how these factors play out to inhibit action in distinct real-world situations, including bullying in school (Chapter 6), sexual misconduct in college (Chapter 7), and unethical behavior in the workplace (Chapter 8). I end by examining how some people are more able to stand up to others and what we can learn from these moral rebels (Chapter 9). In the closing chapter I look at strategies we all can use—regardless of our personality—to increase the likelihood that we will speak up and take action when we are most needed.

My hope is that providing insight into the forces that keep us from acting—and offering practical strategies for resisting such pressure in our own lives—will allow readers of this book to step up and do the right thing, even when it feels really hard. Ultimately, that's the secret to breaking the silence of the bystander—and making sure no one has to wait twenty hours after a serious injury before someone picks up the phone.

Part I

The Silence of the Good People

1

The Myth of Monsters

On August 11, 2012, a sixteen-year-old girl attended a party in Steubenville, Ohio, with some students from the local high school, including members of the school's football team. She drank a lot, became severely intoxicated, and vomited. Students at the party that night described her as appearing "out of it." The next morning, she woke up naked in a basement living room with three boys around her but virtually no memory of the prior night.

Over the next few days, several students who had been at the party posted to social media photographs and videos that vividly illustrated what had happened to the girl: her clothes had been removed, and she had been sexually assaulted. In March 2013 two Steubenville High football players, Trent Mays and Ma'lik Richmond, were found guilty of rape.

When we hear stories like this, most of us assume that these bad acts were committed by bad people. Surely only a bad person would sexually assault an unconscious teenage girl. This belief that bad behavior is caused by bad people is reassuring and comforting. Unfortunately, it's also wrong. As Nasra Hassan, who spent years studying Palestinian terrorists, said, "What is frightening is not the abnormality of those who carry out the suicide attacks, but their sheer normality."[1] Or take it from Sue Klebold. In 1999 her son Dylan, along with his classmate Eric Harris, killed more than a dozen people at Columbine High School in Colorado. "This belief that Dylan was a monster," she said, "served a deeper purpose: people needed to believe they would recognize evil in their midst."[2]

Why do we assume that bad behavior is carried out by bad people? Because that belief reassures us that the good people we know—our friends, our family, even ourselves—couldn't possibly do such things.

But "good people" can and do engage in bad behavior, from bullying in the schoolyard to hazing in college fraternities to sexual harassment in the workplace. So curbing bad behavior is not simply a matter of identifying and stopping the monsters. It is essential to identify the factors that lead otherwise good people to make bad choices so that we can prevent such behavior from occurring—or at least decrease its likelihood. This chapter examines the settings and situations that lead many of us to do things that we know at some level to be wrong. You may not be surprised to learn that we have more of tendency to do harmful things when we are in a group, when a trusted authority figure instructs us to do so, or when we start by taking small steps in the wrong direction. But the reasons underlying these tendencies may not be what you think.

The Hazards of the Herd

As a graduate student at Princeton University, I had a great part-time job living in a residence hall and providing support to junior and senior resident assistants. The job involved eating some meals with students in the dining hall, facilitating dorm-wide social events, and helping students deal with academic and personal concerns. There was one serious downside, however: one evening each year, I was required to serve as a "support person" at the Nude Olympics.

The Nude Olympics started in the early 1970s and was a well-established unofficial tradition until 1999, when it was banned by the board of trustees. Sophomores, both men and women, would run around campus at midnight on the occasion of the first snowfall each year, which typically occurred in January, wearing only running shoes, hats, and gloves. As you might imagine, the participants typically drank large amounts of alcohol in the hours leading up to the run, to help them withstand both the freezing temperatures and the considerable awkwardness inherent in running around naked in front of their classmates.

My role was to stand in the courtyard of one of the colleges wearing a reflective vest and holding a first aid kit, so that any student who experienced trouble—say, falling on ice—would be able to find me. As I stood there each year, fervently hoping I would be able to finish my dissertation and leave Princeton before the next Nude Olympics, I kept thinking to myself, "These students are some of the best and brightest in America. Why are they doing this?" Running drunk and naked at midnight in the snow just doesn't seem like a great idea.

But this story illustrates a fundamental finding in psychology: people will do things in a group setting that they would never do on their own. Although the Nude Olympics was mostly harmless, the same principle holds in cases where people behave really badly. Examples of bad behavior in group settings are abundant:

- In February 2010, Dylan Gifford Yount stood on the fourth-floor ledge of a commercial building in San Francisco as a large crowd gathered below. Many people taunted him, yelling "Jump!" and "Just do it already." After forty-five minutes, he jumped to his death.
- During the 2015–2016 New Year's Eve celebrations in Cologne, Germany, large crowds of men sexually assaulted an estimated twelve hundred women.

- In February 2018, fans celebrating the Philadelphia Eagles' Super Bowl win flipped over cars, removed street poles from the ground, set fires, and broke store windows, causing $273,000 in damages.

What is it about being in a group that leads people to do things they would never do on their own? One explanation is that people in a group believe they won't be held responsible for their actions because they are anonymous. The frequency and severity of aggressive and offensive behavior is greater if people are wearing a mask or hood or operating in the dark, even if they aren't in a group. As the psychologist Philip Zimbardo found, college students who were asked to deliver electric shocks to another student (thinking that they were participating in a study of creativity) delivered significantly longer—and thus more painful—shocks when they were wearing hoods to hide their identity than when they were not.[3]

The same phenomenon has been observed outside the lab. An analysis of violence in Northern Ireland by Andrew Silke at the University of Leicester found that people wearing disguises—masks, hoods, or other clothing to obscure their faces—engaged in more acts of vandalism, harmed more people, and inflicted more serious physical injuries.[4] This helps explain why cyberbullying and other aggressive behavior is so common online, where people can post anonymously.

Groups may also facilitate bad behavior because they create what is called "deindividuation"—the loss of sense of oneself as an individual.[5] When people lose touch with their own moral standards and forget who they really are, which often happens in a pack, the normal constraints against deviant behavior are removed.

The larger the crowd, the worse the behavior. Andrew Ritchey and Barry Ruback at Pennsylvania State University documented this effect by analyzing the behavior of lynch mobs.[6] Examining articles from the *Atlanta Constitution* about lynch mobs in Georgia from 1882 to 1926, they identified 515 victims in 411 separate events. They recorded the size of the mob, the race and sex of the victim, and the amount of violence that had occurred for each case. Although all of the lynchings resulted in death, they defined those in which the victim was also burned, hanged, and/or beaten as having a higher level of violence. Their results indicated that the size of the crowd at a lynching consistently predicted the level of violence.

Although group settings seem to contribute to bad behavior, understanding exactly how they do so is difficult. People may not be conscious of why they chose to do something, so they can't accurately tell researchers what drove their actions. They may also make excuses for their behavior, to make themselves look or feel better.

Recent breakthroughs in neuroscience, however, have provided important tools for helping us explore this behavior. Using neuroimaging techniques, researchers can examine the activity in different parts of the brain while people are in the act of doing certain things. This means we no longer have to rely only on what people say about their motivation. Instead, we can now investigate how being in a group changes patterns of brain activity.[7]

The first study to examine whether neural responses are lower in a group setting was conducted by researchers at MIT. It was prompted by an experience that one of the researchers, Mina Cikara, had when she was in graduate school. One afternoon, Cikara and her husband decided to go to a baseball game between two longstanding rivals, the Red Sox and the Yankees, at Yankee Stadium. Her husband, who wore a Red Sox cap, was relentlessly taunted by Yankees fans. In an attempt to defuse the situation, Cikara put her husband's cap on her own head, assuming that Yankees fans wouldn't target a woman for such verbal abuse.

It turned out she was wrong. "I have never been called names like that in my entire life," she said.[8] She returned from the game

determined to find out why being in a group setting leads otherwise normal people (though, in fairness, they were Yankees fans) to
act so poorly.

Cikara and her colleagues designed a study to test two questions:
Do people think about themselves less when they are participating in
a competitive task as part of a team than when they are acting alone?
And do people who think about themselves less when acting as part
of a team behave more aggressively toward members of the other
team?[9] They hypothesized that competing in a group might cause
people to become less aware of themselves and to lose their ability to
evaluate their own behavior.

In the first part of the study, researchers used an fMRI (functional
magnetic resonance imaging) machine to measure participants' patterns of brain activation while they played a game on their own and
then as part of a team. During the game, participants were shown
statements that described positive or negative moral behaviors about
either themselves or other people, such as, "I have stolen food from
shared refrigerators," or "He always apologizes after bumping into
someone."

The researchers focused on a particular part of the brain called
the medial prefrontal cortex (mPFC), which has been shown to be
more engaged (in colloquial terms, it "lights up") when people
think about themselves—when they consider their own personality
traits, physical characteristics, or mental states—than when they
think about others.[10]

Cikara and her colleagues found that when people played the game
on their own, their mPFC was far more active when they read statements about themselves than when they read statements about other
people. But when they played as part of a team, about half of the
participants showed a much smaller difference in activation in this
part of the brain when they read statements about themselves than
when they read statements about other people. These findings tell us
that some people do in fact think less about themselves when they are
in a group than when they are alone.

But the crucial question for these researchers was not just whether some people have a tendency to think less about themselves when competing as part of a team, but what the consequences are of this reduced self-reflection. They designed another study in which participants were shown six photos of each member of their own team and of the opposing team and were asked to choose one photo of each member, which was supposedly going to be printed in a published report. These photos had been independently rated according to attractiveness, from very unflattering to very flattering. The participants who showed reduced self-referential thinking—as measured by lower levels of mPFC activity—when playing as part of a team tended to choose less flattering photos of members of the opposing team than of their own team. Participants who didn't show lower self-referential thinking chose equally flattering photos of both teams.

The researchers concluded that people who think less about themselves when in a group setting are more likely to act in ways that hurt other people. This behavior may be especially pronounced when people are in groups that are directly competing with one another, as Cikara experienced when she put on her husband's Red Sox cap at Yankee Stadium.

"Although humans exhibit strong preferences for equity and moral prohibitions against harm in many contexts," said Rebecca Saxe, one of the researchers involved in the study, "people's priorities change when there is an 'us' and a 'them.'"[11]

Just Following Orders

One of the earliest—and most famous—research studies demonstrating that otherwise good people can engage in harmful actions was conducted by Stanley Milgram at Yale University. Milgram was interested in whether people would inflict pain on others if ordered to do so by an authority figure. He designed the study specifically to understand the psychological processes that had buttressed the

Nazi Holocaust, when millions of innocent victims were murdered by people who claimed that they were simply obeying orders. "Obedience, as a determinant of behavior, is of particular relevance to our time," wrote Milgram. "Gas chambers were built, death camps were guarded; daily quotas of corpses were produced. . . . These inhumane policies may have originated in the mind of a single person, but they could only be carried out on a massive scale if a very large number of persons obeyed orders."[12]

In a series of experiments, Milgram brought men into his lab at Yale to participate in what was supposedly a study of memory and learning. (His original study was done with forty men; later variations included women.) On arrival, each participant was greeted by a person identified as the experimenter and introduced to another participant, who was really an accomplice planted by the researchers. The experimenter explained that the study was designed to test an important scientific question about the impact of punishment on the speed of learning.

Participants were told that one person would serve as the "teacher" and the other as the "learner," but Milgram rigged it so that the study subject was always the teacher, while the accomplice was the learner. The learner would first be given a series of word pairs and later shown one of the words and tasked with picking out its pair from a list of four options. The teacher, who could communicate with the learner but not see him, was told to administer a shock if the learner gave a wrong answer. The experimenter was supposedly trying to gauge whether the shock helped or hindered the learner. (In reality, no shocks were given.)

The teacher was told to start by giving the learner the lowest level of shock (15 volts) and to increase the shock level each time the learner made a mistake.

At each shock level, the learner responded in a standard way. At the 75-volt level, he began to cry out in pain, and by 150 volts he asked to be let out of the experiment. He also began to claim that his heart was bothering him. If the teacher hesitated or turned to the experimenter in bewilderment asking if he could stop, he received one of four prompts that prodded him to continue: "Please continue," "The experiment requires that you continue," "It is absolutely essential that you continue," or "You have no other choice but to continue." The experimenter kept providing these prompts until the teacher refused to continue or reached the highest level (450 volts, which was marked "XXX dangerous").

Much to Milgram's surprise, the majority of the study participants—65 percent—were willing to give a person whom they believed to be an innocent participant the maximum level of electric shocks. Many people were dismayed by this extremely high rate of obedience, including the psychiatrists Milgram had consulted before the experiment, who had predicted that approximately 1 percent of the participants would follow through to the very end. The Milgram study was conducted more than fifty years ago, but similar experiments recently conducted in both Poland and the United States have found similarly high rates of compliance.[13]

Our willingness to harm others when we are following the instructions of an authority figure has also been demonstrated by studies that more clearly mimic real-world situations. Researchers in one study asked participants to read various test questions to a supposed job applicant, who was actually an accomplice.[14] The applicant was always played by the same person—a well-dressed man about thirty years old. The researchers told the participants that they were interested in examining how job applicants would react under pressure, so they wanted them to harass the applicant by making statements that progressed in offensiveness, including, "If you continue like this, you will fail," and "This job is much too difficult for you." As the "interview" continued, the applicant pleaded with them to stop, then refused to tolerate the abuse and showed signs of tension, and eventually stopped answering the questions in despair. In the control condition, in which there was no authority figure urging them to continue, none of the participants got through all fifteen of the statements. But when the experimenter prodded them along, 92 percent went all the way through the list.

What explains this tendency to obey an authority figure's orders even if it means harming an innocent person? One central factor is the authority figure's willingness to assume responsibility for any negative outcomes. This allows the person who is engaging in the bad behavior to feel absolved of wrong-doing.[15] The tendency to seek absolution on that basis can be found repeatedly in real-world situations, from the American soldiers who abused prisoners at Abu Ghraib in Iraq to business executives engaging in corporate fraud.[16]

Experimental research demonstrates that people who feel less responsible for committing harmful acts are more willing to do so. Participants in a replication of the Milgram study who were made to feel more responsible for inflicting harm—by being told explicitly that they were responsible for the well-being of the learner—stopped the procedure significantly earlier.[17] People who feel more responsible for hurting someone have also been found to be better able to resist explicit instructions to do so. A detailed analysis of the utterances of participants in one of the recent replications of the Milgram study revealed that those who expressed a sense that they were responsible for their actions were more likely to resist the orders and stop delivering shocks.[18]

These findings tell us that feeling less responsible increases the tendency to engage in compliant harmful behavior, but they don't tell us why. Do people blame actions on the instructions of authority figures to avoid facing the consequences of their actions, as in the Nuremberg trials, when Nazi defendants blamed their actions on "just following orders"? Or does the act of following orders actually change the way we process our behavior at a neurological level?

Patrick Haggard, a cognitive neuroscientist at University College London, designed a study with his colleagues to test precisely this question.[19] Students were recruited to participate in what they were told was a study to examine how people interact with each other when they are told what to do, and how they process this experience. The participants were placed into pairs and asked to deliver a "painful but tolerable" electric shock to their partner. In one condition, the participants were told that they had the option to deliver shocks to their partner or not, and if they did, they would receive some additional money. In the other condition, participants were ordered by the experimenter to deliver shocks.

The researchers monitored the participants' brain activity using electroencephalography (EEG). This allowed them to detect what neuroscientists call "event-related potentials," or ERPs—very small voltages that are generated in the brain in response to different sensory, motor, or cognitive events, such as seeing a picture of a face or experiencing a surprise. People who freely choose to engage in an action generally show larger ERP amplitudes—larger brain waves, meaning greater activity and a more intense experience—than those who are instructed to engage in an action.[20] The researchers were interested in finding out whether people who delivered the shocks without being ordered to do so would show larger ERP amplitudes than those who were following orders.

First they confirmed that those who gave the shocks of their own free will felt more responsible (87 percent) than those who were ordered to do so (35 percent). When they looked at the EEG data, they found that the people who had given shocks voluntarily did indeed have larger ERP amplitudes than those who had been ordered to do so. What does this tell us? It seems that people who have been told or coerced into doing something that may be harmful to another person—those who are "just following orders"—experience their action less intensely than those who choose to engage in the same behavior voluntarily.

The lower level of brain response reveals that if you do something that you are ordered to do, at a neurological level it seems to be less meaningful than if you do the same thing of your own volition. This makes it easier for people to feel less responsible for their actions, and thus more likely to engage in bad behavior. It also suggests that the defense of "just following orders" may not be merely a strategy people use to retrospectively excuse their behavior. When a person harms someone at the explicit instructions of an authority figure, their behavior is processed differently in the brain.

A Question of Identity

It is a natural human tendency to look for someone to blame when you are confronted with evidence of having done something wrong. After all, if it wasn't your fault you can convince yourself—and possibly others—that you are really a good person at heart. We've just seen that some data from neuroscience suggest that people who are following orders don't experience their actions as intensely as those who are acting of their own volition. But psychologists have also found that people sometimes come to identify with those who are giving the orders, at which point they may be choosing willingly to engage in bad behavior. We see this especially in the case of charismatic religious or political leaders.

Researchers at the University of St. Andrews and the University of Exeter conducted a study to assess how identifying with a person giving orders would affect people's actions.[21] They recruited people to read about the Milgram study and its variants and to evaluate how much they thought the participants in those studies would have identified with the "experimenter" (who was giving the orders), or with the "learner" (who was receiving the shocks). They chose one group of experts (academic psychologists who were already familiar with the Milgram study) and one of nonexperts (students taking an introductory psychology class who had not yet learned about the study), in case they differed in their assessments (in the end, the results were the same for the two groups). They asked people in both groups to read about the original study and then about fifteen different variations that Milgram had run over the years. These variations tweaked the procedure in small but important ways. In one, the experimenter gave the orders to deliver shocks by phone instead of in person. In another, the experiment was run not at prestigious Yale University but at an office building in Bridgeport, Connecticut.

The psychologists and students were asked to assess how they believed each variant would influence the participants' identification with the experimenter as a scientist and the scientific community he represented, or with the learner and his broader community. The researchers then examined whether these assessments of the nature of the participants' identification in the different variants correlated with the participants' willingness to obey or resist the orders.

Did identification influence obedience? In a word, yes. The variations that pushed participants to identify with the experimenter—and to see their actions as making a valuable contribution to the pursuit of scientific knowledge—led them to follow the orders to deliver shocks far longer. In one of these variations, the learner never gave a verbal complaint: he just pounded the wall in protest. In another, a second experimenter stepped in to give the orders in an attempt to speed up the process.

Variations that invited people to identify with the learner led participants to resist much earlier and more emphatically. In one such variation, two other supposed participants (actually accomplices) refused to continue delivering shocks. In another, two experimenters argued about whether the participant should continue to deliver the shocks.

These findings suggest that people may engage in harmful behavior when they are following orders not simply because they feel absolved of responsibility but because they come to believe that their actions are serving a worthy purpose.

This alternative explanation provides insight into some of the factors that led to the devastating effectiveness of the policies of the Nazis. People were not simply begrudgingly or numbly following orders; in many instances they embraced the broader social vision and mission of fascism. They identified with the dangers that Hitler was articulating, shared his muscular patriotism and nostalgia for a simpler past, embraced his hatred of outsiders, and bought into his vision of a racially pure society.

The question of why some people act badly and others don't is not really about good and bad people. Situational factors and questions of self-identification are far more important than we might imagine.[22]

The Agony of Indecision

As we have seen, most of the participants in the original Milgram study went along and delivered what they believed to be increasingly painful shocks to an innocent person. But what's often overlooked about this study is that the choice to continue obeying the authority was not an easy one for the participants. Videotapes reveal that many participants agonized over what they were doing, even as they continued to deliver shocks. Milgram described one of the troubled participants: "I observed a mature and initially poised businessman enter the laboratory smiling and confident. Within 20 minutes he was reduced to a twitching, stuttering wreck, who was rapidly approaching a point of nervous collapse. He constantly pulled on his earlobe, and twisted his hands. At one point he pushed his fist into his forehead and muttered, 'Oh God, let's stop it.'"[23] This man, like most others, continued all the way to the 450-volt level. But he was hardly a monster who was blissfully and blindly obeying the authority.

The participants in the Milgram study were faced with a difficult—and unusual—dilemma. They had agreed to participate in a study that was supposed to further the goals of science, and they trusted the experimenter who was giving the orders. Then, when the shock levels escalated and it became clear they were no longer administering a "mild punishment," they found it very difficult to extricate themselves.

Most of the participants tried at some point to resist. They turned to the experimenter and asked what they should do. They pushed the experimenter to check on the participant, and many at some point said, "I quit." But they didn't quit. What most participants had trouble doing was actually sticking with their gut feeling and walking out. In other words, they wanted to do the right thing, and they tried, often repeatedly, to do so. But they weren't able to follow through on their decision.

So, who were the people who successfully stood up to the authority figure? Milgram simply divided people into "obedient" and "disobedient," but a recent analysis of audio recordings of the study reveals considerably more nuance.[24] Many people in both groups resisted the orders in some form. Some hesitated to continue delivering shocks, others voiced their concerns about harming the recipient, and still others tried to stop the experiment. Of the "disobedient" participants, who refused to administer the most painful shocks, 98 percent tried to stop participating in the study at an early stage, saying things like, "I can't do this anymore," or "I won't do this anymore." Of the "obedient" participants, those who continued to deliver shocks through to the end, 19 percent did voice some form of direct refusal.

Those who ultimately disobeyed the experimenter did so in varied ways. Participants who called on multiple strategies to try to push back—and challenged the authority earlier—were more likely to quit. This tells us that people who want to do the right thing often don't do so because they lack the right skills and strategies.

Throughout the book I will be providing you with tools and strategies so that when the moment comes and you find yourself thinking, "I can't do this anymore," or "I won't do this anymore," you will follow through.

Gradual Escalation

Another reason we often go along when we are being urged to do something that we know to be wrong is because the situation gets more extreme little by little. Sometimes each small step will feel wrong, but relatively minor. This makes it difficult psychologically to decide not to do it. And then, when the harm escalates, it's hard to change course without explaining one's lack of prior action. This phenomenon, known as "gradual escalation," makes it hard to recognize the problem and extricate oneself early in the process. A good example is Bernie Madoff, a financier who defrauded people of millions of dollars through a massive Ponzi scheme. In explaining how he got started, he said, "Well, you know what happens is, it starts out with you taking a little bit, maybe a few hundred, a few thousand. You get comfortable with that, and before you know it, it snowballs into something big."[25] Other types of bad behavior—from academic cheating to fraternity hazing to sexual harassment—often play out in precisely the same way.

Empirical research demonstrates that small transgressions can put people on a slippery slope; getting away with minor acts makes them more likely to embark on bigger, more serious transgressions. Once you've engaged in a small—but wrong—act, you need to justify having done so while still maintaining a positive view of yourself (as we all like to do). You may explain this small act away by seeing it as not such a big deal, but that shift makes it easier to condone more serious transgressions later on.

To test whether engaging in small acts of dishonesty makes people more likely to engage in larger ones later, researchers conducted a study in which they asked college students to complete a series of math problems, in three separate trials.[26] They randomly assigned the students to one of three payment groups:

Group 1: Students received $2.50 for each correct answer in each of three trials.

Group 2: Students didn't get any money for the first two trials but received $2.50 for each correct answer on the third trial.

Group 3: Students were told they would earn 25 cents for each correct answer on the first trial, $1.00 for each correct answer on the second trial, and $2.50 for each correct answer on the third trial.

Participants were given answer sheets after each trial and were told to check their own work and then take from an envelope the amount of money they were owed. Unbeknownst to the participants, researchers were able to check later to see whether they had calculated the correct amount.

Can you predict what happened? People in the third group, with the gradual increase in reward, cheated the most—at double the rate of those in groups one and two. For people in the third group, the initial lie was very minor—they only received a quarter for lying, so it didn't seem like a big deal. And once they had lied on the first trial, it was easier to continue doing so on subsequent trials in which the rewards for doing so were greater.

Cases of corporate fraud often begin similarly, with small acts of unethical behavior leading to more substantial—and criminal—ones. Executives who have been found guilty of accounting fraud often describe a series of steps that led to the fraud, and they often can't recall exactly when their bad actions began.[27] Fraternity initiation procedures also often follow this pattern of gradually escalating demands: small orders, such as running errands or cleaning someone's car, are followed by more severe ones, such as forced drinking or even physical beatings.

So we have seen that engaging in small transgressions can make it easier for people to engage in larger ones because they are trying to justify their behavior. But another explanation is that people initially experience unpleasant physiological arousal when they engage in bad behavior—because they do recognize that it's wrong—but over time, they adapt and no longer experience such a reaction. In support of this theory, it has been demonstrated that people show lower levels of activation in the amygdala—a part of the brain that processes emotion—after repeatedly seeing negative images (of violence, death, anger, and so on).[28]

Researchers at University College London and Duke University wanted to test whether engaging in small acts of dishonest behavior would lead to reduced brain activation.[29] The researchers used fMRI scanners to monitor people's brains while they completed a series of estimation tasks with a partner (actually an accomplice) that involved guessing how many pennies were in a jar. In one case, they were told that they and their partner would get the greatest reward if they guessed the most accurate number. In another case, they were told that they would get the greatest reward if they lied by deliberately over- or underestimating the number, but that their partner would get less money. The procedure allowed researchers to measure how the brain would respond when people provided intentionally inaccurate estimates.

In the initial trials in which people provided deliberately dishonest guesses, the amygdala showed a strong response, indicating that the person was aware they were telling a lie and felt bad about it. But over time, with repeated trials, the amygdala's activity levels dropped substantially, meaning that the neural response had weakened. Telling small lies, then, appears to desensitize our brains to the negative emotions that typically occur when we do something we know is wrong—which, in turn, makes it easier to engage in bad behavior in the future. These researchers also found that the larger the drop in amygdala activity in one trial, the more likely the person was to lie—and the bigger the lie—on subsequent trials.

Although this study only examined the brain's response to repeated lies, the discovery that neural reactions decrease in response to repeated dishonesty suggests that the amygdala initially reacts strongly to acts that we know to be wrong, but that this emotional response is weakened following repeated bad behavior. "When we lie for personal gain," explained one of the study's authors, "our amygdala produces a negative feeling that limits the extent to which we are prepared to lie. However, this response fades as we continue to lie, and the more it falls, the bigger our lies become. This may lead to a 'slippery slope' where small acts of dishonesty escalate into more significant lies."[30]

We already know that good people typically don't set out to engage in bad behavior. But this research shows that if—for whatever reason—they take a small step in the wrong direction, it can lead to bigger and bigger steps in the same direction.

This finding helps to explain the very high rates of obedience in Milgram's study, which started with the delivery of only very small shocks. Most people felt fine about obeying the experimenter's request at first, and they continued to do so many times before the growing demands of the procedure became clear.[31] They started by giving 15 volts, and then 30, and then 45, all of which seemed like no big deal. They thought they were doing this in the interest of science and that they were helping respected professors determine the relationship between punishment and learning. But this gradual escalation of intensity meant that they had no easy way to justify a decision to stop giving shocks later on. And as they continued to give shocks, their physiological and neurological responses would have weakened. Most people would be unwilling to give a 450-volt shock—marked XXX dangerous—right off the bat, even if ordered to do so by a respected authority. But if it was OK to give a 100 volt shock, what makes it not OK to give a shock of 115 volts? How do you decide when to stop?

But here's the good news: some people did decide to stop. And understanding what enabled them to resist gives us insight we can use to help people stand up to social pressure of all kinds.

Examination of the audio recordings has revealed some of the factors that allowed some participants to disobey. It turns out that the sooner a person started to question the orders out loud, the more likely he was to ultimately disobey.[32] Those who questioned the orders explicitly found it harder to rationalize what they were doing.

In all variations of Milgram's studies, participants who stopped obeying orders did so when they reached 150 volts.[33] What is unique about this voltage level? This was the first time the victim himself asked to be released. That request changed the dynamic of the interaction. Those who disobeyed the experimenter apparently prioritized the victim's desire not to continue over the experimenter's instructions to do so.

Participants who defied the authority in the Milgram studies were ordinary people who chose to deliberate about what they were being asked to do—and that deliberation allowed them to defy the situational pressures and disobey. So what exactly were they doing differently from the other participants? And is there something we can learn from them?

Understanding Silence and Inaction

So far, I have focused on examples of good people doing bad things and at some of the situational factors that facilitate such behavior. Understanding these factors is important. It reminds us that we can all be influenced by them—and it can help us develop approaches to resist the pull. For example, researchers have found that people who understand the importance of questioning orders from authority figures or resisting pressure to engage in small acts of dishonesty are less likely to fall prey to these forces.

I started this chapter by describing the sexual assault of a teenage girl by two high school boys. Here's a fuller picture of the incident. The two students who were found guilty were far from the only people who had engaged in bad behavior that night. Two students had carried the girl—who was completely unresponsive—by her wrists and ankles. Several students had photographed her while she was naked and unconscious; they shared these images with other students and even posted them on Twitter, Facebook, and YouTube. Not a single student tried to help her by intervening to stop the assault, removing her from the unsafe situation, or calling 911.

Clearly the two students who raped the girl did something terrible. But it's equally clear that many others had the power to intervene in some way but chose not to do so. At some level their inaction allowed the assault to take place.

Unfortunately, both historical and present-day examples demonstrate that very few people overcome the pressures that inhibit action, even in situations where something unambiguously bad is happening. Sherrilyn Ifill, author of a book on the legacy of lynching, reminds us that the lynchings of African Americans in the United States were often carried out in the public square, with hundreds and sometimes thousands of people watching.[34] Surely not all of these observers were celebrating. Some were likely horrified, but very few tried to intervene.

Examples of bad behavior by a few that are ignored or overlooked by many are as common today as they were back then. Why did so many people fail to call 911 when a nineteen-year-old student fell down a flight of stairs after a fraternity hazing event at Penn State University? Why do so many Republican leaders ignore President Trump's offensive remarks, such as calling Mexicans rapists and murderers? Why did the Catholic Church choose to protect priests who were molesting children? Why did so many people—from coaches and administrators at Michigan State University to officials at USA Gymnastics—fail to act on information suggesting that Larry

Nassar had been sexual assaulting young gymnasts for years? In all of these examples, a small number of people actually engaged in the bad behavior, but many others failed to do anything to stop it.

The single biggest factor that allows bad behavior to continue is not so much individual bad apples as it is the failure of good people to stand up and do the right thing. Martin Luther King Jr. remarked on this tendency in a 1959 speech: "History will have to record that the greatest tragedy of this period of social transition was not the strident clamor of the bad people, but the appalling silence of the good people."[35]

But here's some encouraging news: understanding the factors that too often lead good people—like us—to stay silent and do nothing can provide the tools needed to encourage us to step up and act. We may recognize bad behavior but not feel responsible and hope others will do something instead, as we will see in the next chapter. Or we may fail to interpret ambiguous behavior as bad, as we will see in Chapter 3. We may think that intervening will be too costly, either physically or socially, as covered in Chapter 4. Perhaps most important, we may fear the personal, professional, and social consequences of standing up to members of our own social group, as discussed in Chapter 5. But each one of these forces can be counterbalanced, if you know what to do.

2

Who Is Responsible?

On April 9, 2017, David Dao, a sixty-nine-year-old doctor, was forcibly removed from a United Airlines flight at O'Hare International Airport after refusing to give up his seat on an overbooked flight. He was dragged down the aisle of the plane by three security officers from the Chicago Department of Aviation, who in the process hit his head against an armrest and knocked him unconscious. Dao suffered a concussion and broken nose, and lost two teeth.

This incident generated considerable publicity, as multiple passengers filmed the incident and posted videos on social media.

Many people who heard the story—and saw the video—focused on the poor treatment of Dao. What they ignored was something that immediately struck me: a plane full of silent passengers. These passengers clearly recognized what was occurring: many took out their phones and filmed the scene, and later expressed their outrage loudly on social media. Yet at the time, only one woman said anything, yelling out, "What are you doing?" No one confronted the officers or intervened to prevent what was clearly inappropriate behavior.

At some level, this is hardly surprising. As numerous studies have shown, we are less likely to intervene when other people are present. We assume that others will do something and we don't have to. Ironically, this tendency, which psychologists refer to as "diffusion of responsibility," means that the chance that a victim will receive help is inversely related to the number of people present. Psychologists call this phenomenon the "bystander effect." As we will see at the end of this chapter, however, this is not a hard-and-fast rule; sometimes people in groups are able to break out of the bystander role.

What factors contribute to the bystander effect? How does the presence of other people affect our response to an emergency situation? And what explains some people's ability, at least in some situations, to do something different—to step up, even in the presence of a group?

The Birth of the Bystander Effect

Research on the topic of bystander inaction took off following a famous case that occurred in Queens in 1964, when a young woman by the name of Kitty Genovese was murdered outside her apartment building. The *New York Times* investigated her murder and published an article that was seen as an indictment of city living and a clear demonstration of its dehumanizing effect.[1] The article recounted the events of the night and claimed that thirty-eight witnesses saw or heard the attack, but not one of them came to Kitty's assistance or called the police during the assault. More recent research has revealed some errors in this story, but the case prompted a flurry of research in psychology on a phenomenon that came to be classified as the bystander effect.[2]

In one of the earliest studies triggered by the Kitty Genovese case, John Darley of New York University and Bibb Latané of Columbia University created a realistic emergency in an experimental setting so that they could assess how the presence of other people would influence participants' responses.[3] The question they asked was, Will people behave differently in a situation where they believe they alone are responsible for getting help than in a situation where they believe others share the same information and could also help? Participants, who were all college students, were told that the study involved an examination of common personal problems faced by students and that to protect their confidentiality, each participant would be in a private room and the experimenters would not be listening in on their conversation. Each participant was taken to one of a series of small rooms connected by intercoms, and was instructed to use the intercom to communicate with the other five participants. The researcher then asked each person to introduce themselves. One participant, John, who was the researcher's accomplice, mentioned that he'd had some trouble with a seizure disorder, which was sometimes triggered by stress. He said that if he started to slur his words, it was really important that someone go and get help.

The researchers then introduced a key aspect of this study. Half of the participants were told that all group members could hear the other members' contributions to the conversation through the intercoms. The other half were told that John's intercom wasn't working correctly and that they were the only one who could hear what he was saying, so they should repeat whatever he said for the whole group to hear.

As you can probably guess, a few minutes into the start of the conversation, John's speech became slurred, and he asked for help.

Who stepped up to help him? First, the good news: 85 percent of the participants who were told that they alone could hear John left the room immediately to get help. (One wonders what the other 15 percent were thinking.) These people apparently believed they were the only ones who knew that John was on the verge of having a seizure, so they felt responsible and knew they needed to act.

But the bad news is that for those who were told that all group members could hear John, the rate of helping was substantially lower. Of the participants who thought four other people could hear John, only 31 percent left the room within six minutes. They must have assumed that someone else would get help and not felt responsible for doing so themselves.

Darley and Latané's study was designed to create an experimental paradigm that mimicked what often happens in the real world, when bystanders confront an emergency and know those around them are aware of it, but don't know how to react. They found that people are more likely to be helped if the emergency takes place in front of just one person—who then clearly recognizes it is their responsibility to act—than if it takes place in front of a larger group, in which case each person will likely wait to see if someone else will step up.

But the more important finding from this landmark study was that even though most people in the group setting didn't go get help, neither did they fit the stereotype of the callous and apathetic bystander ignoring an emergency. When the experimenter entered the room at the end of the study, many of the participants expressed concern about John, asking if he was "all right" and "being taken care of." They also showed signs of physical arousal, such as trembling hands and sweating. If they were so concerned and anxious, why didn't they act?

Darley and Latané posited that the participants who didn't get help had not in fact decided definitively that they would not do so. Rather, they seemed to be in a state of indecision. Participants in the group setting may well have played through a variety of possibilities in their minds as they tried to decide what to do. Because they did not have to act, they probably began to think of reasons not to. Perhaps someone else had already gotten help, in which case their own action would just create more chaos. Perhaps calling for help would be an overreaction and they would feel embarrassed. Perhaps leaving the room would mess up the experiment in some way. Those who were alone didn't weigh these variables, since they understood that they were the only person who could help. As a result, their responsibility was clear.

This finding—that people are far less likely to provide help when they are in a group setting—has been shown repeatedly in real-world emergencies. Here are a few recent examples:

- A group of teenagers in Cocoa, Florida, watched a man drown in a pond. No one tried to help or called for help.[4]
- A student at Florida State University passed out after drinking large amounts of bourbon and was carried to a couch. He lay unconscious as fraternity members continued drinking, partying, and playing pool around him. He was found dead the next morning.[5]
- A man tried to grab a Muslim woman's hijab from her head in a crowded shopping area in London. A number of shoppers observed the attack, but no one stepped forward to help.[6]
- A two-year-old girl in China was run over by a car and lay bleeding for more than seven minutes as at least eighteen people walked directly around her.[7]
- A woman was raped in India in broad daylight. Many people walked by while the assault was underway and did nothing to stop it.[8]

In all of these instances, bystanders could have—and arguably should have—provided help.

We find this tendency toward group inaction even in young children. Maria Plötner at the Max Planck Institute for Evolutionary Anthropology and a group of colleagues designed a study to test whether young children were susceptible to the bystander effect and to investigate what factors drove their behavior.[9] In this study, five-year-olds were told to color in a picture and were then presented with a situation in which the experimenter needed help.

In order to test whether a child's likelihood of helping was influenced by diffusion of responsibility (feeling less pressure to help because someone else could also do so) or social factors (feeling uncertain about whether the situation required help, or shy about stepping up to help in front of others), the researchers set up three conditions: (1) the child was alone; (2) the child was in a group with two other children who appeared to be physically able to help (the bystander condition); or (3) the child was in a group with two other children who were physically unable to help (the bystander-unavailable condition) because they were seated behind a low wall. Unbeknownst to the child being tested, the bystander children had been told in advance that they should not help the experimenter.

About thirty seconds after the child began drawing, the experimenter "accidentally" knocked over a glass of water, spilling it on the floor. She made her distress clear, saying "oops" and groaning, and gestured toward some paper towels that were lying on the floor—in sight of the child, but just out of reach. The experimenter measured how quickly, if at all, the child came over to help her wipe up the water.

The researchers found that children who were alone with the experimenter were far more likely to help, and to do so much faster, than those who were in a group with other kids who also appeared to be able to help. This is the traditional finding from bystander intervention research with adults. But what happened in the third condition, when children were in a group with others who were unable to help? These children helped just as fast as the children who were alone.

To further understand the dynamics at play, a researcher briefly talked to each child at the end of the study. She asked them whether the experimenter had really needed help, whose job it was to help, how they had known who should help, and whether they had known how to help the experimenter.

In all three conditions, most children recognized that help was needed. But children did not feel equally responsible for providing that help: 53 percent of the children in both the alone and bystander-unavailable conditions reported that it was their job to help, compared with only 12 percent of the children who were in a group with other potential helpers. The researchers also found a difference in children's reports about whether they knew how to help. Nearly half—47 percent—of the children in the bystander condition reported not knowing how to help, compared with only 10 percent of those who were alone and none of the children in the bystander-unavailable condition. Given that the help necessary was pretty straightforward—handing the experimenter some paper towels—it seems likely that the children who said they did not know how to help were trying to explain their inaction to the researcher and/or to themselves. Even these five-year-olds appear to have understood that they probably should have provided help and struggled to find a way to justify their behavior.

"The children in our study helped at very high levels only when responsibility was clearly attributable to them," concluded Plötner. "These findings suggest that children at this age take responsibility into account when deciding whether to help."[10] But when other people were available who could also have provided help, they were quite willing to sit back and wait for others to help instead. Young children, this study showed, are naturally helpful as long as they feel responsible.

As any parent of multiple children knows, kids often feel less responsible when other potential helpers are available. Each child is significantly more helpful if the others are not around. After all, why sweep up the broken glass if your brother could do it?

The Hazards of Social Loafing

The failure to act when we are in a group setting, even in most emergencies, is related to a broader human tendency to reduce our effort when we believe our action—or lack thereof—will be less apparent.

This tendency to minimize our own contribution when our effort is combined with others is known as "social loafing."[11]

Social loafing shows up in many different settings, from the classroom to the workplace to the political arena. It explains why so many college students hate group projects: they fear they will be forced to do all the work without getting credit for it, while the other students slack off. It also explains why restaurants often impose a mandatory service charge for groups of six or more. Left to their own devices, individuals in a large party tend to tip poorly, assuming that their own contribution will not be noticed and that others will contribute more to compensate.[12] In other words, people socially loaf at least in part because they believe they can hide in the crowd and that their lack of effort will go unnoticed.

Social loafing is especially likely to occur when our own contribution is not clear or measurable. Researchers at Purdue University, for example, found that college swimmers on a relay team swam faster when their individual time was announced than when only the total relay time was announced.[13] Similarly, when asked to clap or cheer "as loud as they can," people exert much less effort when they're in a group—and their lack of effort is not apparent—than when they're alone.[14] This lack of effort isn't limited to physical tasks: people who simply imagined being in a group setting later pledged less money to a charitable organization than those who imagined being with just one other person.[15] Social loafing also explains why so few people turn out to vote, even if they have strong political views.

Although the examples I've given so far are pretty inconsequential, the tendency to believe that others will pick up the slack can have substantial consequences in work situations. Researchers at the Berlin Institute of Technology conducted a study in which participants were told they had to monitor and cross-check an automated system in a chemical plant to make sure it was operating properly.[16] It is often assumed that having multiple people monitor the same machine increases the odds of spotting a problem—aren't four eyes better than two? But this theory—that putting several people in charge of the same task will yield better outcomes—ignores fundamental research showing that humans have a tendency to withdraw effort on group tasks.

The study on monitoring confirmed this truth. It found that people who were working with a partner performed significantly fewer checks than those who were working alone, and that they found fewer automation failures. Those who were working alone detected almost 90 percent of the failures. But people who were working with a partner detected only about 66 percent. The combined team performance was significantly worse than the performance of participants who were working alone.

But studies of social loafing have yet to examine an important question: Why do people choose to exert less effort in a group setting? One possibility is that people explain away their lack of effort as being justified. Someone might rationalize leaving a small tip because others in their party ordered more expensive food, or were better off. Another possibility is that people actually feel less control over the outcome when they are in a group, and this lack of perceived control leads them to exert less effort.

To test this theory about lack of control, researchers at University College London invited people to perform a somewhat risky task either alone or with a partner.[17] Study participants started with a certain number of points, which would be converted to money at the end of the experiment. They were told that their job was to stop a rolling marble from falling off a tilted bar and crashing to the floor. They could press a button to stop the marble at any time. (This was all done virtually, on a computer.) The farther the marble traveled, the fewer points would be deducted—thus incentivizing delay. But if the marble rolled onto the floor, they would lose a large number of points. When playing with a supposed partner (in reality a pre-programmed computer), if the participant stopped the marble, the participant would lose points but the partner would lose none; if the partner stopped the marble, the partner would lose points but the participant would lose none. The study was designed to set up a different calculus depending on whether a participant was playing alone or with a partner. Participants playing alone simply had to decide how much risk they were willing to tolerate. Those playing with a partner also had to take into account how much risk the partner would tolerate.

The researchers evaluated three distinct aspects of behavior: if and when participants stopped the marble, how much control the participants reported feeling over the outcome, and how their brain responded. They used electroencephalography to measure event-related potentials (ERPs), which are types of brainwaves. The particular ERP component they were interested in is called feedback-related negativity (FRN). The size of the FRN response has been shown to indicate how much control people feel they have over the outcome of their actions. The FRN response is smaller when people work together on a group task than when they work alone, presumably because they feel less control over the outcome when they are working with others.[18] The more involvement others have in the task, the smaller the FRN response. In the marble study, the FRN response was measured when participants learned how many points they had lost on each trial and were faced with the consequences of the choice they had made.

When the researchers analyzed their results, they found that people stopped the marble on average somewhat later when they were playing with a partner than when they were playing alone. This makes sense: if their partner stopped the marble, the participant would lose no points. Thus, they were willing to wait until the last minute to see if their partner would act first.

People who played with a partner reported feeling significantly less control over the outcome. This finding also makes sense: those playing alone had full control over when the marble stopped, whereas those playing with a partner had to think about when their partner might stop the marble.

The analysis of neural activity provided additional evidence that working with others reduces a person's feelings of control. In line with prior research, the FRN response was lower when people were playing with a partner than when they were alone. In this scenario, as in many real-life bystander situations, participants had a perception of less control when with a partner, even though they still had the option to act at any time.

This study extended prior work on diffusion of responsibility in important ways. It showed that people working with a partner tend to process and experience the consequences of their actions in different ways, as shown both subjectively—through self-reported ratings of perceived agency—and objectively—through the EEG data. When deciding whether to act, they felt less responsible for the outcome of their action if they were working with another person than if they were engaged in the task alone.

When we work with others, it seems, our sense of control over our actions and their consequences is reduced, decreasing our sense of urgency to do something.

Overcoming the Bystander Effect

So far, I have described studies that help explain the natural human tendency not to act when we are in a group (especially if those around us are also doing nothing). But inaction is not inevitable. The good news is that we are sometimes able to overcome this tendency. And it turns out that becoming aware of the factors that help us do so may enable us to step up even when others do not—especially when it is hard.

Public Self-Awareness Matters

Although most of us become social loafers when we're in a group, we are less likely to do so if we know we are being watched. All of us like to think of ourselves as good people who usually do the morally right thing. This desire to appear to be good is heightened when we know that other people are evaluating our behavior. Research by Marco van Bommel at the University of Amsterdam revealed that even small cues that increase our public self-awareness can dampen our tendency to reduce effort when in a group. There are several ways to increase such self-awareness.

In one experiment, researchers created an online chat room and told participants that they were studying online communication.[19] Students logged in to the chat room and were then shown messages expressing distress that had supposedly been posted by other people in the chat room. One expressed a desire to commit suicide, another was from a person with anorexia, and a third was from someone whose partner had cancer. Participants could respond to these messages with some form of emotional support, but they were told it was entirely their choice whether to do so or not.

In the first version of this study, each person could see their name on the screen as well as that of other members of the chat room. All of the names were in black. In some cases, thirty other people were logged in to the chat room; in others they were the only person logged in. Just as prior research on the diffusion of responsibility would predict, participants were less likely to respond to the message when they thought that many people were logged in than when they thought they were alone.

But in a second version of the study, the researchers deliberately tried to increase feelings of public self-awareness. Now the participant's name appeared in red, while the others were still in black. This simple shift reversed the typical findings: suddenly participants were more likely to post a reply when there were many people in the chat room than when they were alone.

Why did this seemingly small change make such a difference? Basically, when we are highly aware that our identity is known by others in the group, we don't want to look like a jerk for failing to respond to someone in need. The same psychological factors that can decrease our contributions in a group setting—we don't want to look like a fool for doing all the work on a group project or over-tipping to make up for others' meager contributions—can lead us to be more helpful if we believe that not doing so would make us look bad.

The researchers repeated this study with a different approach to highlighting public self-awareness. This time, half of the people were told at the start of the study to be sure the indicator light of their webcam was turned on, even though the camera was only going to be used in the second part of the study. Others weren't told anything about the webcam. Those who weren't told about the webcam were less likely to respond if there were more people in the chat room. But for those whose public self-awareness was more pronounced because they had first checked the camera, larger groups led to more responses.

This study offers us valuable information about why the bystander effect occurs—and what we can do to overcome its influence. In large groups, we often feel we can hide within the crowd. We don't need to make an effort to step up, since no one will notice our inaction. But when we are conscious that others will notice our actions—or lack thereof—we do help, because we want to make a good impression. In fact, people are more likely to help in an emergency when they are in a large crowd of friends than in a smaller one.[20] Why? Most likely for the simple reason that we want to look good in front of our friends.

Being in a crowd, then, doesn't always stop us from helping; it only does so when the crowd provides us with a cloak of anonymity.

Because we care about our social reputation, we may be more likely to help when we are in a larger group than a smaller one if the people in the group know our identity.

This insight has been particularly useful when it comes to considering group behavior on campus or in the workplace, where people tend to be surrounded by friends and colleagues. It turns out that students and colleagues can spur themselves to collective action, at least in cases where providing help doesn't involve interfering with members of their group. (We'll return to this in Chapter 5.)

Responsibility Matters

Another factor that influences social loafing is whether you believe your efforts will make a difference.[21] If you act, will it matter? People who are asked to perform a difficult task that they believe they can do better than others do not generally withdraw effort, even when their individual output won't be evaluated. In this case, they feel that they can make a unique and important contribution to the group's success. Researchers have also found that people step up more quickly to help in an emergency when they are in the presence of children—who presumably won't be as capable of helping—than when they are in the presence of adults.[22] This is true even when they don't know the children and so are not concerned about setting a good example.

This also helps explain why people with specialized training tend to step up and help in an emergency. They don't succumb to the normal feelings of diffusion of responsibility. In fact, those who have some type of specialized skill, like doctors, nurses, soldiers, or volunteer firefighters, feel more responsible to act—and usually they do.

In one study, researchers recruited students from both a nursing program and a general education program to participate in what they were told was a simple questionnaire study.[23] Half of the students were placed in a room alone to work on their questionnaire; the others were in a room with another student (who was actually the researchers' accomplice). As they were working, they heard a man fall from a ladder outside the room and scream out in pain.

Education students who were alone were much more likely to help than those who were with another person. This is precisely what prior research on diffusion of responsibility in a group setting predicts. But the percentage of nursing students who helped was the same whether they were alone or not. This doesn't mean that nursing students are nicer people—though maybe sometimes they are. It reflects the fact that they knew what to do, and therefore felt a greater responsibility to act.

People also feel more responsibility if, instead of possessing special skills, they are in a position of authority. Research participants who were randomly assigned to serve as a group leader in a psychology study were more likely to assist a fellow student who appeared to be choking than were those who did not have a leadership role.[24] Being randomly assigned a leadership position reduced the normal diffusion of responsibility that occurs in a group setting.

In some instances, the person with the specialized knowledge isn't the person with authority. Even so, they may take charge. During my senior year of college, I was sitting in a classroom on the fourth floor of a building when the room suddenly started swaying back and forth. The 1989 Loma Prieta earthquake had just struck Northern California. The students all turned to the authority—the professor—to figure out what to do.

Her response was not what we had expected: she grabbed the edge of the table and yelled, "I'm from New York!" Her statement clearly indicated that she had no idea what to do.

Another student then yelled, "I'm from California," establishing his credibility in this emergency. Then he said, "Get under the table."

Connection Matters

In January 2019, Divyne Apollon, a thirteen-year-old African American ice hockey player, was competing in a tournament in

Maryland when members of the opposing team began to shout out racist remarks. Some made monkey noises, others told him to get off the ice and go play basketball. At least one used the N-word. None of the adults present—coaches, referees, parents in the stands—intervened. But Divyne's teammates did. At the end of the third period, they started yelling at the players on the other team and a fight broke out. Even though Divyne's teammates were all white and weren't personally subjected to the racist slurs and taunts, they came to his defense on the ice. Their sense of connection as a team overrode the bystander effect.

How exactly does feeling connected to a person in need help us overcome our natural human tendency to stay silent? According to what is known as "self-categorization theory," our self-identity is connected to our group identity, whether it be our gender, race, or nationality, our school affiliation, sports team, or line of work.[25] This sense of shared identity can make us more likely to help, even in group settings where we would normally hang back. We tend to feel greater connection to members of our own group, so failing to act feels worse: when someone in our group needs help, we step up.

Research by Mark Levine and colleagues has shown that even a very simple shared identity—an affinity for the same sports team—can increase people's willingness to extend help.[26] In one experiment, the researchers recruited fans (all male) of the soccer team Manchester United to take part in what they were told was a study of crowd behavior during sporting events. The participants completed brief questionnaires about their support for their team and were then told they had to go to another building to watch a video.

As they were outside walking to the other building, they were confronted by a staged emergency: a person slipped and fell on the grass, then grabbed his ankle and cried out in pain. The man was wearing either a Manchester United jersey, a jersey of a rival team

(Liverpool), or a plain shirt with no team identity. Can you guess who they were more likely to help?

The Manchester United fans were much more likely to help if the person who stumbled on the grass was wearing a jersey of their team. Over 90 percent of them stopped to help the injured man wearing a Manchester United jersey. Only 30 percent helped the man in the Liverpool jersey, and 33 percent helped the man in the plain shirt. This study and others by the same authors demonstrate that even seemingly superficial types of shared identity—like attending the same college or rooting for a certain team—can make a big difference in helping behavior.[27]

Feeling a sense of shared identity can even prompt people to intervene in violent situations, when the cost of getting involved is substantially greater. Research using an immersive virtual environment—for ethical reasons, the only practical way to experimentally study bystander behavior in dangerous situations—revealed that people were more likely to intervene to stop a violent incident when the victim was a fan of a team they supported than when he wasn't.[28]

So it's easier to overcome our natural human tendency toward inaction in a group setting if we feel some connection to the person in need of help. This helps explain why the young hockey players responded to the racist attacks on their teammate instead of staying silent. Their shared sense of identity made them feel they had to do something. (Their action ended up starting a local movement to combat racism in sports.)

It also helps explain the true story of Kitty Genovese's death. Newspaper reports at the time claimed that there were dozens of witnesses, all of whom did nothing. But later research revealed that at least two people had called the police, and one woman did much more. Sophie Farrar, who was a friend of Kitty's, was called by a neighbor about the attack; she immediately phoned the police and then raced to Kitty's side, even though it was the middle of the night and she had no way of knowing whether doing so would put her own life at danger.[29] Sophie was holding Kitty in her arms when the ambulance arrived.

Sophie Farrar may have feared for her own life, but there was no question that Kitty needed help. In less black-and-white cases, the decision about whether to intervene is harder. As you'll see in the next chapter, acting is particularly hard in situations in which we aren't really sure what's going on.

3

The Perils of Ambiguity

In February 1993, two ten-year-old boys abducted a toddler, Jamie Bulger, from a shopping mall in Liverpool, England. The three of them walked two and a half miles together. Jamie had a bump on his forehead and was crying the entire time. Although they were seen by three dozen different people, most did nothing to intervene. Two people did approach the older boys, but the boys said Jamie was their younger brother, or that he was lost and they were taking him to the police station. No one called the police.

The older boys took Jamie to a secluded place by a railroad track and proceeded to beat him to death. His body was found two days later.

Jamie Bulger's tragic story illustrates a fundamental challenge we've all faced at some point in our lives. Sometimes we notice that *something* is wrong, but we aren't sure exactly what we are seeing or hearing. Is that comment at the office a harmless joke, or is it racist and offensive? Is that spat a minor quarrel, or a serious case of domestic violence? Is that person splashing in the pool in real trouble, or just horsing around? Ambiguous situations like these make it harder for people to step up and act.

In this chapter, I describe how uncertainty about what exactly is happening, coupled with a tendency to rely on others' behavior to help us interpret a situation, will often keep people from taking action, especially when they are in a group, at times with tragic consequences. I also review recent developments in neuroscience, which suggest that this kind of inaction can be detected in patterns of brain activation.

Ambiguity Drives Inaction

One summer during college I had a job in downtown Atlanta. My roommate and I walked home one night from work and saw a man passed out on the front steps of our apartment building. We were naturally concerned about whether he was OK, and we called 911. The ambulance arrived a few minutes later. The driver and an attendant went over to the man and started laughing. Apparently, he was well known in the community as a drunk and was simply sleeping off a long night of drinking. How did we feel? Embarrassed. Stupid. Naive.

This experience illustrates the psychological challenge of stepping up in an ambiguous situation. Our attempt to do the right thing is complicated when we don't understand what's going on. We are often inhibited from acting because we are anxious that others might judge us as stupid or overly sensitive. Psychologists call this "evaluation apprehension." Larger crowds tend to increase our concern about making a bad impression—after all, there are more people to witness our embarrassing behavior. This condition is known as "audience inhibition."

Imagine you see a couple arguing loudly in a public area, and it seems the fight may turn physical. You may think, "Maybe I should do something." But you may also feel that you shouldn't get involved in a personal argument. A study conducted by R. Lance Shotland and Margret K. Straw at Pennsylvania State University demonstrated precisely this dynamic.[1] As participants began completing a survey in a waiting room, the researchers staged a fight between a male–female couple (who in reality were actors from the school's theater department). First, a loud argument was heard from behind closed doors, in which a man accused a woman of picking up a dollar that he claimed to have dropped. The couple then entered the room, and the man began violently shaking the woman, who struggled and screamed, "Get away from me!" In one case, she added, "I don't know you," and in the other, she added, "I don't know why I ever married you." The couple continued to struggle for forty-five seconds, at which point a researcher arrived and broke up the fight if the participant hadn't yet stepped in. The researchers measured any action by the participant—from calling the police, to shouting at the man to stop, to directly intervening physically.

In this study, the participant was always the lone bystander, so there was no question about who was responsible to help. But rates of intervention varied substantially based on the couple's relationship. Sixty-five percent of people actively stepped in to stop the man from assaulting a woman if they thought they were strangers. But only 19 percent intervened if they believed they were watching a fight between a married couple.

What explains this difference? For many people, interfering in a potentially violent conflict between strangers seems like the right thing to do. But interfering in a domestic dispute has the potential to lead to awkwardness and embarrassment for all parties.

This concern about how we appear to others can also be seen in children, though work by the psychologist Ervin Staub suggests that the effect may vary with age. In a study where children heard another child in distress, young children (kindergarten through second grade) were more likely to help the child in distress when with another child than when alone.[2] But for older children—in fourth and sixth grade—the effect reversed: they were less likely to help a child in distress when they were with a peer than when they were alone.

Staub suggested that younger children might feel more comfortable acting when they have the company of a peer, whereas older children might feel more concern about being judged by their peers and fear feeling embarrassed by overreacting. Staub noted that "older children seemed to discuss the distress sounds less and to react to them less openly than younger children." In other words, the older children were deliberately putting on a poker face in front of their peers.

Social psychologists have found that one of the consequences of the fact that people are more willing do something when they don't fear judgment is that they are far more likely to take action in the case of a clear emergency than in an ambiguous situation.[3] In one study, researchers created an ambiguous incident—participants heard a loud crash in another room—and an unambiguous emergency—a loud crash followed by groans of pain.[4] Everyone who heard the crash and groans helped, regardless of whether they were alone or in a group. Fewer people helped when they heard only the crash, but they were more likely to help if they were alone than in a group.

These results provide insight into what might at first seem like a puzzling real-world finding. Contrary to what we so often hear, in some kinds of emergencies, people absolutely do step up and help. In Chapter 2 we saw some situations in which people in groups tend to help (for example, when they feel more responsibility); another situation is in the case of a real, unambiguous emergency.

During the morning rush hour on July 7, 2005, suicide bombers set off a series of coordinated attacks in London's transit system, killing fifty-two people and injuring hundreds more. Although this was clearly a serious emergency in which those who helped victims might risk injury themselves, eyewitness accounts repeatedly described people providing first aid and consoling strangers.[5] One survivor described her experience in a subway station: "These guys helped me up on the platform and then this woman came and asked if I was alright and then held my hand as we walked up the platform together. And um got the lift up to the tube station and sat down for ages and ages and then this really nice woman came and sat with me and put her coat round me [and] kind of looked after me."[6]

Similar accounts of spontaneous outpourings of support from total strangers came after the 2013 Boston Marathon attack, the 2013 mass shooting at the Westgate Mall in Nairobi, Kenya, and the 2017 terrorist attack in Barcelona.

What accounts for the discrepancy between our natural tendency toward inaction and these examples of people putting their own lives at risk to help a total stranger? When bombs explode or shootings occur, the immediate question of whether the situation is an emergency is clearly answered. There is no ambiguity. This means that people have far less fear about looking stupid or feeling embarrassed for overreacting. Indeed, empirical research has shown that in situations of high potential danger, people are just as likely to help whether they are alone or in a crowd.[7]

Results from a recent cross-cultural study document cases of this kind of help. A team of researchers examined closed-circuit television footage of 219 public fights, including arguments and assaults, in three different cities: Amsterdam, Netherlands; Lancaster, United Kingdom; and Cape Town, South Africa.[8] They reviewed video recordings of each fight, as captured by security cameras, and recorded witnesses' behavior. In 91 percent of the cases, at least one person intervened in some way, such as gesturing for the aggressor to calm down, physically blocking or pulling the aggressor away, or consoling or providing help to the victim. (There was no statistically significant difference in the rate of intervention among the three cities.) The greater the number of bystanders, the greater the likelihood that the victim would get help. So in these emergency situations, some people did step up to help. But not all of them.

The researchers—whose areas of expertise included psychology, sociology, anthropology, and criminology—proudly proclaimed that they had proven that there is no such thing as the bystander effect. They suggested that the truism in the psychology community about bystander apathy in group settings doesn't hold up to scrutiny. But remember, these researchers were examining a very specific type of behavior—people intervening to stop a public fight. As we have seen, emergency situations do tend to elicit more helping behavior. And a meta-analysis has confirmed that bystanders tend to act in certain situations, including dangerous ones where the risks are physical rather than social.[9]

Unfortunately, many situations lack the type of clarity that seems to prompt action. Is that intoxicated college student willingly going into that guy's dorm room, or is this a potential sexual assault? Is that parent appropriately disciplining their child, or is it child abuse? Similarly, it can be difficult to tell for sure whether a particular joke or comment is offensive. An inappropriate comment may seem positive on the surface—think of "Asian people are naturally good at math," or "That dress really shows off your legs."[10] Even if we recognize that a comment is problematic, we often wonder whether it is harmful enough to merit a response. People who hear offensive remarks—in the workplace, at school, in public settings—often stay silent because they just aren't sure whether or how to respond.

The Hazards of a Poker Face

When facing an ambiguous situation, our natural tendency is to look to others to figure out what's going on. We expect that their behavior will give us information about what they are thinking or feeling, which we can then use to guide our own reaction. But here's the problem: if everyone is looking to others for guidance, no one may actually acknowledge what is going on.

In a famous study conducted in 1968, John Darley of New York University and Bibb Latané of Columbia University investigated how other people's reactions influence our own interpretation of a situation. Students were brought into the lab to fill out a simple questionnaire.[11] Some were asked to complete the questionnaire in a room alone; others were placed in a room with two other people (accomplices who had been told not to respond in any way to the emergency that was about to be created). A few minutes after the students had begun filling out the questionnaire, smoke started pouring into the room. The researchers were interested in seeing what they would do in the face of this seemingly obvious emergency.

Darley and Latané found that 75 percent of the participants who were alone in the room stood up to investigate the source of the smoke and then left the room to report it to the experimenter.

But when they were not alone, only 10 percent of the students got up to get help over the course of the next six minutes (at which point the researchers ended the experiment). The smoke was not subtle: by the end of the six-minute trial, it was so thick that the students were constantly having to wave it away from their faces just to read the questionnaires. But still they kept at it. Why?

When the researchers asked the nonresponding students if they had noticed the smoke, they all readily admitted that they had, and then offered a number of different explanations for it. One said he thought it was air conditioning, another said "steam," and two suggested "truth gas." The lack of response from the others in the room led them to interpret the smoke as not indicating anything serious.

This study established a classic principle of social psychology: that people who are alone will readily recognize a situation as an emergency and act appropriately, but in a crowd of nonresponding individuals, they do not. In a group of nonresponders, most of us will do nothing.

Conversely, when one person reacts to a situation, others are much more likely to follow. In one study, male students were asked to complete a questionnaire in a room alone, but they could see another person—really an accomplice of the experimenter—through a glass partition in an adjacent room.[12] While the participants were completing the questionnaire, they heard a woman screaming and objects falling. Participants were much more likely to stand up and try to find out what was going on when the accomplice appeared to be agitated and concerned than when that person didn't react at all. In another similar study, Ervin Staub found that when an accomplice identified an initially ambiguous sound as an emergency and told the study participant to go get help, every single person did so.[13] Both studies provide evidence that in ambiguous situations, we often depend on people's reactions to help us evaluate what's happening and determine our own response.

The fact that people in a group will look to one another's behavior to determine what they should do contributes to our tendency to fail to act in an ambiguous situation. If each person is looking to the person next to them to figure out what to do, and no one wants to be seen as the person who overreacts (and risks feeling foolish and embarrassed), the person in need may receive no help at all. The members of the group may all collectively assume that because others are not reacting, there is no emergency. In other words, inaction breeds inaction. Each person may privately believe an emergency is in fact occurring, while publicly they show no concern.

This condition, in which a majority of group members privately hold one belief, but incorrectly assume that most others hold a different belief, is known as "pluralistic ignorance." Pluralistic ignorance sometimes contributes to inaction in the face of life or death emergencies, as when people don't react to a fire alarm because no one else seems to be doing anything. But this condition is also common in daily life. When students or employees hear sexist, racist, or homophobic comments, for example, they will generally look to see how others are responding to determine how they should react. If others do not seem to be bothered, they will infer—perhaps wrongly—that their friends or colleagues support such language. But it is possible that everyone is just as bothered by the comment.

Pluralistic ignorance helps explain why we often feel more out of synch with other people than we actually are. Researchers in one study asked college men to report how comfortable they were with sexist remarks, and then to report how comfortable they believed other male students were likely to be with the same remarks.[14] Here was one scenario: "You and some male friends are walking down campus walk, as a woman that you have never seen before walks past. After you pass her, one of your friends says, 'I'd bend that over and nail her in a heartbeat.'" The college students reported themselves to be significantly more uncomfortable with such language than they believed other men would be. The researchers got the same result when they tested the men in a room with several friends and asked them to compare their level of comfort with that of their friends (rather than men in general). The researchers concluded, "Men who are familiar with one another are no more accurate at predicting their peers' attitudes than men who are relative strangers."

Understanding Common Misperceptions

Why do we so consistently misinterpret other people's thoughts and feelings? One reason is that certain types of behavior are more visible than others. Our attention is more likely to be drawn to students who are laughing as the bully taunts a victim than to the many others who are watching in silence, quietly horrified by this behavior.

Jonathon Halbesleben conducted a study to examine whether seeing someone respond approvingly to offensive behavior—such as laughing at a sexist joke—would lead a person to believe that other nonresponders were more comfortable with that behavior than they themselves were.[15] College students were asked to read a series of sexist jokes. They were then asked (1) how comfortable they were with the joke and how funny they found it; and (2) how comfortable they thought their peers would be with the joke and how funny they were likely to find it.

As Halbesleben predicted, students consistently believed that others were more comfortable with the jokes than they themselves were and that the others would find the jokes funnier than they themselves did. But students who were asked to rate the jokes in a room with other people, where they could hear scattered laughter, showed an even greater self–other gap. As obvious as it is, it bears mentioning that action is more visible than inaction. Laughter registers more than silence.

We tend to believe that other people's behavior reflects their true thoughts and feelings, even when we are aware that our own behavior does not. Thus, if other people aren't acting as if there is an emergency, we imagine they must really think there isn't an emergency.

You've undoubtedly heard the tale of the emperor's new clothes. In this story, two weavers promise the emperor a handsome new outfit that will be invisible to stupid people. When the emperor parades through town in his "outfit," all the townspeople see that he is naked, but no one wants to be the first to point it out and confirm their stupidity. It takes a young boy, who is unconcerned with his image, to yell out, "The emperor has no clothes!"

This story perfectly illustrates the idea that even when people recognize that their own actions and words don't match their thoughts, they believe that other people's do. Think of a time when you heard a lecture in school or a presentation at work, and the professor or presenter asked, "Are there any questions?" Perhaps you did have a question—maybe even many questions—but chose not to raise your hand. Perhaps, as you scanned the room, you noticed few—if any—hands were raised. If I were to ask you why you didn't raise your hand, you would probably say you didn't want to look stupid in front of your peers. But if I were then to ask you why others had chosen not to raise their hands, there is a good chance you would have a very different answer: that they understood the material and didn't have any questions. This is a classic illustration of pluralistic ignorance in action. People don't raise their own hand because they are embarrassed; but they think others aren't raising their hands because they don't have questions.

Dale Miller at Princeton University and Cathy McFarland at Simon Fraser University conducted a study to examine this issue.[16] They asked participants to read an article in groups of three to eight, to prepare for a discussion. The article was deliberately written in a confusing manner and was virtually incomprehensible. Students were told to come to the experimenter's office to ask questions if they had any trouble understanding the paper. After finishing the article, they completed a questionnaire in which they were asked how well they understood the paper, and how well they thought the other students understood it. Not a single participant in the study asked the experimenter a question, and they thought that the other students understood the paper better than they did. The researchers concluded that participants believed their own behavior was motivated by fear of embarrassment, but that they believed the other students' behavior reflected their greater understanding of the article.

This misperception of the factors that drive our behavior and others'—even when that behavior is identical—can be seen in a variety of settings. We may think that our reluctance to express interest in a potential romantic partner is driven by fear of rejection, while seeing our would-be partner's reluctance as indicating a lack of interest.[17] Similarly, both white and black people report that they want to have more contact with members of other racial groups, but they believe others are not interested.[18] Once again, members of each group explain their own inaction as caused by fear of rejection, but see others' inaction as caused by a lack of interest. (In Chapter 5, we'll see how pluralistic ignorance is especially common when we want to fit in with a valued social group.)

The discovery that social awkwardness and fear of rejection sometimes impede our ability to act helps explain why our willingness to

respond to an emergency is increased when our inhibitions are reduced. Later we will see that people who are less concerned about
fitting in with the crowd are more likely to intervene, and we will
look at what we can do to nurture that tendency—but for now it is
enough to consider what impact social awkwardness might have on
our actions.

Researchers in the Netherlands designed a study to test whether
people who had lower social inhibition as a result of drinking alcohol would be quicker to offer help.[19] They invited people who
were drinking at a bar in Amsterdam to participate in a brief study.
After asking the participants to join them at the end of the bar, one
of the researchers dropped some items on the floor. They then measured how long it took before the person helped the researcher pick
up the items, either when they were alone with the researcher or
when they were in the presence of two other accomplices.

People who were relatively sober took longer to help in the presence of bystanders than when they were alone, as we would expect.
But those who had consumed a fair amount of alcohol, it turned out,
helped more quickly when they were in a group than when they were
alone. The researchers posit that the alcohol helped reduce their inhibitions and dampened any possible apprehension about the potential social risks of helping in front of others.

The Neuroscience of Acting in a Crowd

Explanations of the bystander effect have usually focused on the cognitive processes that lead people to hesitate when an emergency
occurs in a group setting. Perhaps we don't help because we don't
feel responsible, or because we don't want to look stupid if it turns
out not to be an emergency, or because we think others don't see
the situation as an emergency. All of these explanations involve
people's thoughts and feelings, and their interpretation of the nature
of the situation.

But some researchers have proposed that when a person observes someone in distress, it should prompt an automatic desire to help that person. According to the "perception-action model" developed by Stephanie Preston and Frans de Waal, seeing someone in need of help activates parts of the brain that are responsible for action.[20] Some research supports this theory: in response to emotional scenes that cause distress, people do show activation in parts of the brain (such as the motor cortex) that prepare for action.[21] Could it be that when we witness an emergency, the mere presence of other people around us reduces this type of automatic neural response?

To examine this question, Beatrice de Gelder, director of the Cognitive and Affective Neuroscience Laboratory at Tilburg University in the Netherlands, examined how the number of people present during an emergency influences patterns of brain activity. In one study, she and her colleagues showed people videos depicting a real-world example of an emergency and measured their brain activity with an fMRI machine.[22] In everyday life, we are usually busy with something else when a crisis occurs. So the researchers told the participants that their task while in the machine was to look at three dots and signal whether they were the same or different colors. Then in the background they showed a video, which they did not mention to the participants. The video showed a woman falling to the floor. In some cases, no one else was present. In others, one, two, or four people walked by the woman after she had fallen.

The study revealed two key findings. First, the larger the number of people shown observing the emergency, the greater the increase in activity of the parts of the brain that process visual perception and attention (the superior occipital gyrus, lingual gyrus, cuneus, middle temporal gyrus), indicating that the participants were paying close attention to what these observers were doing. This was presumably because the actions or reactions of others helped them interpret the situation: Did the woman faint, or did she just slip? Is she really hurt?

But at the same time, as the number of observers increased, the parts of the brain that are in charge of preparing us to take action—the motor and somatosensory cortices—became less active.

The presence of a group, then, seems to undermine—at a neural level—our spontaneous inclination to help a person in need. When we are alone, our brain automatically prepares us to intervene. The calculus in this case is easy: someone needs help, and it's up to us to provide it. But when others are present, our brain instead focuses on what these other people are doing, and interpreting their actions takes time. This may explain why we are slower to provide help (and less likely to do so) when other people are around.

Strength in Numbers

So far, we have looked at how ambiguous situations inhibit people from intervening in the face of bad behavior of all kinds. But I want to end by describing how, at least in some cases, we are able to act even when we aren't sure exactly what's going on.

Psychologists have consistently found that people are more likely to stand up to bad behavior—and risk the costs of doing so—if they don't have to stand alone. As Jean Lipman-Blumen writes in *The Allure of Toxic Leaders,* "Bonding with others in the same situation can create trust, strength, and collaborative practices that will serve you well as an organized group of resisters."[23] In other words, find a friend.

Although those who overhear an ambiguous situation—such as a woman falling and crying out in pain—are less likely to help when they are with another person than when they are alone, pairs of friends have been found to help significantly faster than pairs of strangers.[24] Perhaps friends are less inhibited from acting because their fear of embarrassment is lower. Friends may also be more willing to talk about the situation and thus be less likely to misinterpret the thoughts and feelings of their co-witness.

This helps explain a recent event that had a very different outcome from that of the tragic story of Jamie Bulger that started this chapter.

On March 12, 2003, Alvin and Anita Dickerson were running errands in Sandy, Utah, when they spotted a man walking down the street with two women. Something about the man's face seemed familiar to Alvin, and he mentioned to his wife that the man looked like the street preacher suspected in the disappearance of Elizabeth Smart, a teenager who had been kidnapped from her home nearly a year earlier. The couple decided to call the police to report what they had seen. They waited for the police to arrive, and then returned home. Later that day, they received a call alerting them to the fact that their action had helped lead to Elizabeth's rescue.

The Dickersons didn't see their action as heroic or even particularly unusual. As Anita Dickerson put it at a news conference, "I'm just glad we did make the call, so she can be reunited with her family."[25]

Although the specific factors that led the Dickersons to choose to call the police aren't clear, one factor may well be that they were together and could discuss how to interpret what they had seen. As a married couple, they were less likely to worry about feeling stupid for sharing their thoughts. This opportunity to openly express what we see with someone we trust may go a long way toward helping us make sense of ambiguous situations.

What else can help? Having another person deliberately remove any ambiguity and offer clear instructions for what to do.

Shortly after the 9/11 terrorist attacks, when concerns about additional airplane hijackings were very real, a United Airlines pilot is said to have delivered an unusual announcement to his passengers.[26] Once the plane had pulled away from the gate, he came on the loudspeaker and gave them the following instructions:

First, I want to thank you for being brave enough to fly today. The doors are now closed and we have no help from the outside for any problems that might occur inside this plane. As you could tell when you checked in, the government has made some changes to increase security in the airports. They have not, however, made any rules about what happens after those doors close. Until they do that, we have made our own rules and I want to share them with you.

Once those doors close, we only have each other. The security has taken care of a threat like guns with all of the increased scanning, etc. Then we have the supposed bomb. If you have a bomb, there is no need to tell me about it, or anyone else on this plane; you are already in control. So, for this flight, there are no bombs that exist on this plane.

Now, the threats that are left are things like plastics, wood, knives, and other weapons that can be made or things like that which can be used as weapons.

Here is our plan and our rules. If someone or several people stand up and say they are hijacking this plane, I want you all to stand up together. Then take whatever you have available to you and throw it at them. Throw it at their faces and heads so they will have to raise their hands to protect themselves.

The very best protection you have against knives are the pillows and blankets. Whoever is close to these people should then try to get a blanket over their head—then they won't be able to see.

Once that is done, get them down and keep them there. Do not let them up. I will then land the plane at the closest place and we *will* take care of them. After all, there are usually only a few of them and we are 200+ strong! We will not allow them to take over this plane.

I have no idea whether this pilot had ever taken a class in social psychology, but his message perfectly conveyed what we know helps people step up in an emergency. He told passengers it was their responsibility to act if a hijacking occurred, he told them exactly what they should do, and he created a sense of shared identity. And although the passengers on this flight did not face an emergency, the pilot's announcement certainly would have helped had someone been foolish enough to try to hijack his plane.

Unfortunately, in most real-world situations, we have no such guidance to help us make sense of what's going on and guide our response. Instead, we're on our own to weigh the costs of action versus inaction.

4

The Considerable Costs of Helping

On May 26, 2017, Rick Best, a technician for the City of Portland, Oregon, was heading home on a commuter train when a man began shouting racist and anti-Muslim slurs at two teenage girls—one black and one wearing a hijab. Rick and two other men confronted the attacker, who pulled out a knife and stabbed all three, killing Rick and one of the other men.

We've seen how psychological factors make it hard for us to figure out whether an emergency is occurring and muddy our sense of responsibility. Even in an obvious emergency, it can be hard to intervene if we think that acting to stop bad behavior may pose a significant or even life-threatening risk to us. We also fear the less tangible costs of calling out bad behavior, such as impeding career advancement or creating social awkwardness. Unfortunately, this fear and anxiety can lead to substantial consequences. We see this when someone chooses to laugh at a sexist joke or to observe bullying without intervening.

This chapter looks at how these inhibitions prevent most of us from standing up to bad behavior, and considers the rational calculations we make about the relative costs and rewards of acting before we decide to do something.

Weighing the Costs of Helping

Imagine that you are in a hurry to get to an important appointment when you happen to notice someone in need of help. Do you stop, even if doing so will likely make you late?

One of the earliest studies to test our willingness to help in an emergency set up precisely this situation. John Darley and Daniel Batson asked students at Princeton Theological Seminary—all aspiring ministers—to prepare a short talk on the parable of the Good Samaritan (Luke 10:25–37).[1] This parable describes a person who helps a wounded man lying on the side of the road and illustrates the moral value of aiding strangers who are in need.

After giving each student a few minutes to prepare, the researcher returned, told him that he would be walking over to a neighboring building to give his talk, and delivered one of three messages:

- In the "low hurry" condition, the student was told that the professor would be ready in a few minutes, but he might as well go ahead and start walking over to the next building.
- In the "intermediate hurry" condition, the student was told that the professor was ready for him to deliver the speech, so he should head over right now.
- In the "high hurry" condition, the student was told that the professor was waiting and he should hurry over, since he was already late.

As each student walked to the building where he would give his speech, he passed a man who was slumped in a doorway with his head down and his eyes closed, coughing and groaning. (This was actually an accomplice working with the experimenter.) Now we come to the key part of the study: Who will stop and help?

Remember, all of the participants in this study were theology students. They had also just prepared a speech on the importance of helping others. Yet the major factor that predicted who stopped and helped was how much of a hurry they were in. Nearly two-thirds—63 percent—of those in the "low hurry" condition stopped and helped, as did nearly half—45 percent—of those in the "intermediate hurry" group. But of those in the "high hurry" group, only 10 percent did.

Although these findings may seem surprising—shouldn't aspiring ministers help regardless of time pressure?—they are exactly what social psychologists' models predict. According to the "arousal/cost-reward" model, people experience unpleasant physiological arousal when they see other people who are experiencing pain and suffering.[2] In other words, we feel bad when we see someone in need—say, a homeless person asking for money for food, or a person standing by a car with a flat tire. We want these bad feelings to go away, and the way to accomplish that is to help the person.

Helping definitely does have benefits—it makes us feel good about ourselves, and we may be recognized by others for our virtue. But in many cases, it also has costs—in lost time, embarrassment, personal safety. So before deciding to act, we conduct a subconscious cost-benefit analysis. If the benefits outweigh the costs, we help. But if the costs outweigh the benefits, we don't.

The result is that sometimes the people who are most in need of help are the least likely to receive it. We see this in situations of extreme conflict, such as the Rwandan genocide of the 1990s and mass shootings, when people may want to help but are uncertain about how best to do so, and when the costs of even attempting aid may be substantial. During the shooting at Marjorie Stoneman Douglas High School in Parkland, Florida, in February 2018, the armed school resource officer heard shots but did not enter the building and apparently retreated while the massacre was going on. His inaction makes sense according to the arousal/cost-reward model. The potential cost of trying to stop a shooter with an assault rifle is very high, while the benefits are uncertain.

Researchers at the University of Wisconsin–Madison conducted a clever study on a subway car in Philadelphia to directly test whether people are indeed less likely to provide help to someone in need if the potential costs are high.[3] An accomplice of the experimenter walked to the end of the car using a cane and then fell down. In some cases he lay still on the floor; in others, he lay still and appeared to start bleeding from the mouth. (In reality he just bit into a red dye packet to simulate blood.) Another accomplice then timed how long it took for someone to help him.

Can you predict what happened? Blood is clearly a sign of a serious problem: everyone would agree that a person who is bleeding is in more need of help than someone who is not. The presence of blood means that bystanders don't have to wonder whether this is an emergency, as they do in more ambiguous situations, so they shouldn't fear social awkwardness for overreacting. But blood also imposes greater costs on helpers—at a minimum, requiring a greater investment of time; more seriously, risking infection with hepatitis, HIV, or another serious disease.

Just as the researchers anticipated, people were significantly less likely to help when the man was bleeding, and if they did help, took longer to do so.

We all like to think of ourselves as moral and good people who would help someone in need. The message that we should do so is a mainstay of most faiths. But highly religious people are no more likely to intervene in the face of bad behavior (and in some cases, religiosity may even encourage bystander inaction, as I'll describe later on). Circumstantial factors play a far more important role in determining our actions than we may like to acknowledge.

People's calculations about the costs and benefits of helping are affected by many other factors besides the severity of the emergency. Data on bystanders' willingness to use cardiopulmonary resuscitation (CPR) has suggested that geographical location may have an influence. The American Heart Association has a program to train people in CPR, a procedure that can be performed by a bystander when a person collapses from a heart attack. Quick action is extremely important in the case of cardiac arrest. But data gathered by the association reveals that bystanders provide CPR in only about 40 percent of cases, and that rates vary considerably by neighborhood. One 2010 study of over fourteen thousand people who experienced cardiac arrest in twenty-nine different cities found that CPR was delivered twice as often in wealthier, predominantly white neighborhoods as in low-income, predominantly black neighborhoods.[4] Another study found lower rates of bystander CPR in low-income neighborhoods (where cardiac arrest is actually more frequent), regardless of race.[5]

Although the CPR data suggest that people in affluent neighborhoods are more likely to give help, it could be because more of them have training in CPR. To test the possible effect of training, Erin Cornwell and Alex Currit at Cornell University examined all types of bystander help in over twenty-two thousand medical emergencies in different neighborhoods across America.[6] Many of the helping activities—offering water, covering someone with a blanket, providing a cold compress—required no special skill. The researchers noted each neighborhood's socioeconomic status (based on median household income, education level, and rate of poverty) and density (based on number of people living in a square mile). They also noted whether the person in need of help was white or black (there were too few victims of other ethnicities in the data set to measure).

Cornwell and Currit found that both neighborhood and race affected helping behavior. People living in high-density areas were less likely to get help than those living in less crowded environments, once again suggesting that the presence of more people in an emergency is not necessarily good news for the victim. But neighborhood affluence had an even greater effect than density: people living in poor areas were significantly less likely to get help. And black victims fared worse than white victims in all neighborhoods, suggesting bias, whether explicit or implicit, also plays a role.

The neighborhood effect could be related to levels of mistrust. Sociologists have found that in neighborhoods with few resources and high levels of disorder and crime, people tend to develop a general sense of mistrust and to believe that others are more likely to hurt than to help them.[7] Greater mistrust means that the cost of helping seems higher, and so bystanders are less willing to step up and act in an emergency.

In line with this study are data showing that people living in rural areas are more likely to offer help of all kinds—giving change for a dollar, picking up a dropped item, providing directions—than those living in urban areas.[8] Although many factors may contribute to this difference, including the difficulty of noticing a person in need in a crowded urban environment, and the relative lack of anonymity and greater social cohesion in a rural environment, it's plausible that the cost-benefit analysis is also a factor.

The Social Costs of Speaking Up

For several years, I regularly had lunch with a male colleague. We shared many interests—we liked the same novels and had similar political views and teaching philosophies—and I enjoyed his company. But on a few occasions, he made comments that felt somewhat inappropriate. Once he noted that I'd lost weight and said I "looked really good." On another occasion he suggested that if I was ever lonely on a business trip, I should let him know and he'd come with me. These comments consistently made me uncomfortable, but I never mustered the courage to tell him to cut it out.

At the time, I was a tenured professor, and he had no power over my career trajectory. And yet I said nothing. I laughed off these and other comments, and just stopped having lunch with him. I didn't want to make things awkward between us, or have him accuse me of overreacting. It was just easier for me to say nothing.

That's what most of us do when we find ourselves in a situation that makes us feel uncomfortable. We fear the interpersonal cost of calling out bad behavior, and most often we do nothing. This fear can be amplified when we are a witness of, rather than the victim of, bad behavior, since in this case we are also worried about the reactions of the other people around us.

Think about a time when you've heard an offensive remark, a gratuitously derogatory put-down, or a racist or sexist slur. How did you respond? Did you say something and risk appearing overly sensitive or creating social awkwardness? Or did you keep your thoughts to yourself? Even when we know we should say something, it's a lot easier not to.

In the late 1990s, when reality TV shows were first being introduced to an eager public, researchers at Pennsylvania State University recruited women to participate in a study that involved selecting the twelve people—from a list of thirty—who they thought would be most likely to survive on a desert island.[9] Unbeknownst to the participants, the researchers were not actually interested in understanding how people made their selections—they were using this set-up to test how women would respond to sexist remarks. The researchers recruited several men (whom the women believed to be other participants in the study) and instructed them to make sexist remarks, including "Yeah, we definitely need to keep the women in shape," and "One of the women can cook." At the end of the study, participants were asked for their impressions of the other group members. Most of the women—91 percent—reported having negative thoughts about the man who had made the sexist remark. But only 16 percent of the women directly responded at the time, saying something along the lines of "Oh my God. I can't believe you said that!"

The women probably did not call out the offensive remarks because they didn't want the men to see them as overly assertive or politically correct. And they weren't wrong: one study found that men like women less when they call out sexist remarks than when they stay silent.[10] So in practice, even if we want to confront offensive behavior, we may say nothing out of the (realistic) fear of triggering negative repercussions.

Confronting someone who uses offensive language or engages in derogatory behavior takes cognitive and emotional energy. Even in more egregious cases, most people tend to stay silent. Researchers in one study brought students into the lab to work with two other students, one white and one black, both of whom were accomplices of the experimenter.[11] They then exposed the students (none of whom were black) to either a moderate or an extreme racial slur. In the moderate slur condition, the black man accidentally bumped the white man's knee as he left the room. After he had left, the white man said, "Typical, I hate it when black people do that." In the extreme slur condition, the white man said, "clumsy 'N-word.'" In a third, control, condition, the white man said nothing.

Next, after the black man returned to the room, the experimenter asked the student to choose which person they wanted to work with: the black person or the white person. In the control condition, 53 percent chose the white person, but in both of the conditions in which a racist slur was said, 63 percent chose the white person as their partner. This finding, that people were somewhat *more* likely to choose the white person as their partner after he had made an offensive remark, was unexpected and seems counterintuitive. Why would participants be more interested in working with someone who appeared to be racist?

The researchers did a companion study to explore not how people respond to actual incidents of racism, but how they *think* they will respond to them. They asked participants to predict how they would react to a situation like the one just described, after reading about it or seeing a video reenacting the situation. When forecasting what they would do, only 25 percent of those who read about the incident, and 17 percent of those who saw the video, stated that they would choose to work with the white person who had used the racial slur. The level of emotional distress they predicted they would experience was also greater than that reported by the people who experienced the actual scenario.

This discrepancy tells us that although people imagine they will be very upset if confronted with a racist comment, when it actually happens, they probably won't be. It appears that people may harbor more unconscious racism than they are willing to admit. Why else would so many of the participants in this study want to work with the person who had insulted the black man? The researchers concluded that those who witnessed the racist behavior may have justified it to themselves by recasting the comment as just a joke, which meant they did not have to diminish their assessment of the person responsible.

"People do not think of themselves as prejudiced," concluded Kerry Kawakami, the lead author of this study. "They predict that they would be very upset by a racist act and would take action. However, we found that their responses are much more muted than they expect when they are actually faced with an overtly racist comment."[12]

These findings point to the fact that time and time again, we think that we will do the right thing—speak up when an interviewer asks inappropriate questions, call someone out for using a racist slur, and so on—but when push comes to shove, our actual behavior is considerably less impressive.

What many of us fail to appreciate is that our natural reluctance to speak out actually perpetuates the bad behavior. Silence conveys a lack of concern, or tacit acquiescence, making it far more likely that it will continue.

Social Rejection Feels Bad in the Brain

The desire to avoid calling out bad behavior when doing so would impose social costs appears to reflect a fundamental human desire to prevent pain of all types. Neuroscientists have recently found that the brain responds in precisely the same way to social pain—breaking up with someone or being socially rejected—as it does to physical pain—twisting an ankle, slicing a finger.[13]

In one of the first studies to demonstrate the neurological similarity between social and physical pain, Naomi Eisenberger and Matthew Lieberman at UCLA and Kipling Williams at Macquarie University in Australia set up an interactive virtual ball-tossing game called Cyberball.[14] Participants completed the game while in an fMRI scanner, and they were told that their two adversaries were also playing from scanners. (Unbeknownst to them, the game was actually a preset computer program.) In the first round of the game, the participant and two other (computer) players tossed and received the ball equally. In the second round, the two others initially included the participant—for seven throws—but then they exclusively threw the ball back and forth to each other for the remainder of the game, which came to about forty-five throws. Questionnaire data collected at the end of the study revealed, not surprisingly, that participants felt excluded and ignored.

The researchers then examined activity patterns in the brain to see how social ostracism was being processed. When participants were excluded from the ball-throwing task, two parts of the brain—the dorsal anterior cingulate cortex (dACC) and the anterior insula—showed increased activity. This pattern is very similar to what is seen in studies of people who are experiencing physical pain. The dACC is thought to operate as an alarm system for the brain, basically indicating "something is wrong here." The anterior insula is involved in regulating pain and negative emotion.

To further explore the neurological link between feelings of social exclusion and physical pain, researchers asked participants to report how acutely they experienced social pain—feeling invisible and rejected—during the Cyberball game. Those who reported feeling more excluded and uncomfortable showed greater activity in precisely those parts of the brain that process physical pain. Although this groundbreaking study was the first to demonstrate that experiencing social exclusion activates the same parts of the brain that respond to physical pain, subsequent studies have supported and extended these results, as we'll see in Chapter 9.

If social pain is really experienced in the same way as physical pain, then you might think that medication used to reduce headaches and muscle aches would also reduce social pain. To test this hypothesis, Nathan DeWall and his colleagues asked sixty-two undergraduates to keep a daily record for three weeks of how much they experienced having their feelings hurt.[15] All participants were given a pill to take each day. Half received acetaminophen, the active ingredient in Tylenol or paracetamol, and the other half a placebo. (People didn't know which pill they had been given or what the pills were.) Over the course of the three weeks, those who were given the acetaminophen showed decreasing levels of hurt feelings, suggesting that a simple over-the-counter drug that reduces physical pain can also reduce social pain. (Before you start encouraging a socially anxious teen to start popping acetaminophen on a daily basis, it is worth remembering that it can have serious side effects.)

A more recent study demonstrated that this popular pain reliever also decreases our ability to feel other people's pain.[16] Psychologists at Ohio State University and the National Institutes of Health gave college students one of two drinks: one contained 1,000 mg of acetaminophen, the other a placebo solution. An hour later, after the drug had taken effect, the students read eight stories about someone experiencing social or physical pain. In one story, a person's father died; in another, someone suffered a severe knife cut. The students rated how much the person in each story felt hurt, wounded, or in pain. Students who had taken the painkiller consistently rated the protagonist's pain and suffering as less severe than did those who had taken the placebo.

In a second study, the researchers again gave one group of students acetaminophen and the other a placebo. They then asked them to imagine other students experiencing two different types of pain: one physical—receiving a loud blast of white noise—and one social—being excluded in an online game. Once again, ratings of others' pain were lower among students who had received the painkiller.

"These findings suggest other people's pain doesn't seem as big of a deal to you when you've taken acetaminophen," concluded Dominik Mischkowski, the lead author on this study. "If you are having an argument with your spouse and you just took acetaminophen, this research suggests you might be less understanding of what you did to hurt your spouse's feelings."[17]

So it seems that common painkillers have psychosocial side effects, interrupting our capacity to empathically connect with other people's painful experiences. Quite literally, acetaminophen reduces your ability to feel another person's pain.

We know that the possible social consequences of calling out bad behavior—rejection or ridicule—feel really bad. What these studies tell us is that people can't ignore social pain—or even fear of social pain—any more than they can ignore the pain of a twisted ankle or severe headache. As we'll see in Chapter 5, this pain is even harder to ignore when we are ostracized as a result of calling out bad behavior committed not by random strangers, but by members of our own social groups—classmates, teammates, colleagues, or members of our own religious community or political party.

Overcoming the Costs

The arousal/cost-reward model describes a rational calculation that most people use when determining whether to act. This decision-making process leads us to inaction if we come to the conclusion, consciously or subconsciously, that the risks of acting are too high. But sometimes people intervene even when the costs are high. What is different about these people?

Ted Huston and his colleagues at Penn State interviewed thirty-two people who had intervened in a dangerous situation—a mugging, robbery, or bank holdup—and compared them with those who hadn't intervened.[18] They found that those who stepped up were far more likely to have been trained in some type of life-saving skill, such as first aid. In fact, 63 percent of those who intervened had received life-saving training. They weren't different in personality—but they were equipped with different skills.

Even relatively low-level training can give people the courage to act in an emergency. In May 2013, Ingrid Loyau-Kennett jumped off a London bus to help a man who lay bleeding in the street, then stayed and engaged the two men who had murdered him in conversation for ten minutes until the police arrived.[19] She attributed her actions to the training in first aid that she had received as a Cub Scout leader. In March 2017, Stewart Graham performed CPR on a man who had collapsed and fallen off his exercise bike while working out near him at a YMCA in Maine.[20] Graham credited a CPR course he had taken three years earlier with his ability to act quickly and ultimately save this man's life.

These examples point to the role of training in increasing people's willingness to do something when they are faced with true life-or-death emergencies. But training can also give people the skills necessary to step up in more mundane daily life situations, from high school students telling a bully to stop, to fraternity brothers resisting pressure to haze pledges, to hedge fund managers punishing traders who engage in insider trading. What does this training involve? I'll describe some specific approaches that have been found to be effective in later chapters. But first let's look at what happens when people feel pressure to conform.

5

The Power of Social Groups

On February 4, 2017, nineteen-year-old Timothy Piazza, a sophomore at Penn State University, was given eighteen drinks in eighty-two minutes as part of a hazing ritual at his fraternity. At around 11 P.M., he fell head-first down a flight of stairs. Timothy was unconscious and had signs of severe injury, including a large bruise on his abdomen, and many members of the fraternity were aware that he was in very bad shape. But it was not until more than twelve hours after his fall that someone called 911. When Timothy finally reached the hospital, he was found to have a lacerated spleen, severe abdominal bleeding, and brain injuries. He died the next day.

Timothy Piazza's death is a tragedy. But it is not unusual. Virtually every year a college student dies as a result of a fraternity initiation. Fraternity hazing is carried out by normal young men who are good members of their college communities. In fact, Timothy decided to join that particular fraternity because so many of its members were serious students—engineering and biology majors. The fraternity was also involved in community service activities. Fraternities are not full of callous psychopaths. Yet in case after case of deaths caused by hazing, the story is the same: multiple young men are aware that someone is in serious trouble and in need of medical attention—and do nothing.

Chapter 4 examined the costs of calling out bad behavior. The social costs of speaking out can be even greater when this behavior is committed by members of our own social group. These social costs are what inhibit most of us from speaking out against members of our community, from fraternity brothers who are hazing freshmen recruits to colleagues who are laughing at an offensive remark. The cost is so high that we will even ignore a member in need in order to protect the others. Why is it so hard to challenge members of our community? Recent research in neuroscience has shown that our tendency to conform to the norms of our social group is hardwired into our brains. For virtually all of us, it is far more comfortable to fit in than to stand out.

The Social Pressure to Conform

In the 1950s, Solomon Asch, a pioneering psychologist who is best known for his studies demonstrating the effects of social pressure on conformity, recruited people to participate in what they were told was a study on "visual discrimination."[1] The design of the experiment, which has since become famous, was simple: Participants were asked to look at a target line, and then at three other lines, and to determine which of the three comparison lines was the same length as the target line. This is an easy task, and when people do it on their own, they make virtually no errors.

Asch was interested in determining whether people would give what they knew to be a wrong answer in order to fit in with the group. He recruited male college students to do this task in groups of eight, but in reality, only one person wasn't in on the game. The others were all accomplices. Each person gave his answer out loud, with the participant coming last.

In most of the line judgment trials, everyone gave the correct answer. But in a few cases, the accomplices had been told to all give the same wrong answer. Imagine the situation: the first person identifies what is clearly a wrong answer, and you almost laugh because it is so obvious that it is wrong. But then the next person gives the same answer, and so does the next. At this point, what do you think? More importantly, what do you do?

Over one-third (37 percent) of the time, the test subjects gave the wrong answer in order to conform with the rest of the group. Half of them gave the wrong answer at least half the time.

What's remarkable about these findings is that the participants had no particular need to fit in with the other people. They weren't friends, or fraternity brothers, or colleagues. Yet still, even in this group of strangers, college students gave answers that they knew to be wrong in order to conform. Asch himself was disturbed by the results. "That we have found the tendency to conformity in our society so strong that reasonably intelligent and well-meaning young people are willing to call white black," he wrote, "is a matter of concern."

Although Asch's study and the many efforts to replicate it provide strong evidence that people will sometimes give what they know to be a wrong answer simply to fit in with a group, this experimental paradigm is admittedly artificial, and the consequences of giving a wrong answer are minor. Most people aren't going to be particularly bothered if the experimenter thinks they aren't very good at judging line lengths.

Are we less likely to conform if the stakes are higher? Or if the thing that we are being asked to evaluate is more important to us and closer to our sense of self? The answer, briefly, is no. Subsequent studies have shown that our social group influences all types of attitudes and behaviors, from the songs we like to the foods we eat.

Sociologists at Columbia University were interested in looking at how social norms influence teenagers' taste in music.[2] Over fourteen thousand teenagers were recruited from internet sites and asked to participate in a study of music preferences. Half of them were asked to listen to obscure rock songs and download the ones they liked. They received no information about the songs, which were taken from a website where unknown bands post their own music. The other half were asked to listen to these same obscure songs, but they were also shown how many times the song had been downloaded by others (a measure of its popularity). Knowing that many people had downloaded a particular song significantly increased participants' likelihood of downloading that song themselves, clearly indicating that the teenagers had relied on others' ratings when deciding which songs to download.

So we care what other people think. But we don't value all opinions equally. As countless studies have shown over the years, we are particularly influenced by the opinions of those in our in-group. Suzanne Higgs from the University of Birmingham and Eric Robinson from the University of Liverpool found that college women who learn that other college women dislike orange juice will later report liking orange juice less themselves.[3] The knowledge that college men dislike orange juice had no impact on their ratings, however. We care about fitting in with people in our group—other college women, in this case—and are willing to shift our own views to conform.

The pressure to conform can be very powerful; people who deviate from the norm often experience negative consequences such as embarrassment, awkwardness, or hostile behavior from others.[4] Even watching someone else experience rejection—which presumably reminds us of how unpleasant it feels—can lead to greater conformity.

In a powerful demonstration of how fear of rejection can drive conformity, researchers randomly assigned college students to watch one of three humorous videos.[5] In the first video ("other-ridicule"), one person made fun of another person's appearance, saying, "His acne was so bad as a teenager we used to call him 'pizza face.'" The second video ("self-ridicule") showed a person making fun of themselves, saying "My acne was so bad as a teenager they used to call me 'pizza face.'" The third video (the control condition) featured a comedian making jokes that weren't directed at anyone.

All participants were then shown some cartoons and asked to rate how funny each one was. The cartoons had previously been rated by other students as either very funny or not funny at all. Right before they rated the cartoons, participants were told how their peers had supposedly rated them—but they were told the opposite of the actual ratings. What would their own ratings show?

Those who had watched the other-ridicule video conformed much more to their peers' supposed ratings than did those who had watched the self-ridicule and control videos: they rated the unfunny cartoon as funny, and vice versa. So we see that anything that reminds us of being ridiculed—a form of social rejection—increases our tendency to conform. The study also provides some insight into how bullies, through their taunts and jibes, are able to elicit greater conformity.

We are actively motivated both to learn and to adhere to the norms of our group, and we tend to fear the consequences of calling out bad behavior, especially when it is perpetrated by members of our own social group. This inhibits us from speaking up in all kinds of situations—when a fellow student circulates a list rating female students' bodies, when a relative uses a homophobic slur at the Thanksgiving dinner table, or when a colleague makes an offensive comment during a meeting. It also helps explain how members of religious and political groups come to tolerate behavior that many of those outside the group would find intolerable.

Why Conforming Feels So Good

Neuroscientists have found compelling evidence that underlying neurological factors drive our tendency to follow the crowd. A study by researchers at University College London analyzed brain activity when subjects believed their own music preferences were—or were not—in line with those of experts. The researchers asked participants to list twenty songs they liked but did not own.[6] They then placed each person in an fMRI machine and played one song from their list and one obscure song that they had not listed. They were asked to pick which of the two songs they preferred, and then they were told which of the songs two supposed "music experts" had rated higher.

The results provide strong evidence that being told that others share our views—especially when these people are said to be knowledgeable—feels good. Study participants who learned that one of the music reviewers shared their preferences for a particular song showed greater activation in the ventral striatum, a part of the brain that processes rewarding experiences, than when an expert preferred a different song. (This is the same part of the brain that is activated when we win money or eat chocolate.) Activation was even stronger when both experts agreed with their song preference. This study was one of the first to reveal that neural mechanisms play an essential role in creating social conformity.

Another study revealed that the brain also responds in distinct ways when our opinions are validated by those of our peers. Anna Shestakova and her colleagues at Saint Petersburg State University in Russia asked women to rate the attractiveness of over two hundred women based on photographs of their faces.[7] After reporting their own rating, the participants were told the average ratings supposedly given by other women. In some of the trials, participants were told that their ratings were very similar to those of others, and in others they were told that their ratings were very different. The researchers assessed the participants' response to learning that others did or did not share their ratings by using electroencephalography to measure event-related potentials (ERPs)—small voltages generated by the brain in response to different stimuli. The participants were then given a chance to re-rate the images, again while their brain activation patterns were measured.

As predicted, when the participants believed that others disagreed with their ratings, they changed their ratings to be more in line with those of the group. What was more surprising and revealing, however, was their neural response. When women were told that their ratings conflicted with those of others, their ERPs were significantly more negative than when they learned that their ratings were in line with those of others. When their views conflicted with those of the group, a neural response was triggered that indicated an error had occurred that needed correction.

Research using fMRI data—which examines the activation of different parts of the brain, not just electrical activity at the surface—has revealed comparable findings. In a study using a similar procedure to the one just described, researchers asked women to rate other women's facial attractiveness and then showed them how others had rated these same women.[8] The fMRI data showed that when the participants discovered that their ratings differed from those of others, the rostral cingulate zone and the ventral striatum were activated. These parts of the brain process outcomes of behavior, social learning, and rewards. The patterns of neural activation found in this study were similar to those seen when someone makes a mistake while learning. This pattern of brain activity is basically the brain's way of saying, "You've made a mistake; please correct it."

When participants in this study recognized that their assessments were not shared by others, they tended to adjust their ratings to bring them in line with those of the group. The larger the neural signal indicating an "error," the larger the shift in ratings. As Vasily Klucharev, the lead author on this study, notes, these findings show that our brain "signals what is probably the most fundamental social mistake—that of being too different from others."[9] This helps explain why we conform: conforming feels good, and deviating from the group decidedly does not.

Peer Pressure Is Real, Especially for Teens

You probably won't be surprised to hear that the drive to conform is especially strong among teens. But why is it so strong then? One obvious explanation is that the prefrontal cortex, the part of the brain responsible for impulse control and judgment, is not fully developed until we are in our early twenties.[10] The lack of maturity of the prefrontal cortex is one reason why teenagers are more likely to make impulsive decisions and engage in risky behavior. It also appears to make them particularly prone to adopting the behavior of their peers, without thoughtfully evaluating the consequences of their choices.

But the relative immaturity of the prefrontal cortex is not the whole story. Teenagers are highly focused on belonging to a group. They frequently adopt the dress, attitudes, mannerisms, and behavior of their peers. This adherence to group norms helps them form an identity that is distinct from members of other groups, in a process that psychologists refer to as "normative regulation." Adolescents care more about fitting in with their social group to avoid rejection than adults do: studies have found that compared with adults, they feel worse after being excluded by their peers, and they feel better when they are socially accepted.[11]

Teenagers are especially likely to look to their peers for information on how to interpret an ambiguous situation. Researchers in one study asked visitors to the London Science Museum to rate the riskiness of everyday situations, such as crossing a road on a red light or taking a shortcut through a dark alley.[12] They were told the average riskiness rating by adults and by teenagers and were then asked to re-rate each situation. In reality, the researchers randomly assigned whether the ratings were supposed to have come from adults or teenagers.

In line with what we have seen about conformity, people of all age groups changed their ratings after receiving information about others' ratings, altering them to align more with those of others. Teenagers were more likely to shift their ratings than adults were, however, and they shifted them more dramatically. Most people adjusted their ratings to conform more with adults' views. But one group deviated from this general trend: adolescents between twelve and fourteen were far more likely to change their ratings to conform with those of teenagers than with those of adults. For young teenagers, who are in the process of forming and defining their own identity, fitting in with peers matters more than just about anything else.

Unfortunately, this desire to fit in can lead to serious—even life-threatening—consequences. Researchers at Temple University recruited adolescents (thirteen to sixteen years old), young adults (eighteen to twenty-two), and adults (twenty-four and up) to play a video game called Chicken.[13] The game asks you to decide when to stop a car once a traffic light turns from green to yellow, potentially risking a crash if the light switches to red and another car moves through the intersection. Half of the people in each age group played the game alone; the other half played it with two other participants watching and giving advice about when to stop. Although people generally made riskier choices when playing in a group than when they were alone, this effect was much greater for adolescents and young adults.

Given the general propensity for risk-taking among adolescents, the concern about fitting in often leads them to engage in riskier behavior when they are with their peers than when they are on their own. For example, teenage boys with passengers in the car are nearly six times as likely to perform an illegal maneuver—running a stop sign or doing an illegal U-turn—and twice as likely to drive aggressively—speeding or tailgating—as those driving alone.[14] This type of risky behavior is even more likely if they are driving with another male passenger.[15]

But what makes teens particularly susceptible to social influence? Neuroscientists have found that adolescent brains are hardwired to pay close attention to their peers' attitudes and behavior.[16] They posit that the hormonal changes brought on by puberty lead to physiological changes in the brain that increase teenagers' focus on social information.

In one study, researchers showed teenagers (ages thirteen to eighteen) various photos while they were in an fMRI machine.[17] Some were neutral images of food and people, while others, such as images of cigarettes and alcohol, were associated with risk. Each photo showed the number of likes the image had supposedly received from other teenagers. Half of the photos had a high number of likes and half had a small number. (In reality, the number of likes on a given photo was randomly assigned.) Researchers showed the same photo to two groups of teenagers and asked them to click "like" if they liked the image or "next" if they did not. The teens' assessments were highly influenced by those of their peers. For both types of photos, they were more likely to click "like" if the image had a large number of likes next to it than if it didn't.

This drive to conform was also clearly evident in the brain. When teenagers saw photos with a large number of likes, certain regions of their brain lit up, including areas that process social cognition, social memories, and imitation (the precuneus, medial prefrontal cortex, hippocampus, and inferior frontal gyrus). Also active was the ventral striatum, part of the brain's reward circuitry. This tells you something about what is going on in the brain when kids are on Snapchat or Instagram. When teenagers see photos they believe their peers like, their brain is telling them, "Pay attention, remember this, do this again," and "This feels good." But their neural responses also differed depending on what kind of image they were looking at: regions of the brain associated with cognitive control were less active when they viewed the risky images than the neutral images. The researchers speculated that this decrease in cognitive control might lead to an increase in the teens' likelihood of engaging in risk-taking behaviors.

Some evidence suggests that the desire to fit in and be accepted by peers may be especially strong for girls, probably because adolescent girls are more sensitive to social signals than boys, and more focused on the dynamics of social interactions.[18] Boys are more attuned to larger group relationships and to their relative dominance. Girls' greater concern about peer evaluation and social approval—and overall level of interpersonal stress—may also help explain why they show higher rates of depression and anxiety.[19]

To examine the neural processes underlying gender differences in susceptibility to peer approval, researchers at the National Institutes of Health and Georgia State University recruited preteens and teens—ages nine to seventeen—to participate in what they were told was a study on teenagers' use of internet-based chatrooms.[20] They asked study participants to look at forty photographs of potential partners for their chat and to rate their interest in interacting with each one. They then divided these partners into "high interest" and "low interest" groups. In the next phase, researchers scanned participants' brains while they again saw all forty photos and had to rate how likely they believed it was that each person would want to interact with them.

The results showed that the girls were especially conscious of how they were seen by others. When older girls thought about how their peers would rate them, the ventral striatum, insula, hypothalamus, hippocampus, and amygdala—brain regions associated with the social processing of emotions, rewards, memory, and motivation—were activated; these activation levels were even greater when they imagined how peers with whom they were particularly interested in interacting were likely to judge them. This neural response was greater in older girls than in boys of any age, suggesting that with age, girls become more focused on how they are seen by others. Girls' increasing focus on intricate social dynamics during adolescence is clearly seen in patterns of brain activation, indicating that they pay more attention to their peers and worry more about what their peers think of them.

The Consequences of Misperceiving Social Norms

It's human nature to want to fit in with our social group. But our tendency to stay silent to avoid appearing deviant can create an illusion of support for behavior that most members of a group actually oppose. As we saw in Chapter 3, we may privately disagree with our friend or colleague's behavior, but when we look to others to validate or shape our own reactions, we see only support for the status quo. This dichotomy between what people feel and how they act can lead us to conform to a norm that in reality does not exist. A vivid example of the power—and consequences—of perceiving norms that don't exist plays out with unfortunate regularity on college campuses.

Many college students feel personally uncomfortable with excessive alcohol use on campus, but they tend to believe that other students—including their friends—are more comfortable with the amount of drinking going on than they themselves are.[21] Unfortunately, this state of pluralistic ignorance (as described in Chapter 3), in which a majority of group members privately hold one belief but incorrectly assume that most others hold a different belief, can be very harmful. Because students believe that others approve of heavy drinking, they may express public support for drinking and talk about times when they've been out partying and gotten drunk, but they will not mention times when they chose not to drink a lot. This tendency to express views that are wrongly believed to be widespread leads people, in turn, to assume that these views are more common, and more fully accepted, than they actually are.

I have seen this in my own students and have carried out several studies to probe the psychological factors that lead them to publicly express support for behavior that they don't actually believe in. When I started working on this topic, I decided to look at women's body images and conceptions of their weight and compare them with broader campus norms. In a study I conducted with colleagues at Princeton University, we asked college women in all years various questions related to body image and weight, including how often they exercised, their motivation for exercising, and their current height and weight.[22] We also showed them a scale portraying nine different drawings of a female figure—ranging from very thin (figure 1) to very heavy (figure 9)—and asked them to pick which figure best matched their own ideal body. We then asked them to report their perceptions of the views of other women at their university on these same measures.

We found that women's own attitudes and behaviors were quite different from what they thought their peers' were. For starters, they reported exercising about four hours a week on average, but they believed that other women exercised around five and a half hours a week. They also saw other women's exercise as more motivated by external reasons—to be attractive, lose weight, and tone their bodies—than their own exercise, which they reported to be motivated more by internal reasons, such as to cope with stress, improve their health, or increase their stamina.

The most remarkable thing we found in this study was that the students didn't just misperceive others' attitudes and motivations: they misperceived their actual physical size. We asked women to report their own height and weight and their perceptions of the average height and weight of their peers on campus. We then computed the BMI, or body mass index—a crude ratio of weight to height—for both sets of numbers. The women had an average BMI of 22, but they believed that other women had a BMI of 20.5. In addition, the gap between women's own BMI and their perceptions of other women's BMI was smaller for first-year students than it was for older students. This same pattern held for the data assessing women's ideal body size on the pictorial scale. First-year women had a small gap between their own ideal body size and their perception of other women's ideal body size: 3.1 versus 2.7, respectively. For upper-class women, the gap was larger: 3.0 versus 2.3.

The discovery that women felt more out of whack in terms of body shape and size the longer they spent on campus was, frankly, puzzling. This study was conducted at Princeton University, where virtually all students live on campus and regularly interact with their peers in the classroom, dining hall, gym, and dorms. These women had lots of exposure to other women's actual shapes and sizes. You might expect that as they spent more time there, their assessments would become more accurate, not less so. Why did women persist in seeing their classmates not only as thinner than themselves, but as thinner than they actually were? And why did this tendency get worse over time?

The reason probably has to do with the focus on thinness in our society, which leads women to publicly express attitudes that are in line with this norm, even if those attitudes don't reflect their own true feelings. They might, for instance, choose to tell their friends how little they've eaten ("I've been so busy today that all I've had to eat is an apple") or how much they've exercised ("I just spent forty-five minutes on the treadmill"). They are much less likely to describe times when they sat alone eating Oreos and couldn't bring themselves to go to the gym, or even when they ate a healthy serving of enchiladas and just took a short bike ride. Women's tendency to publicly share certain types of behavior and not others creates a false impression of the true norm—a fact that has been further exacerbated since the time of our study by social media.

And it's not just that women express attitudes in line with the thinness norm—they also behave in public in ways that suggest that they have embraced this norm. At many residential colleges, women are consciously aware of the foods they eat in public (a phenomenon known as "tray gazing"). They stack up their tray with salad, nonfat yogurt, and Diet Coke, knowing—or imagining—that others will be watching their choices.

The irony in all of this public expression of the thinness norm is that many students fail to recognize that others around them are doing the same thing. They know that they themselves talk the talk and walk the walk in the dining hall and other public places—but privately enjoy a bag of Doritos or a scoop or two of ice cream in their dorm rooms later on. They feel ashamed and isolated, without realizing that almost everyone else is wolfing down chips in private, too. Because eating only salad, nonfat yogurt, and Diet Coke leaves you feeling pretty hungry later on.

These misperceptions could be heightened in the college environment, at least at residential schools where people are surrounded by public presentations of other women's eating and exercise behavior. To examine whether this tendency is limited to college settings, one of my former students and I conducted an almost identical study, but this time with high school students.[23] We collected the same data as we had in the study of college students for three private, single-sex high schools in the United States and the United Kingdom. The results were virtually identical to what we found in the previous study: students underestimated their peers' BMI and body size, and misjudged their motivation for exercise.

Feeling like one doesn't fit in with the norms of one's group can have substantial negative consequences, even if this perceived discrepancy is an illusion. Women who feel that they do not conform to norms of thinness may go to considerable—and unhealthy—lengths to try to meet the perceived ideal. In both of these studies—the one with college women at Princeton and with high school girls in the United States and the United Kingdom—the bigger the gap between a woman or girl's reported size and her perception of that of others, the greater the chance of her reporting symptoms of eating disorders, ranging from an extreme focus on thinness to binge eating and purging.[24]

Our findings are mirrored by research on other types of health-related behavior. Students who believe (wrongly) that other students consume more alcohol than they themselves do often increase their drinking.[25] They also tend to feel alienated from campus life and report less interest in attending college reunions later on. As we'll see in Chapter 7, men who believe that other men endorse common myths about rape are more likely to behave in a sexually aggressive way.[26] In other words, people change their behavior to adhere to their perception of a norm, but their perception is often wrong.

The Power of Correcting False Norms

So we've seen that people want to fit in with prevailing norms. But here's the good news: the drive to conform can also be used to influence behavior in a positive way by teaching people that their ideas about certain norms are wrong. This approach has been used repeatedly in high schools and colleges to improve health by providing students with more accurate information about alcohol use and body image.[27] This approach has also been used to decrease rates of sexual assault, as we will see in Chapter 7.

Here's one example of the benefits of correcting false norms. Christine Schroeder and Deborah Prentice at Princeton University randomly assigned 143 first-year students to watch a seven-minute video depicting alcohol-related social scenes and then participate in a discussion about alcohol use.[28] Some students were given information about common alcohol norm misperceptions and told why people think alcohol use is more common on campus than it actually is, and how these misperceptions affect campus drinking culture. Other students were given information about the hazards of excessive alcohol consumption and offered strategies for drinking responsibly. When Schroeder and Prentice surveyed the students six months later, those who had received information on norm misperceptions reported having consumed far fewer drinks each week on average than those who had simply been encouraged to adopt healthy drinking habits.

My own research has also shown that correcting perceptions of norms can reduce rates of disordered eating. One of my students, Jenny Mutterperl, and I measured first-year college women's rates of disordered eating and then randomly assigned them to read one of two brochures.[29] The first brochure provided general information on how to maintain healthy eating and exercise habits. The second described common misperceptions college women hold about their peers' eating and exercise habits—thinking that they want to be thinner, eat less, and exercise more than they actually do—and explained why these misperceptions occurred. We then contacted the participants again three months later to see if either brochure had changed their behavior.

Receiving information that dispelled common misperceptions about other women's drive for thinness did seem to help—at least for some women. For those who didn't initially place a strong emphasis on achieving the thin ideal commonly portrayed in magazines and on television, receiving the norm misperception brochure led to higher actual and ideal body weights and lower frequencies of disordered eating. These women appear to have formed more accurate perceptions of the weight of other women on campus, which led them to feel less pressure to lose weight. Unfortunately, these benefits did not carry over to the women who at the start of the study were already focused on achieving the ideal body image peddled in the popular press. We believe these women weren't actively comparing their own bodies to those of their fellow students so much as to images they'd seen in magazines and on television. This meant that learning more accurate information about campus norms had less influence on their behavior.

My most recent line of research examines misperceptions among college students about mental health, and in particular their tendency both to underestimate how many of their peers struggle with mental health issues and to overestimate the social stigma around seeking therapy.[30] My student Kate Turetsky and I randomly assigned college students to attend one of three fifteen-minute workshops. One workshop focused on correcting misperceptions about campus mental health use and outlined how these misperceptions can reduce their likelihood of seeking help. Another provided general information about mental health disorders and myths. And the third focused on improving mental health through stress management. Two months later, we measured the effects of all three workshops on students' attitudes.

We found that students clearly benefited from receiving accurate information about campus mental health use. This workshop was just as effective as the general education workshop at improving attitudes toward seeking professional help for mental health issues, and was more effective than the stress management workshop. Although our study did not find evidence that receiving accurate information about mental health norms led to an increase in actually seeking help, our follow-up period of two months may have been too short to see such an effect. Prior studies demonstrating the role of attitudes in predicting behavior suggest that these students might be more willing to seek therapy for mental health issues in the future. And given the epidemic of suicides among undergraduates, this kind of behavior change could well help save lives.

The Power of Outsiders

As we've seen, the pressure to conform to our social groups is very strong and is clearly reflected in patterns of brain activation. The push to stay silent in the face of bad behavior is particularly strong when people convince themselves that their silence is in service of the greater good provided by an institution they value, such as their church, fraternity, or political party. We saw that people were more likely to go along with the request to deliver painful shocks when they identified with the goal of the researcher in variations of the Milgram experiment, and this tendency can cause them to sublimate their personal sense of right and wrong to support institutions they revere, from the police to the church.

The decision to ignore or actively cover up bad behavior by group members is, sadly, not uncommon. We have seen it in the sex abuse scandal in the Catholic Church. A grand jury report described how church leaders in Pennsylvania looked the other way when more than three hundred priests sexually abused over a thousand children during a period of seventy years: "Priests were raping little boys and girls, and the men of God who were responsible for them not only did nothing; they hid it all. For decades." "Church leaders," the report stated, "preferred to protect the abusers and their institution above all."[31] And we saw it in the case of Larry Nassar, the doctor for the USA Gymnastics team, who abused hundreds of young women. Rachael Denhollander, the first gymnast to speak publicly about the abuse, told the *New York Times:* "Predators rely on community protection to silence victims and keep them in power. Far too often, our commitment to our political party, our religious group, our sport, our college or a prominent member of our community causes us to choose to disbelieve or to turn away from the victim."[32]

This unwillingness to speak out against members of our own group helps explain why outsiders are often the ones who actually do take action. Perhaps you recall the two Swedish graduate students who were biking to a party and stopped to intervene when they saw Stanford University student Brock Turner sexually assaulting an unconscious woman.

I started this chapter by describing Timothy Piazza's fraternity hazing and the general lack of concern shown by his fellow fraternity members. But that isn't the complete story of what happened that evening.

Videotapes reviewed after Timothy's death revealed that one student, Kordel Davis, pleaded with the others to get help. Kordel told

ABC News: "I started freaking out. Tim fell and he's just lying on the couch. If Tim fell, he does not need to be on the couch . . . he needs to go to the hospital. We should call 911."[33] Kordel was only a freshman, and his repeated pleas were ignored. He was shoved up against a wall, accused of overreacting, and told that the situation was under control.

What led Kordel Davis to step up and try to get help for Timothy that evening, risking embarrassment and ridicule from the older members of the fraternity? One factor no doubt was that Kordel had himself experienced a serious injury after a fall during a fraternity party earlier that year. Despite his head injury, and profuse bleeding, no one had called 911. So he may well have felt more empathy with Timothy Piazza because of their shared experience of injuring themselves during a fraternity social event.

But another factor may also have played a part. Kordel was the only black member of the fraternity and may have felt in some ways like an outsider. This meant that he would have felt less pressure to conform. Although his attempt to help didn't save Timothy's life, it provides evidence that there are certain factors that can push people to overcome group pressure. We'll return to this issue of what prompts people to act in the final two chapters of this book, but first let's look at three areas where silence and inactivity are rife—at school, at college, and in the workplace—and consider what might be blocking people from speaking up, and what changes or training might make a difference.

Part II

Bullies and Bystanders

6

At School: Standing Up to Bullies

On June 14, 2017, Mallory Rose Grossman, a sixth grader at Copeland Middle School in New Jersey, died by suicide.[1] She left behind her parents, three siblings, and a large extended family. Although many factors contribute to suicide, the cyberbullying that Mallory experienced over the course of the school year clearly played a substantial role. Her classmates had been after her relentlessly for months—sending messages by text, Instagram, and Snapchat—telling her she was a loser and had no friends. One message even suggested she kill herself.

Painful though it is to believe, Mallory's experience is not rare. A study of teenagers who were admitted to a hospital for mental health concerns revealed that a history of bullying was strongly linked with thoughts of suicide. Teenagers who had been subjected to verbal bullying were 8.4 times more likely to have thoughts of suicide, and for cyberbullying, that number shot up to 11.5 times.[2]

Bullying may seem like an inevitable aspect of school life, but it doesn't have to be. In this chapter we'll examine the psychological factors that contribute to bullying as well as those that enable some children to stand up to such behavior. Then we'll review strategies that parents and schools can use to change school culture to eliminate the type of behavior that contributed to Mallory's death.

Understanding—and Misunderstanding—Bullying

When he was ten or eleven years old, my son Andrew came home from hockey practice one day and confided that one of his teammates was repeatedly taunting another kid on the team in the locker room. I asked Andrew if he had told the bully to cut it out. Andrew was horrified at my question and said he hadn't wanted to butt in. Why? Because he didn't want that kid to then start bullying him.

This story plays out in locker rooms and on playgrounds and school buses with great regularity. Andrew knew that what his teammate was doing was wrong, but he didn't have the courage to stand up to him because of the consequences he feared he might face. Research on bullying shows that most students who are present in bullying situations passively watch, and that more students actively join in than try to intervene.[3]

Researchers from York University videotaped playground interactions between children aged five to twelve at several elementary schools in Toronto.[4] They then examined fifty-three distinct bullying episodes to see how other children responded. Most bullying, they found, occurs in the presence of other children: in 80 percent of the episodes, at least one other child saw the incident, and on average four children witnessed it. In over half of the cases—54 percent—other children passively watched the bullying. In 21 percent of the cases other children joined the bully and engaged in some type of physical or verbal aggression. Older boys—those in grades four to six—were more likely to actively join the bully than younger boys, or girls of any age.

In only 25 percent of the cases did any of the children intervene to stop or discourage the bullying. Girls and younger boys—in grades one to three—were more likely to intervene than older boys. Although this study didn't directly examine the factors that led to these age and gender differences in rates of intervention, other research has shown that children's empathy for victims of bullying decreases with age and that girls are more likely than boys to notice bullying events, interpret them as emergencies, and intervene.[5]

This reluctance to support targets of bullying or confront bullies is not surprising, since bullies are often at the top of the social pecking order. One study of middle school students in Los Angeles found that bullying behaviors increased children's social status and popularity, and that those who were identified by their peers as the "coolest" were the most likely to behave aggressively. Jaana Juvonen, a professor of psychology at UCLA, summed up the situation: "The ones who are cool bully more, and the ones who bully more are seen as cool."[6]

Bullying also continues because students believe that their peers are comfortable with such behavior. Many students are quietly horrified when they see other kids being bullied, but they misinterpret others' silence as a lack of concern or even tacit support, following the mistaken logic outlined in Chapter 2. Marlene Sandstrom and her colleagues at Williams College asked 446 fourth and eighth graders to describe their own attitudes about bullying as well as their perception of their peers' attitudes.[7] The children were also asked how they would respond if they witnessed an episode of bullying. As predicted, students consistently underestimated their peers' opposition to bullying and believed that they personally held more negative attitudes toward bullying—seeing bullying as wrong and respecting students who stood up to bullies—than their peers did.

This perceived self–other gap was greater among eighth graders than fourth graders, a result in line with other findings showing that the underestimation of peers' opposition to bullying widens during the teenage years. Students who see their peers as more approving of bullying than they themselves are will be less likely to defend the victim and more likely to join in. The tendency to respond passively to bullying also increases with age, in part because teenagers worry more about the social consequences of deviating from their peers.[8]

Researchers found that students who believed their peers would intervene to stop bullying were much more likely to do so themselves.[9] In fact, one study of over five thousand middle and high school students revealed that perceived social norms were a stronger predictor of intentions to intervene than students' own reported belief that they would do so.[10] It's much easier to engage in behavior that conforms to group values than to defy the group and invite negative social consequences.

This research on bullying and norms suggests that the most effective strategy for reducing bullying may not be to emphasize the negative consequences of bullying so much as to tackle norms head on—to give students accurate information about how their peers feel about bullying. Many students worry that they will face social rejection if they stand up to bullies, or that they will be seen as a "snitch" if they report what they've seen or heard. Helping students understand why they may imagine that their peers are less bothered by bullying than they actually are—by explaining how and why people behave in a way that doesn't match their true feelings—should allow them to form more accurate beliefs about prevailing norms. And students who understand that other students oppose bullying and respect those who stand up to bullies may feel more empowered to do so themselves.

Who Stands Up to Bullies?

In the fall of 2007, a ninth-grade boy at Central Kings Rural High School in a small town in Nova Scotia chose to wear a pink shirt on the first day of high school. This choice did not go over well: several students called him gay and threatened to beat him up. Two twelfth-grade students, David Shepherd and Travis Price, heard about the bullying and decided to do something to stop it. "I just figured enough was enough," said David.[11] They organized what they called a "sea of pink." They bought fifty pink shirts at a local discount store, sent an email to classmates describing their anti-bullying campaign, and handed the shirts out to their classmates at the start of school the next morning. When the bullied student arrived at school, he saw hundreds of students wearing pink. Travis described the bullied boy's reaction: "Finally, someone stood up for weaker kid. . . . It looked like a huge weight was lifted off his shoulders." David and Travis's intervention clearly made a difference: the bullies weren't heard from again.

This story illustrates a consistent finding in research on who stands up to bullies: students with some kind of social capital, which involves a combination of peer support, teacher support, and social skills. One study of bullying in sixth graders found that those who defended victims of bullying were usually the highest in status.[12] Although the specific factors that led David and Travis to take action are not known, these boys were seniors, a privileged position in high school. Such students are less concerned about the consequences of taking action, such as retaliation and a loss of popularity, because their status in the school social hierarchy is well established. This comfort with their social position gives them the courage to stand up to bullies.

Now, you might be trying to reconcile this finding—that popular kids stand up to bullies—with the statement earlier in this chapter that bullies tend to be popular. Research by Robert Faris at the University of California, Davis, and Diane Felmlee at Penn State have examined precisely this issue.[13] They used data from a longitudinal study of over thirty-five hundred students in nineteen middle and high schools in North Carolina to examine the connection between bullying and students' status. Bullying in this study included physical acts, such as hitting and shoving, as well as more subtle behaviors, such as spreading rumors and name-calling.

First, the good news: two-thirds of the students weren't bullied during the three-month period in which data were collected.

Now, the not so good news: starting at about the middle of the school's social hierarchy, as students' rank in the hierarchy increased, up to the top 95th percentile, the odds of being picked on by their peers increased by more than 25 percent. Above that level, rates of bullying were much lower. What explains these findings? These researchers believe that students use bullying as a way to gain—or at least maintain—social status and power, and they do so by tormenting their (somewhat) popular peers. But once they get to the top, they don't need to defend their position anymore. "If status were money, they would be like Bill Gates—their positions are secure," says lead author Robert Faris. "They don't need to torment their peers in an effort to climb up the social ladder—a tactic commonly used among those battling for position—because they are already at the top, and they aren't being victimized because they are out of reach and have no rivals."[14]

In the words of the anti-bullying activist Rob Frenette, "Bullying tends to be a social tool."[15] Only the few students at the very top of the social ladder are secure in their popularity and can therefore risk standing up for those who are bullied. These acts of kindness may even solidify their social status.

What else predicts a willingness to stand up to bullies? Self-confidence. People with high levels of self-efficacy, meaning a confidence in their ability to successfully carry out their goals, are more likely to intervene in bullying situations.[16] At some level this is not surprising. Social self-efficacy includes confidence expressing opinions in a group setting and making friends, which are especially important predictors of teenagers' willingness to support peers who are bullied. Students who feel confident that their efforts to stop a bully would be successful should be more likely to act. Self-confident kids may also have less concern about being the targets of bullies themselves.

Finally, students who are confident in their own social skills are better able to stand up to bullying behavior. Researchers at Eastern Illinois University examined factors common to middle school students who reported defending victims of bullying behavior.[17] Nearly three hundred students answered questions about how often during the previous thirty days they had defended someone, for example, by telling other students that a rumor was false. They were also asked to evaluate their confidence in their own social skills, including communication, assertiveness, and empathy. Students who perceived that they had more support from their peers reported intervening to support victims of bullying more frequently. These students experience less social risk from challenging bad behavior, and thus may feel more comfortable calling out bullies.

Another characteristic of those students who counteracted bullying was confidence in their own social skills. This makes sense: standing up to bullying isn't easy. In fact, it requires several different types of skills, including an ability to feel empathy for the victim, act assertively toward the bully, fend off ridicule, and communicate effectively why the bully's behavior needs to stop.

Strategies for Reducing Bullying

All three of my children attended a summer camp that had the motto "The Other Fellow First." There were—and are—many great things about this camp, including the "no electronics" policy, but this motto was, at least for me, one of the highlights. And it wasn't just a motto used in marketing to anxious parents. It really epitomized the determination of the camp to help children and young adolescents take another person's perspective. The most effective anti-bullying programs try to create precisely this sort of climate, in which students feel true empathy for one another and thus avoid engaging in bullying themselves and speak up if they witness such behavior.

Let's consider some strategies parents and schools can use to give children the tools—and the disposition—to stand up to bullies. In the film *Chocolat*, Père Henri, a young priest newly arrived in a small village, delivers an Easter sermon designed to bring people together, in contrast to the divisive message that his predecessor had favored. His words perfectly capture the tremendous value of shifting the way people find worth—from excluding others to including them: "I think that we can't go around measuring our goodness by what we don't do—by what we deny ourselves, what we resist, and who we exclude. I think we've got to measure goodness by what we embrace, what we create, and who we include." Schools that have eliminated—or at least drastically reduced—bullying foster a philosophy and school culture that aligns with this concept of inclusion and positive action.

Provide Bystander Training

Bullying is far too prevalent in many schools, but it isn't inevitable. Schools districts that have implemented comprehensive antibullying programs have seen substantial improvement. One analysis of twelve school-based bully prevention programs, which involved nearly thirteen thousand students from kindergarten to twelfth grade, revealed that programs that specifically addressed the role of bystanders led to increases in students' intervention behavior.[18]

Researchers at the Berlin Institute of Technology looked at rates of bullying in fifth, sixth, and seventh grade classes in Luxembourg, comparing twenty-two classes that had received a structured classroom-based bystander intervention training program to twenty-six classes that had not.[19] The training described the hazards of bystander inaction, fostered empathy and social responsibility, and taught kids how to respond to aggressive behavior by using practical activities and roleplays. Regular classroom teachers—who received a sixteen-hour training course—delivered the training, which was designed to be given during two classes each week, for a total of sixteen to eighteen hours.

Both before and after the training, students answered questions about how frequently they had witnessed verbal, physical, and relational aggression. They were also asked about their intentions to intervene if they witnessed bullying, using various scenarios. One example was: "Imagine you come for recreation to the school yard. You see a boy of your age who stands alone by himself. Suddenly, another boy comes along and starts shoving the first boy around. He falls down several times but does not defend himself. As he tries to walk away, the second boy seizes him and starts hitting him hard." Researchers also evaluated how much time teachers actually spent on this material during class—some spent only two to four hours, whereas others spent as much as thirteen to eighteen hours—and how well the teachers felt they covered the material provided in the training manual.

First, the good news: students in classes that received a longer and more in-depth version of the training program reported lower rates of victimization at the three-month follow-up. They were also less likely to report passive bystanding, like ignoring or walking away, when observing bullying.

Now, the not so good news: even intense and lengthy training didn't help students actually confront the bully. Although this finding is disappointing, it points to the difficulty of getting people to risk the social—and perhaps physical—consequences of challenging a bully's bad behavior.

In what is decidedly more encouraging news, training programs seem to be more effective when they target subtle forms of aggression or intimidation that are often a precursor to bullying. This type of relational aggression, such as teasing, name-calling, rumor-spreading, and other ostracizing chitchat, can feel just as painful to students as physical bullying, but it may not be identified by teachers or students as particularly harmful.

Researchers at Wichita State University and the University of Washington examined the effectiveness of an anti-bullying program called Steps to Respect, which emphasizes the importance of resisting subtle forms of bullying such as malicious gossip and social exclusion.[20] This program includes training for both students and teachers on how to respond when they witness relational aggression. Students are taught that retaliation can often escalate bad behavior, so a better choice is to assertively tell the bully, "Knock it off." They are also taught to understand that silent bystanders can inadvertently suggest support for the bully—even if they actually disapprove of what is going on. Palm Pilots were used to electronically record second-by-second observations on the playground of third- to sixth-grade students in six different Seattle-area elementary schools for ten weeks in the fall, and again for ten weeks in the spring, after implementation of the program. The researchers counted all acts of slander or derogatory talk about other students, like, "Is the cootie girl in your class?" or "Did you hear Dan cheated on the exam?"

What they found was extremely heartening: rates of malicious gossip overall dropped 72 percent. This meant that there were 234 fewer instances of gossip and 270 fewer instances of a student being the target of rumors. Encouraging children to respond to low-level types of bullying may help them gain skills that make it easier for them to respond more effectively (and to be more willing to respond) to more overt acts of bullying. It may also change the school climate to one where fewer students feel ostracized and there is less bullying later on.

Change the School Culture

I have mostly focused thus far on the role of social norms in inhibiting people from standing up to bullying, but norms can also be used to reduce bad behavior itself. Wesley Perkins and his colleagues at Hobart and William Smith Colleges used a poster campaign to change bullying norms in five diverse public middle schools in New

Jersey.[21] Students at these schools consistently misperceived both the prevalence of bullying and what their classmates thought about it: they thought that pro-bullying norms and actual bullying were more common than they really were. Students who believed that such norms were more common held more pro-bullying attitudes themselves and were more likely to engage in bullying.

To try to combat these misperceptions, researchers hung large posters around the school showing what students actually reported they felt about bullying at each of the schools. The information on the posters—with the school name replaced by a blank here—was simple and clear:

- Most _____ Middle School students (3 out of 4) do NOT exclude someone from a group to make them feel bad.
- 95 percent of _____ Middle School students say students should NOT tease in a mean way, call others hurtful names, or spread unkind stories about other students.
- Most _____ Middle School students (8 out of 10) think that students should tell a teacher or a counselor if they or someone else are being bullied at school.

Data collected after these posters were hung revealed substantial positive effects of this simple anti-bullying strategy, with fewer reports of bullying behavior and of students feeling victimized. The changes were most pronounced in schools in which more students recalled seeing the posters: bullying was reduced by an estimated 35 percent in the school in which the most students remembered seeing the posters, versus 26 percent in the school in which the fewest said they saw the posters. These findings suggest that one strategy to reduce school bullying may therefore be simply to change the perceptions and attitudes of students about what their peers think about bullying.

Social norms within a school can also be changed by tailored programs that target only a small number of carefully selected students.

A team of researchers from Princeton, Rutgers, and Yale examined whether training particularly influential students within a school setting—so-called "social influencers"—would be effective at changing bullying norms.[22] Their hope was that if these students could be convinced to adopt strong anti-bullying attitudes, they would shape their peers' attitudes and beliefs.

The researchers randomly assigned middle schools in New Jersey to receive a peer-based anti-bullying program called Roots either at the start of the school year or at the end (so that it could be implemented the following year). They used a technique known as social network mapping to identify the kids with the most connections to other students at their schools. Students were asked to list up to ten students with whom they spent the most time; the researchers were then able to identify which students had the broadest social network. These are not so much the most popular kids as the ones who are most broadly connected to other kids. The most influential students were by and large linked to a more socially mature social network, and they came from wealthier backgrounds.

Next, twenty-two to thirty of these social influencers at each school were invited to participate in the Roots program, which provides training in managing peer conflict and supports the creation of school-wide messaging campaigns. Roots has a strong emphasis on personal agency, and students were given templates for anti-bullying campaign materials that they then designed themselves. One group created the hashtag #iRespect on Instagram to emphasize tolerance and hung colorful signs with this hashtag around school. Another group created brightly colored rubber wristbands with the Roots logo. Each time a Roots member saw another student intervening to stop a conflict or help another student, he or she gave the student a wristband with a tag that said, "A Roots student caught you doing something great." Yet another group organized a one-day Roots Day festival in which students promoted Roots through posters, wristbands, and giveaways, and encouraged students to sign a petition stating that they would do something nice for someone else at school. All of these activities served to bring students together and highlighted the benefits of showing positive behaviors.

At the end of the year, researchers compared rates of student conflict in the schools that had implemented the Roots program with those that had not.

Their results showed that the program was very successful: middle schools that had used Roots saw a 30 percent reduction in student conflicts and disciplinary reports, even though the program provided training to only about 10 percent of the students. Elizabeth Paluck, a psychology professor at Princeton who was the lead researcher on this study, noted, "You can target specific people in a savvy way in order to spread the message. These people—the social referents you should target—get noticed more by their peers. Their behavior serves as a signal to what is normal and desirable in the community."[23]

Here's another great thing about the Roots program: it's far easier for schools to implement than most other approaches, since it doesn't require delivering anti-bullying messages to all students. Instead, the Roots program relies on training a relatively small number of specially selected students—say, 5 to 10 percent of the student population—and then letting them create and deliver schoolwide messages. Similar approaches, in which a small number of well-liked people in a given community are trained to deliver a message, have been shown to foster other types of social change, such as safer sexual behavior and reductions in prejudice.[24]

The KiVa Program

So if you can get the cool kids to make bullying seem uncool, you can turn around a school culture. But another way of stopping bullying doesn't really address bullying at all. It just involves being nice.

One of the most well-known programs to reduce bullying is the KiVa program, which was developed in Finland. (In Finnish, the phrase "Kiusaamista vastaan" means "against bullying," and the word "kiva" means "nice.") This program, which includes discussion, group work, and short films, is designed to reduce negative bystander behavior and boost defender behavior by increasing students' empathy, self-efficacy, and anti-bullying attitudes. It includes role-playing exercises designed to increase students' feelings of empathy as well as computer games and simulations that require students to think through how they would intervene in certain circumstances. Students control cartoon avatars who encounter various bullying situations and have to choose whether and how to act. In one exercise, students are asked to imagine seeing one kid shoving another up against a locker and then to describe what they would do. In another, they are asked to think about what they would do if a new student was trying to make friends. This approach allows students to try out different options and gain confidence in knowing what to do in future bullying situations, and it fosters empathy and support for victims.

Most important, it works. In fact, a meta-analysis of fifty-three anti-bullying programs worldwide found that the KiVa program was one of the most effective.[25] Students in schools without this program were nearly twice as likely to report being bullied as those in schools with it. Although this program began in Finland, it's now being used more widely—in Italy, the Netherlands, the United Kingdom, and the United States.

The KiVa program has also led to improvements in mental health more broadly. One study of more than seven thousand students attending seventy-seven elementary schools in Finland compared rates of self-esteem and depression in students at schools using the KiVa program to those at schools that provided them with some information about how to reduce bullying, but in a much less comprehensive way.[26] The KiVa program was associated with higher levels of self-esteem and lower rates of depression, and particularly benefited students who experienced the highest rates of bullying. Although this was unexpected, researchers believe that this program improves teachers' ability to deal with bullying as well as students' ability both to empathize with and to stand up for victims of bullying, which in turn leads these students to feel more supported in their school environment. "The beauty here is that this school-wide program is very effective for the children who most need support," said Jaana Juvonen, lead author on this study.[27]

Build Strong Relationships

Another effective strategy that has been found to reduce bullying is to foster strong connections between students and teachers. Students who feel supported by adults are more likely to report bad behavior, making it possible for staff and teachers to intervene early on.[28] Students who feel that their teachers support, encourage, and accept them are also more likely to defend victims of bullying.[29] Schools should therefore prioritize helping teachers build warm and caring relationships with their students.

When adults ignore or overlook bad behavior, students see no reason to report it—they have no reason to think anyone will act to stop it—and bullies feel empowered to keep bullying.[30] Teachers who believe bullying is the norm, a fact of life in the early teenage years, are less likely to intervene. This attitude models inaction for their students.[31] Their students in turn experience more bullying. Teachers who believe victims should assert themselves foster a classroom atmosphere in which students feel less empathy for victims and report less inclination to intervene. Teachers' views about bullying, then, can create a ripple effect throughout the school, for better and for worse.

In a vivid illustration of how school culture influences students' response to bullying, researchers collected data from sixth graders and ninth graders in middle- to low-income public schools in the southeastern United States about their relationships with family members, peers, and teachers.[32] They asked them to read eight different scenarios that described some type of aggressive act, such as cyberbullying, rejection by a social group, or teasing and mean-spirited gossip. For each scenario, students were asked to rate how acceptable the behavior was and how acceptable it would be for them to intervene in some way. They were also asked to estimate how likely they would be to respond to each act and what they would do. Would they directly confront the person who engaged in the behavior? Would they walk away? The students also answered a series of questions about their families and schools. Did they have a lot of rules at home? What happened when they broke the rules? Did they like their teachers, and were they treated fairly at school?

Students' relationships with others had a major impact on how they reported they would respond. Those who felt discriminated against by teachers and/or excluded by their peers were less likely to say that they would intervene and help victims of bullying, and more likely to say that they would ignore it. Those who felt they had good relationships with teachers were far more likely to say they would step up and act. These findings are in line with those from other studies indicating that feeling a sense of connectedness increases high school students' willingness to intervene to stop bullying. Creating a greater sense of connectivity at school—actively fostering mutual respect, shared responsibility, and social inclusion—may therefore go a long way toward combating the widespread apathy of high schoolers.[33] Fostering a supportive school environment with trusting teachers helps students feel comfortable reporting bullying to adults, but also gives them the courage to challenge bullies themselves.

This research also points to the value of positive relationships at home. Students who reported feeling close to their families were more likely to say they would intervene to stop a bully. Having good relationships with adults, whether at home, at school, or elsewhere, seems to increase teenagers' willingness to step up. "The study tells us that both home and school factors are important for recognizing bullying behavior as inappropriate and taking steps to intervene," said Lynn Mulvey, a professor at North Carolina State and the lead author on this study. "It highlights the value of positive school environments and good teachers, and the importance of family support, when it comes to addressing bullying."[34]

This chapter started with a description of Mallory Rose Grossman's bullying, and how it was widely ignored by students, staff, and administrators at her school. Imagine how different the outcome of that story would have been at a school in which students felt comfortable telling teachers about the acts they were witnessing and stepping up to the bullies themselves. A change in school culture might well have saved Mallory's life.

7

In College: Reducing Sexual Misconduct

The Delta Kappa Epsilon (DKE) fraternity, founded at Yale in 1844, is one of the oldest fraternities in the United States. DKE is proud of its culture of community service and leadership; many important politicians and businessmen have been members, including six presidents of the United States, five vice presidents, and four Supreme Court justices. Presidents George H. W. and George W. Bush and Supreme Court Justice Brett Kavanaugh belonged to the Yale chapter.

Yet numerous members of this fraternity at chapters across the country have engaged in highly publicized acts of bad behavior over the years, from urinating on pledges to assaulting (and even raping) women. In October 2010, DKE pledges stood blindfolded outside the Yale Women's Center chanting, "No means yes, yes means anal," and "Fucking sluts!" Following this incident, the fraternity was banned from campus for five years.

In 2016, when DKE returned to Yale, members spoke about the valuable lessons they had learned from this experience. As Luke Persichetti, then president of DKE, told a reporter for the *Yale Daily News*, "I believe the sanctions had a positive impact on the culture of our fraternity. Our current members understand the history of the ban and have played an important part in the cultural shift that has taken place since then."[1]

These positive lessons appear to have been short-lived. Only five months later, Yale suspended Persichetti for three semesters after a disciplinary hearing found him guilty of "penetration without consent" following an incident with a woman in his bedroom at the DKE house. Eight other women complained of sexual misconduct by members of the DKE fraternity in a two-year period following the lifting of the ban.

At some level, reports of all-male groups—fraternities, athletic teams, bands, the military—engaging in bad behavior are hardly surprising. What's perhaps more surprising is that this bad behavior continues even when many—maybe even most—individual members of the fraternity or team don't support it. Research suggests that only a very small number of men actually commit sexual assault.[2] The problem is that their peers rarely intervene. This chapter describes factors that lead men to wrongly perceive that their peers both support and engage in sexual misconduct and looks at strategies that universities and high schools can use to help students think differently and act to stop it.

The Hazards of All-Male Groups

The link between all-male groups and sexual violence toward women is well established.[3] Men who participate in all-male organizations— most notably athletic teams and fraternities—report more positive attitudes toward sexual violence, greater acceptance of rape myths, and more sexually aggressive behavior. They are more likely to use alcohol, drugs, and verbal coercion to have sex with reluctant or nonconsenting women, and are also more likely to commit sexual assault.[4] One study of thirty NCAA Division I universities found that male athletes accounted for 19 percent of all sexual assault cases on campus even though they represented only 3 percent of the student population.[5]

Researchers at a large public NCAA Division I university in the southeastern United States recruited male undergraduates to complete an online study on attitudes toward women, rape myth acceptance, and sexual behavior.[6] Compared to nonathletes, athletes had more traditional views about gender roles, such as believing that women should worry less about having equal rights and more about becoming good wives and mothers. They also believed more strongly in myths about rape, such as that if a woman is drunk or doesn't fight back, it isn't rape. Most important, athletes were more likely to engage in sexually coercive behavior (insisting a partner have sex when they didn't want to, or using threats or force): 54 percent of the athletes reported engaging in this behavior, versus 38 percent of the nonathletes.

Why are athletes and members of fraternities so disproportionately predatory in their relations with women?

One explanation is that men who view women in more objectifying ways will naturally tend to gravitate toward such groups. Researchers at Kenyon College took photos of all of the images of women—including posters, advertisements, and computer screensavers—displayed in the bedrooms of men who were or were not in fraternities.[7] They found that fraternity men displayed significantly more images of women in general, and more sexual and degrading images in particular. Many of these images were from magazines like *Playboy, Maxim,* and *Stuff* that portray women as sex objects. Male college athletes also tend to hold more conservative, traditional attitudes toward women than do nonathletes.[8]

It's hard to say which comes first—the demeaning attitudes or the membership in the fraternity or athletic team. Either way, preexisting proclivities don't explain everything. Psychologists have found that spending time in an all-male group increases a young man's likelihood of engaging in sexually aggressive behaviors. By their junior year, men who had joined a fraternity in their first year at a large state university reported a greater increase than non-fraternity men in peer pressure to engage in sex, and they were more likely to believe that others would approve of engaging in sexually aggressive behaviors such as getting a woman drunk to sleep with her.[9] So it's not just that men who tend to objectify women gravitate toward all-male groups: time spent in these groups also matters.

Yet another explanation for the link between membership in an all-male group and the development of an approving attitude toward sexually aggressive behavior is the pressure such groups place—directly and indirectly—on exaggerated ideals of manliness. A meta-analysis of twenty-nine studies examining the link between athletic participation, fraternity membership, and sexual aggression among college men revealed that involvement in either type of male-only group was associated with higher rates of masculinity ideals.[10] These ideals include engaging in risk-taking, avoiding anything stereotypically female, and being tough and aggressive.[11]

Membership in fraternities or athletic teams appears to foster the impression that particular kinds of behavior are valued. Men who belong to these groups may as a result feel greater pressure to objectify women and engage in risk-taking behavior such as drinking large quantities of alcohol and having sex with multiple partners.[12] A study of students attending a large state university in the Southeast found that 25 percent of fraternity members believed that more than ten of their friends had gotten a women drunk or high as a way to have sex with her; fewer than 10 percent of men who weren't in a fraternity held this belief.[13] Men in frats were also much more likely than those not in frats to believe that their friends would approve of their having sex with many women during the school year (70 percent versus 53 percent) and less likely to believe their friends would disapprove (8 percent versus 19 percent).

Adherence to traditional masculinity norms also appears to legitimate various forms of sexual aggression. Researchers at the University of Michigan compared pressure to adhere to masculinity norms and attitudes toward sexually aggressive behavior in undergraduate men who did or did not belong to a fraternity.[14] The results were pretty depressing: on every measure tested, men who belonged to fraternities held more objectifying attitudes toward women than those who didn't. They more strongly agreed with traditional masculine norms ("If I could, I would frequently change sexual partners," "I would be furious if someone thought I was gay") and felt more pressure from their friends to adhere to these norms (including pressure to "act like I want sex all the time," "avoid doing anything that is girly," and "do shots of alcohol"). They were more supportive of objectifying women ("It is okay for a guy to stare at the body of an attractive woman he doesn't know," "It is fun to rate women based on the attractiveness of their bodies") and more accepting of myths about rape ("When a girl goes to a guy's house on the first date, it means she is willing to have sex," "Girls have a secret wish to be raped"). They were also more willing to engage in sexually deceptive behaviors, such as having sex with someone just so they could tell their friends about it, or telling someone "I love you" in order to have sex with them.

The push toward risky behavior as a way to demonstrate masculinity leads many college men to overdrink, which may facilitate sexual assault, since alcohol reduces inhibitions.[15] A survey of men at four colleges and universities in the northeastern and mid-Atlantic regions of the United States found that those who both conformed to more masculinity norms and drank heavily engaged in the most sexually aggressive behavior.[16] Other research has demonstrated that men who show greater increases in their frequency of binge drinking—having five or more drinks within two hours—during their first year in a fraternity also engage in more frequent sexual aggression. Another explanation for the higher rates of sexual assault committed by men in fraternities may, therefore, be their substantially higher rate of risky alcohol use.

The strong emphasis placed on traditional masculine ideals in certain groups helps explain why sexist and sexually aggressive behaviors are more widespread among members of sports teams and fraternities than other all-male groups. Although sexist attitudes tend to be more common in all-male groups than in mixed ones, the prevalence of such beliefs varies considerably depending on the nature of the group. We don't hear much about sexual violence by men in all-male singing groups, and even within all-male sports teams, research shows higher rates of sexual coercion among men on some teams—football, ice hockey, basketball—than on others—golf, tennis, swimming.[17] It appears that in all-male groups that place less of an emphasis on adopting and adhering to masculine norms, men don't feel as much pressure to adopt objectifying attitudes toward women, binge drink, engage in sexual coercion, and so on.

The tendency to adopt more sexist attitudes and engage in more sexually aggressive behavior when in all-male groups is, sadly, not limited to college students. A 2017 survey conducted by the Pew Research Center found that women whose workplaces were male-dominated were less likely to feel that they were treated fairly and more likely to experience gender discrimination than those who worked primarily with women or with a mix of men and women.[18] Women in mostly male workplaces were also more likely to identify sexual harassment as a problem: 49 percent in workplaces that were mostly male versus 34 percent in those that were gender-balanced, and 32 percent in mostly female ones.

In their book *The Silent Sex: Gender, Deliberation, and Institutions,* the political scientists Christopher Karpowitz and Tali Mendelberg argue that inappropriate norms tend to develop in all types of male-dominated institutions.[19] One example is the US Senate. Kirsten Gillibrand, one of only twenty female senators, has recounted numerous instances of sexism on the part of her male colleagues.[20] After she lost fifty pounds, one male colleague squeezed her stomach and said, "Don't lose too much weight now. I like my girls chubby." Another encouraged her to keep working out "because you wouldn't want to get porky." At a fundraiser, Senate Majority Leader Harry M. Reid referred to her as "the hottest member of the Senate."

Similar reports of sexist attitudes and behavior in other male-dominated environments, such as at hedge funds and in Silicon Valley, are also common. Women in asset management have experienced sexual harassment from clients, colleagues, and bosses.[21] One male asset manager noted, "There are still an awful lot of sexist and derogatory remarks happening when there are only men in meetings." Reports from Silicon Valley are nearly identical.[22] Women in construction and other male-dominated trades also report rampant harassment.[23]

There's no question that sexual misbehavior is common, especially in all-male groups. But as we will see, it may not be as common as we think—and correcting that misperception, along with providing skills training, can help reduce bad behavior and help people step up when they see it.

The Challenge of a Few Loud Voices

When I was an undergraduate at Stanford University, I attended a dorm presentation on date rape, which focused on the importance of giving and receiving consent prior to engaging in any sexual activity. The workshop leaders explained that if your partner said "No" or "Stop" but you proceeded to go ahead and have sex anyway, it was considered rape.

A high-profile athlete on campus raised his hand and said, in utter disbelief, "That can't be right. By that definition, everyone I've ever had sex with I've raped."

I was horrified by his comment—and made a mental note to avoid him—but most students laughed. He clearly saw nothing wrong with the view he'd expressed, presumably because he believed it was widely shared.

Yet considerable research shows that ideas like "no means yes" and "if women dress provocatively they are asking for it" are not widely shared by either women or men in most Western countries. Many men privately find sexually aggressive behavior offensive, but (wrongly) believe that others endorse it.[24] Researchers at the University of Mary Washington asked men to rate their own beliefs about women and their level of discomfort with sexist behavior, and then to assess other men's attitudes on these same measures—those of either other men at their school, or of a friend with whom they completed the questionnaire. In both cases, men overestimated how much other men held sexist beliefs and underestimated their level of discomfort with sexist behavior. Men estimated the average male score at about 17.1, the mid-point of the scale assessing discomfort with sexism (with 35 points being the most discomfort). But in reality, the average score was 23.5. Men also saw their friends as somewhat more comfortable with sexism than they actually were: their mean rating for their friends was 21.6, but their friends' actual score was 23.6.

Why do men see even their close friends as holding more sexist views about women than they actually do? One factor may be their reluctance to openly counter such views, due to a fear of ridicule, judgment, or ostracism. Interviews on campus revealed that the most common reason male students gave for failing to intervene in situations involving sexual violence was evaluation apprehension—a fear of being laughed at or ridiculed—and, in particular, a desire not to appear weak to other men.[25] Men who underestimate their peers' discomfort with sexist attitudes and sexually aggressive behavior may fear the consequences of calling out offensive comments and inappropriate behavior and thus stay silent, which creates a perception that such views are widely shared, when in reality they are not. This tendency to say nothing may be particularly powerful for men in fraternities and on all-male teams, who may fear being ostracized.

Researchers in another study asked undergraduate men to complete surveys assessing their beliefs about women, rape, and sexually aggressive behaviors, alongside one of their close friends.[26] Both students rated their agreement with common myths about rape, such as, "When girls go to parties wearing slutty clothes, they are asking for trouble," "If a girl doesn't physically fight back, you can't really say it was rape," and "If a girl goes to a room alone with a guy at a party, it is her own fault if she is raped." They also indicated whether they had engaged in various forms of sexually coercive behaviors with women. They were then asked to complete the same questionnaire based on how they thought their close friend would answer, and again for an average male college student.

The results provided further evidence that college men have skewed views of what those around them—even their close friends—are thinking when it comes to sexism and sexual assault. Most students saw their classmates as holding more negative attitudes toward women and more strongly endorsing rape myths than they themselves did. This is a classic case of pluralistic ignorance: if you ask any student in particular, they will tell you that they are not comfortable with objectifying attitudes toward women and sexually aggressive behavior, but they believe their peers are perfectly comfortable with such attitudes and behavior.

Men who report having committed sexual assault have been found to believe that others are more accepting of such behavior. A study of sexual aggression found that 54 percent of men who had committed sexual assault said they thought their close friend had done so too, compared with only 16 percent of men who had not.[27] It is tempting to believe that this difference in perception reflects reality—perhaps men who have committed sexual assault are more likely to have friends who do so, too. But that turns out not to be true. Men who had engaged in sexual assault were nearly three times as likely to wrongly believe their friends had done the same than were those who had not. This misperception can have serious consequences, as research indicates that men who believe other men approve of forced sex are more likely to engage in such behavior themselves, even years later.[28]

What does this tell us? The small number of men who actually hold attitudes and beliefs that are supportive of sexual assault—and who commit assault—vastly overestimate support for such behavior. This leads them to feel quite comfortable expressing these views. Their willingness to share sexist beliefs unfortunately leads others to believe that these attitudes are more common than they actually are, especially if the sexual aggressors are in high status positions, as members of athletic teams and fraternities frequently are.

Believing that other men are generally accepting of sexually aggressive behavior has been found to inhibit one's willingness to intervene to stop such behavior. In 2003, researchers at Western Washington University examined college men's and women's beliefs about the importance of consent and their willingness to intervene to prevent sexual assault, as well as their perceptions of their peers' beliefs about both measures.[29] They found that both men and women said they placed a high priority on obtaining and honoring consent in sexual interactions. But college men consistently underestimated the importance their male peers placed on consent. Although there were no differences between men's and women's self-reported beliefs about the importance of intervening to prevent sexual assault, men once again underestimated their male peers' willingness to intervene in such situations. This is in line with prior research showing that men tend to see other men as less concerned about sexual consent and less willing to intervene than they themselves are.

Unfortunately, this misperception decreases their own willingness to act. Men's perceptions of their peers' attitudes are a stronger predictor of their willingness to intervene than their own stated attitudes about sexual aggression.[30] When in the presence of other men who demonstrate offensive behavior toward women, they are especially likely to stay silent.

Researchers at Georgia State University designed a clever experiment to measure willingness to intervene in a sexually aggressive situation.[31] College men were recruited to participate in a study that they were told examined gender, emotions, and attitudes toward foreign film. Each participant was told that he would be working in a group with three other men, and that the group would choose a film clip to be shown to a woman. Clips from two different films were shown—one sexually explicit and one not. The participant had to choose which film clip he would like the woman to watch. He was told that the final choice would be made randomly from among the choices of the four men in the group. He was further informed that the woman's profile stated that she did not like to watch sexually explicit material.

After making his selection, the student was led to a new room where he was joined by the three other men, who were in reality all accomplices of the experimenter. The woman (also an accomplice) briefly entered the room, ostensibly by mistake. After she left, one of the accomplices made either an objectifying comment ("Man, I'd hit that"), which the other two agreed with, or a neutral comment ("Man, that girl looks just like my roommate's sister"). The researcher told the group that the sexually explicit film had been randomly selected, that they would be watching the woman's reaction through a webcam, and that they could stop the film at any time by pressing a key on a keyboard that was next to the participant. (In reality, the men were watching a pre-recorded video of the woman.) The researchers then measured whether the participant would choose to stop the film and if so, when.

The students who had heard the objectifying comment were significantly less likely to stop the video: 35 percent of the men who heard a neutral comment intervened, but only 15 percent of those who heard the objectifying comment did. Those who did stop the video also took longer to do so. During the debriefing, some of the men indicated that pressure to appear masculine in front of their peers played a role in this decision. "The girl looked very uncomfortable," one participant noted. "I knew I had the power to stop it, which I eventually did, but there is more pressure when there is a room full of guys. Part of me felt like they were saying, 'a real man would enjoy watching this.'"[32]

The presence of male peers engaging in "locker-room talk," it appears, can inhibit other men from allowing themselves to stop sexually aggressive behavior.

Strategies That Work to Reduce Sexual Assault

So far I've focused on the power of all-male social groups to create and maintain sexist beliefs, even when many of their members individually do not endorse them. Why, then, do these norms continue? One of my students—a male varsity basketball player—recently told me that every day in the locker room, someone says something offensive. Then he wondered aloud, "Why do I sometimes say something and sometimes I don't?" He recognized that what he was hearing was offensive, but also that he didn't always speak up. What he probably didn't understand was that in all likelihood some of his teammates also felt uncomfortable with these comments, but they too stayed silent.

In this final section of the chapter, we'll look at some strategies that high schools and colleges can use to help students step up when witnessing problematic behavior by their peers. President Barack Obama remarked on the need for such strategies in a 2014 speech: "We are going to need to encourage young people—men and women—to realize that sexual assault is simply unacceptable. And they are going to have to summon the bravery to stand up and say so, especially when the social pressure to keep quiet or to go along can be very intense."[33]

Correct Norm Misperceptions

Given the consistent evidence that men believe others are more comfortable with sexist attitudes and aggressive behavior than they themselves are, and that this belief inhibits them from speaking up, correcting this misperception would seem to be an obvious place to start if we want to reduce sexual violence. In recent years, several programs have been established that focus on helping men understand that the extreme attitudes and behaviors of a small number of their peers are not the norm. This approach may be especially effective since it is easier to change people's perceptions of others' beliefs—by providing accurate information—than to change their own beliefs. As Michael Haines, director of Health Enhancement Services at Northern Illinois University, put it, "You don't have to change the social norm. You just have to show people what it is."[34]

Encouragingly, these programs have proven to be quite effective at reducing sexist attitudes and beliefs.

Christopher Kilmartin and his colleagues at the University of Mary Washington delivered a twenty-minute presentation to men in an introductory psychology class at a university in the Southeast.[35] They offered general information about social norms and about the factors that lead people to misperceive them, like assuming that someone who laughs at a joke actually finds it funny, instead of just laughing to be polite. They explained that these misperceptions can hinder people from challenging bad behavior and laid out specific steps people could take in order to intervene in a problematic situation.

This brief program led to immediate and positive changes. Three weeks after attending the presentation, the students said they saw other men as holding fewer negative beliefs about women, like, "Women are too easily offended" or "Most women interpret innocent remarks as sexist." They also had come to believe that other men were less comfortable with sexist remarks than they had thought before.

Correcting misperceptions about social norms not only affects attitudes but can actually reduce instances of sexual assault. Christine Gidycz and her colleagues at Ohio University randomly assigned half of the first-year men at a medium-sized midwestern university to participate in a ninety-minute sexual assault prevention program in their dorms. The other men—the control group—simply completed questionnaires.[36] The program included three components: refuting rape myths and fostering empathy by describing the impact of sexual assault on women, increasing awareness of the importance of consent, and correcting norm misperceptions about other men's attitudes and behaviors.

Data collected four months later revealed that even this relatively brief intervention made a long-term difference. Men who participated in the program not only believed that their peers would be more likely to intervene in situations that might lead to sexual assault, but they reported reduced levels of sexual aggression themselves. About 6.7 percent of men who didn't participate in the program reported engaging in sexually aggressive behavior, compared with only 1.5 percent of the men who did.

These programs work in two ways. First, when given more accurate information about what other people actually believe, men tend to feel less inhibited about speaking out and intervening. Second, men who might be at risk of being sexually aggressive may change their attitudes and reduce their inclination to dominate women when they learn that their peers do not actually support such behavior.

This approach to reducing sexual assault works not by changing norms, but simply by telling people what the actual norms are and giving them insight into why and how such misperceptions occur. This is the same approach I've used in my own research to reduce symptoms of eating disorders and improve positive attitudes toward seeking mental health treatment in college students.[37]

Provide Skills Training

As students at Connecticut College, Greg Liautaud and Matt Gaetz took on a unique—and unofficial—role in their campus apartment building. Greg, a junior, and Matt, a sophomore, decided to train their fellow students in how to defuse situations that could lead to sexual assault. How did they know what to do? They'd received training themselves as part of the Green Dot program. This training doesn't involve drastic measures—you don't have to tackle someone, break up a passionate embrace, or call 911. You just have to interrupt potentially problematic situations early on. "It's not really about calling someone a bad person," Greg explained. "It's just defusing the situation." Greg and Matt were both members of the college's ice hockey team—precisely the type of all-male athletic team that people think of as engaging in sexual aggression, not working to prevent it.

The Green Dot program is one of a number of bystander intervention training programs designed to reduce sexual assault that have been rolled out at colleges across the country. Others include Bringing in the Bystander, Step Up! and TakeCARE. The Green Dot program teaches students three strategies for intervening to prevent bad behavior from happening. Let's imagine you see a friend making advances on a woman who has clearly had too much to drink. Green Dot advises students to:

1. Create a distraction. Ask your friend to join you for fast food, or tell them another girl is eager to talk to them.
2. Ask someone else to intervene. This can be another friend, or an older student.
3. Step up. Urge your friend to find another girl to talk to.

The specific content varies, but all of these programs emphasize the importance of taking some action to stop bad behavior early on, before it escalates, and train students in the specific skills they need to do so.[38] They use interactive exercises to model and teach skills in all sorts of different scenarios. In one, students act out what they would do if they overheard a sexist comment. In another, they play out what they would do if they saw a drunk person heading into a bedroom with another person. In a third, they are presented with a situation in which they observe an act of sexual violence. This type of training reminds students that everyone has a responsibility to prevent sexual violence.[39]

These programs can be delivered in a number of different formats, including as workshops, within regular courses, or on the internet.[40] Researchers at the Prevention Innovations Research Center at the University of New Hampshire and the Tiltfactor Laboratory at Dartmouth College created video games to teach college students strategies for intervening in situations of sexual and relationship violence, and deliberately wove this information into more general campus information, pop culture, and entertainment.[41] Researchers at Georgia State University created a web-based program called RealConsent to enhance bystander intervention to reduce sexual violence. Charlene Senn, a professor of psychology at the University of Windsor, chose to embed information about bystander intervention into regular academic classes.

Empirical research suggests that these programs work. Students who participate in them report a variety of positive effects, including a decrease in rape myth acceptance, greater empathy for rape victims, and an increased willingness to help.[42] Students reported feeling more confident in their ability to intervene and more willing to do so. Many also said they had actually engaged in some form of bystander behavior, such as checking on a friend who seemed really intoxicated yet was heading upstairs at a party, or speaking up when they heard a sexist remark (e.g., "She deserved to be raped").[43] Rates of sexual violence are markedly lower on campuses that have implemented a bystander intervention program than on those that have not: an evaluation of the effectiveness of the Green Dot program published in 2015 found that experiences of sexual harassment and stalking were 11 percent lower and that instances of unwanted sexual activity with women who were too drunk or high to stop them were as much as 17 percent lower.[44] It isn't just that people say they intend to behave differently: the program changes their actual behavior.

Another program that seeks to give bystanders the skills they need to intervene effectively is the video-based TakeCARE program. A narrator begins by describing the importance of keeping safe during social activities and outlines how people can take care of their friends to help prevent sexual violence. The video then presents three vignettes to demonstrate responses to incidents of sexual coercion, relationship violence, or other potentially harmful activities. In each case the video suggests specific things a person could say or do to prevent the event from occurring or stop it from escalating, or to provide support if it has already occurred.

In one scene, an intoxicated couple at a party heads into a bedroom together, while another couple observes what is happening. The scene pauses while the narrator describes how this situation could lead to problems for one or both members of the couple. The video then shows bystanders interrupting the couple, sending the male student back to the party, and taking the woman home. The narrator describes other ways in which one could intervene in similar situations to prevent harm and stresses the importance of taking care of your friends. This approach—which focuses on the importance of taking *some* action—is designed to give students the confidence that they could actually intervene in a potentially harmful situation without having to do too much. The video is brief—less than half an hour—and practical for use in large settings.

Can a short video give students the ability to act? The simple answer is yes. College students who watched the video reported an increase in confidence that they could intervene in various risky situations, from expressing discomfort if someone says that rape victims are to blame for being raped to helping a very drunk person who is being taken into a bedroom by a group of people at a party.[45] They also reported that they had intervened more in the month after watching the video.

Despite this indication that an entirely video-based program can lead to short-term increases in students' confidence about intervening, further research is needed to assess its longer-term effects. Do these initial increases in attitudes and behaviors last over time, or do they fade? Are there ways this approach could move beyond passive video watching to include more interactive components that might allow for deeper processing of the material and have more lasting effects? It certainly seems likely that practicing the skills portrayed in the video would lead to even stronger effects. Although these are important questions for future research, it's also worth recognizing the immense practical value a short video-based intervention provides. Many college students would not attend a lengthy program on preventing sexual assault. TakeCARE and other programs like it may therefore have a distinct advantage precisely because they can reach a wide variety of students and thus result in broader changes in campus norms.

Video-based approaches may be equally effective in high school settings. In one recent study, TakeCARE was tested on students at a low-income urban public high school in the southern United States.[46] Compared to a control condition, students who participated in the TakeCARE program reported that they engaged in more acts of bystander intervention six months later. Examples included confronting a friend who made excuses for abusive behavior, expressing concern to a friend with unexplained bruises, and trying to get others to help with a situation involving potential sexual or relationship abuse. This study included a creative virtual reality measure. Students wore goggles and participated in an immersive virtual environment in which they interacted with an avatar to simulate real-world situations involving sexual violence in which they could intervene. In one of these, two drunk friends headed into a bedroom at a party. Another involved a potential case of physical assault in a dating couple. A third involved a male student expressing an intention to get his date drunk so that he could sleep with her. The researchers recorded how students responded to each of these situations and how forcefully they tried to prevent a potentially harmful situation from occurring. Compared with students who viewed the control video, those who saw the TakeCARE video demonstrated more assertive behavior during the virtual reality simulation. They also reported more bystander interventions in real-world situations six months later.

These programs work because many of those who witness bad behavior actually want to intervene but don't know what to do. As we'll see in Chapter 10, training in the specific skills necessary to act effectively can help people overcome their natural tendency toward inaction. Those who have received training generally feel a greater sense of responsibility to act when they find themselves confronted by a situation that is similar to one of the scenarios they were taught about, and they feel more confident that they can do so effectively.[47] In over one-third of sexual assaults, at least one other person is present who potentially could intervene but in most instances chooses not to.[48] What does it take to turn that silent witness into an active obstructer? Knowing what to do and how to do it is a good start.

Create New Norms

Men in tight-knit groups that put a premium on male bonding feel considerable pressure to show loyalty to other group members. This sometimes translates into not calling out bad behavior committed by their peers—sticking together, regardless of right or wrong.[49] But there is a good side to the cohesion of these groups: the same underlying dynamics of peer influence can be used to create more positive beliefs and behavior. Many bystander intervention programs (like Green Dot) focus on shifting group norms: from one of protecting group members by staying silent about bad behavior to one of stepping in to prevent bad behavior in the first place. These programs aim to help students understand that a single bad act by a group member hurts the reputation of the entire group, and that all members of teams, fraternities, and dorms have a responsibility to protect their friends from getting into trouble. David Rowe, a football player at the University of New Hampshire, told the *New York Times* that his goal was to look after his teammates, even if that meant interrupting a potential sexual encounter: "Maybe you don't get the girl, but you'll keep your scholarship and still be on the team."[50]

Individual fraternities and athletic teams differ substantially in their cultures and values, and groups with a lower tolerance for sexual aggression and coercion can pressure group members to adhere to their own norms.[51] A study of first-year men attending a small private midwestern university compared rates of sexual coercion between those who had played an aggressive high school sport—football, basketball, wrestling, or soccer—to those who had played a nonaggressive sport—baseball, golf, cross-country racing, swimming, tennis, or track and field.[52] Those who had played a nonaggressive sport held less sexist attitudes toward women, were less supportive of rape myths, and were less likely to engage in sexually coercive behavior.

One study of a single fraternity by sociologist Eric Anderson at the University of Bath revealed an intentional focus away from the typical masculinity norms.[53] One of the members said, "We expect our brothers not to partake in that macho jock mentality. We want to stand out as being intellectual and athletic, but also as being kind and respectful."

Ayres Boswell and Joan Spade at Lehigh University conducted an in-depth study of fraternity life at a private college in Pennsylvania in which roughly half of the students join a Greek organization.[54] They interviewed students and attended fraternity parties to observe social interactions. Their observations offer clear evidence that not all fraternities are the same.

During parties at a fraternity that women described as "high-risk" for sexual violence, men and women rarely interacted as friends. Gender ratios were often highly skewed, and men and women segregated themselves into different parts of the room. Women often danced alone, and when couples danced, they did so in a very close and sexual way. The men in these frats behaved much more crudely—rating women's bodies using a thumbs up or down gesture, making sexist jokes and comments, and engaging in much more flirtatious and openly sexually behavior. Men openly tried to get women to leave the party and go upstairs to their bedrooms, saying things like, "Want to see my fish tank?" or "Let's go upstairs so that we can talk; I can't hear what you're saying in here."

Parties at fraternities that women described as "low-risk" could not have been more different. Men and women danced together—in couples and in groups—and many couples kissed or showed some type of affection. Roughly equal numbers of men and women attended the parties, and men and women regularly engaged in friendly conservations. Pushing, yelling, and cursing were rare, and if they did occur, apologies quickly followed.

In her book *Fraternity: An Inside Look at a Year of College Boys Becoming Men,* Alexandra Robbins explains that men in all-male groups don't set out to engage in bad behavior. Fraternities provide support for men away from home for the first time, create a safe space for them to share social and academic anxieties, and foster the development of valuable leadership skills. The point of this chapter is not to suggest that every member of a fraternity is a sexual predator or that parents should discourage their sons from joining a sports team. My own sons benefited from the experience of being on a sports team and joining a fraternity. But it takes work to help boys understand what is acceptable. One good place to start is by making sure they choose their social groups wisely and to remind them (more than once) that fewer people endorse sexually aggressive behavior than they might think. Another is to help them understand that being a good friend, fraternity brother, or teammate means intervening before potentially problematic behavior escalates.

8

At Work: Fostering Ethical Behavior

On October 20, 2014, Laquan McDonald, a black teenager, was shot and killed by Jason Van Dyke, a Chicago police officer. Initial police reports filed by Van Dyke and several other officers at the scene suggested that the shooting was justifiable because the seventeen-year-old had been acting crazy and lunging at officers with a knife. But further investigation uncovered a strikingly different story. The autopsy revealed that Laquan had been shot sixteen times. A video further indicated that the first shot had been fired while he was walking away—not lunging at the officers—and that he had been shot repeatedly even after he had fallen to the ground. Based on this evidence, Officer Van Dyke was found guilty of second degree murder and sixteen counts of aggravated battery with a firearm. He was sentenced to nearly seven years in jail.

Although Van Dyke had fired all the shots, he was not the only officer at the scene. Seven other officers who were present filed reports that supported his account that Laquan had been coming toward him with a knife, which is clearly contradicted by the video. Three of these officers were indicted by a grand jury for official misconduct, conspiracy, and obstruction of justice for their role in covering up Van Dyke's actions. All three were found not guilty.

This story—in which one person engages in bad behavior but their colleagues at best ignore it and at worst cover it up—is not unique. Similar incidents occur in all industries, from employees ignoring fraudulent business practices to politicians ignoring illicit use of government funds or offensive language by a leader of their own party. This chapter examines the factors that lead people to stay silent about bad behavior in the workplace and suggests strategies organizations can use to change their work culture to foster moral courage.

Will You Confront Your Boss?

When I was in college, I was with my boss one day when we were driving to a meeting, and he was having trouble finding a parking place. He drove around for a bit, but we were by this point late for the meeting, so he pulled into a handicapped parking spot and parked the car. We got out of the car and he turned to me, grinned, and started limping. I said nothing.

My failure to call out my boss is hardly unique. Most people will do nothing when they witness offensive acts by those in powerful positions. They may wonder, "Will speaking up cost me a promotion? A raise? Will I lose my job or get a reputation as a troublemaker?"

When asked about hypothetical situations, people usually say that they would have the courage to confront bad behavior. But in reality, most of us fail to act when we find ourselves actually facing such a situation. It isn't that we don't recognize right from wrong, or realize, if given an opportunity to evaluate the situation dispassionately, that some intervention is called for. Something appears to stop us from acting on our convictions.

Julie Woodzicka at Washington and Lee University and Marianne LaFrance at Yale conducted a study that allowed them to compare what people say with what they do.[1] They recruited young women (age eighteen to twenty-one) and asked them to read and respond to a written scenario about a job interview. Participants read the following passage: "Imagine that you are interviewing for a research assistant position. You are being interviewed by a male (age thirty-two) in an office on campus. Below are several of the questions that he asks you during the course of the interview. Please read each question and indicate how you would respond and feel. Write how you think you would react, not how you think you should react. Indicate how you would actually behave, think, and/or feel."

The three questions were: "Do you have a boyfriend?" "Do people find you desirable?" and "Do you think it is important for women to wear bras to work?"

Most of the participants (62 percent) reported that they would confront the harasser in some way, either by asking him why he was asking the question or by telling him that the question was inappropriate. Twenty-eight percent of the women reported that they would respond even more forcefully, either by rudely confronting the interviewer or by leaving the interview. And 68 percent reported that they would refuse to answer at least one of the three questions. The results clearly indicated that when faced with sexual harassment, participants assumed that they would feel angry or indignant and be confrontational. But would they really?

In a follow-up study to test this important question, the same researchers recruited another group of women to interview for what they believed to be an actual research assistant job and then subjected these applicants to the same three sexually harassing questions. Not one of these women refused to answer even a single question. Most were nonconfrontational. Those who did raise concerns did so in a polite and respectful way, asking why the interviewer asked that question.

When they thought about the situation in advance, almost two-thirds (62 percent) of women had expected that they would confront the offender. But when they were actually put on the spot only about one-third (36 percent) did so. So even when we imagine that we would take a courageous stand, most of us will fail to act when we are actually confronted by such a situation.

Most women who experience sexual harassment at work choose not to report it. When asked why, the most common reason given is fear—of losing their job, hurting their chances of promotion, or being blackballed in their industry.[2] A meta-analysis of sexual harassment in organizations revealed that only one-quarter to one-third of people who have been harassed at work report it to a supervisor, and only 2 to 13 percent actually file a formal complaint.[3] They are not wrong to fear repercussions. Women who do report such behavior "become troublemakers—nobody wants to hire them or work with them anymore," says Jennifer Berdahl, an expert on gender and diversity in the workplace.[4] And what do you do if the person harassing you is your boss? Silence in the face of bad behavior is particularly common in the case of people who have direct power over us; the cost of calling these people out is pretty clear.

A survey of professional accountants found that 60 percent had observed wrongdoing in their workplace at some point—stealing supplies, misclassifying expense reports, manipulating revenue and expenses—and half of them chose not to report it.[5] Common reasons for overlooking this behavior included thinking that it wasn't serious enough to report, that there wasn't enough proof, or that someone else would report it. But the most common reason for staying silent was concern about losing their job or experiencing an unpleasant work environment.

Unfortunately, this fear of retaliation is not misguided. Researchers at the University of Massachusetts Amherst examined more than forty-six thousand sexual harassment claims reported to the Equal Employment Opportunity Commission and state Fair Employment Practices Agencies from 2012 to 2016.[6] Of the claimants, 68 percent reported some type of retaliation by their employer, and a full 65 percent lost their job within the year. Another study, of over one thousand federal court employees, revealed that two-thirds of those who had complained about mistreatment were either shunned by their coworkers, passed over for a promotion, transferred to a less desirable job, or unfairly given poor performance evaluations.[7] These consequences were especially common when workers made complaints about people in powerful positions, which helps explain why people are especially likely to stay silent in these situations.

Few people are brave enough to confront a person in a leadership position who makes a sexist, racist, or otherwise offensive comment. Leslie Ashburn-Nardo and her colleagues recruited female and male college students to participate in a study that was putatively on distance communication and told them they would be working with two other people in an online chat group to evaluate job applications.[8] Before the group discussion began, participants completed questionnaires that they were told would be used to determine their role in the group. Each participant was told that their responses indicated strong listening and interpersonal skills, and that they would therefore serve as the human resources observer. This role involved listening in on the computer chat between the other two group members, taking notes, and then giving them feedback. In reality, the other group members were fictitious, and the conversation was staged.

During the discussion of a female job applicant, one of the group members typed: "i don't know about women in business positions they are so emotional. i wish there was a pic included. for me to put up with a nagging woman at work, she'd have to be really hot!" (The researcher deliberately used lowercase to simulate the casual style of communication between students.) In one condition, participants were told that the person saying this was just one of the two group members; in the other, they were told that this person had been designated the "boss" and was in charge of determining how much each group member would be paid for taking part in the study. After completing the task, participants were asked about their perceptions of the other group members' comments. They were then asked if they would like to meet and provide feedback.

Can you predict their findings?

First, participants in both conditions recognized that the comment about women was inappropriate and discriminatory. But they were much less interested in confronting the person who said it when that person was the boss: only 43 percent of those who heard the sexist comment coming from the higher-power person wanted to meet and share their feedback, compared with 68 percent of those who heard it from a person without this power.

In a second study by the same researchers, participants were asked to read a scenario describing someone—either a supervisor, a co-worker, or a subordinate—making either a sexist or a racist remark in a workplace setting. The scenario for the supervisor role making a sexist remark was as follows:

> Imagine that you work for a software company. You are attending a lunch meeting regarding budget goals for the upcoming year. After the meeting concludes, your supervisor, who is male, turns to the only female in the meeting and says, "Hey, how about taking care of this lunch mess? Aren't women supposed to be good at this sort of thing? You know, being maids and stuff?"

The script replaced "supervisor" with "coworker" or "subordinate" for trials testing the role of the person making the remark, and "male"/"female" with "white"/"African American" for the racist scenario. Each participant was then asked whether they thought the remark was prejudicial, and whether they would confront the person, either directly or indirectly.

As in the previous study, participants found the comment discriminatory and inappropriate—regardless of the target of the comment or who it was made by. They tended to see the comment as less serious and were less likely to report it if it was sexist than racist. When the person making the comment was a supervisor (rather than co-worker or subordinate), participants felt less responsible for intervening, were less able to decide what they would do, and saw the costs of confronting the person as greater. Not surprisingly, they were also less likely to say that they would confront the person who made the comment.

Many people are reluctant to call out problematic behavior committed by people in powerful positions, even if that behavior can have extremely serious consequences. Researchers in one study examined this issue within a medical setting, where a failure to speak up when a colleague makes a mistake or uses an unsafe practice may mean the difference between life and death.[9] Interns and residents at two large northeastern academic medical centers were asked to complete a survey assessing medical courage. They indicated how much they agreed with the following statements:

- I do what is right for my patients, even if I experience opposing social pressures (e.g., opposition from senior members of the healthcare team, medical guidelines, etc.).
- When faced with ethical dilemmas in patient care, I consider how both my professional values and my personal values apply to the situation before making decisions.
- I do what is right for my patients, even if it puts me at risk (e.g., legal risk, risk to reputation, etc.).
- My patients and colleagues can rely on me to exemplify moral behavior.

Next, they were asked how many times in the previous month they had seen some type of patient safety breach, such as poor hand hygiene or an improper technique for sterilization, that could increase the risk of patient harm. If they reported that they had observed at least one such breach, they were asked whether they had brought this up with the person involved.

As predicted, participants who scored higher on the moral courage scale were more likely to report speaking up when witnessing a patient safety breach. However, interns were less likely to call out bad behavior than residents, regardless of their level of moral courage. (Interns have less training and authority than residents.) These findings are in line with those from other studies showing that people often fail to speak up in medical settings if doing so requires challenging a person of higher authority. Medical students and nurses are by and large reluctant to challenge doctors.[10]

One of the first research studies to demonstrate how hard it is for people to confront those in powerful positions was designed by the psychiatrist Charles Hofling and carried out in a hospital in the 1960s.[11] On twenty-two separate days, a man called the nurse who was on the floor in the evening (a different nurse each time) and said that he was a doctor on staff, but gave a fictitious name (meaning the nurse did not know him or recognize that he was a doctor at that hospital). He then asked her (all were women) to check whether the drug Astroten was on hand. This was a fictitious drug, actually just a harmless sugar pill that had been placed in the supply room earlier that day. When she reported that the drug was there, he instructed her to immediately administer 20 mg of the drug to a patient (using the actual name of a patient on her floor) and said that he would sign the order when he arrived at the hospital later on. The maximum dosage listed on the bottle was 10 mg.

Keep in mind that giving the medication in the dosage requested would violate three rules: accepting orders over the phone, accepting orders from an unknown doctor, and giving a dose above the maximum noted on the bottle. What did the nurses do? Twenty-one nurses—95 percent—were stopped by the researchers as they walked into the patient's room with the too-high dosage of medication.

Now, this study was published in 1966, and it's certainly reasonable to assume that the doctor–nurse power imbalance may be less extreme today than it was more than fifty years ago. Nurses might feel more comfortable challenging dubious orders, especially when they could have serious consequences for patients. But are we certain that is the case?

To see whether the situation has changed, researchers from VitalSmarts, a leadership training company, examined reports filed from 2,383 registered nurses regarding times in which they had trouble speaking up or getting others to listen about a potential problem at work.[12] Most nurses—58 percent—reported experiencing a situation when they felt that it was unsafe to speak up, or when they did speak up but were unable to get others to listen. Seventeen percent of the nurses said they had experienced this situation at least a few times a month. Many of these problems involved their colleagues taking dangerous shortcuts, such as not washing their hands long enough, failing to change gloves, or neglecting to perform a safety check. Although 84 percent of nurses reported seeing colleagues take dangerous shortcuts, and 26 percent of them believed that these shortcuts led to patient harm, only 31 percent had fully shared their concerns with the person who had engaged in this behavior.

Bad behavior of all types continues in part because most people are afraid that any challenge would be costly. This cycle of silence plays out again and again, as fear of retaliation keeps us silent even in the face of egregious behavior. Many of the young gymnasts who experienced repeated sexual abuse from Larry Nassar worried that complaining about—or even questioning—their treatment at the hands of the team doctor would hurt their chances of making the Olympic team. And they were probably right.

Professional Benefits of Staying Silent

Even when retaliation is unlikely, people sometimes have personal motives for overlooking bad behavior. Where corporate fraud is involved, they may directly benefit from ignoring unethical behavior in others. As Kurt Eichenwald revealed in *Conspiracy of Fools,* many leaders at the energy company Enron, including managers, lawyers, and advisers, were aware that the company was hiding billions of dollars in debt to maintain high stock prices, but they failed to speak out. Several executives at Arthur Andersen, an acclaimed accounting firm hired by Enron to conduct regular audits of its financial statements, recognized that fraudulent practices were being used to hide loses. Exactly how much any one person knew depended on their position, but many of them were benefiting financially from looking the other way. In the end, sixteen people—including Enron founder Kenneth Lay, CEO Jeffrey Skilling, and CFO Andrew Fastow—pleaded guilty to financial crimes, and five more people were also found guilty. But many more had some knowledge of what was going on and did nothing to stop it.

Enron's implosion received a great deal of attention, but it is hardly the only case of white-collar crime that goes unreported for years. In 2005, the two top executives of the private security company Tyco—CEO Dennis Kozlowski and CFO Mark Swartz—were convicted of misappropriating more than $400 million from the company. They committed various financial crimes, including stock fraud and unauthorized bonuses, and used company funds to maintain lavish lifestyles featuring massive estates, expensive jewelry, and over-the-top parties. In 2018, Dr. Jorge Zamora-Quezada was arrested and charged with federal health care fraud. He is accused of filing more than $240 million in false health care claims, including falsely diagnosing patients with serious and even terminal illnesses in order to prescribe expensive medications and procedures. This fraud enabled him to buy numerous residential properties, luxury cars, and a private plane.

But unethical business behavior isn't restricted to cases that make headlines. It occurs all the time in businesses of every size. Expense reimbursement fraud, such as submitting fictitious receipts or filing reimbursements for personal expenses as if they were business expenses, accounts for 11 percent of fraud cases in large businesses (those with over 100 employees) and 21 percent of cases in small businesses.[13] A few years ago a colleague of mine regularly charged various personal items to the college, including his kids' school supplies, stamps for his family's holiday cards, and costs of a family vacation in Florida.[14] (This practice finally ended after college officials became involved.)

Politicians around the world often claim personal expenses as business expenses. Members of Parliament in the United Kingdom have been caught charging the government for a massage chair, a Kit Kat bar, and the clearing of the moat at the family estate.[15] California Republican congressman Duncan Hunter was accused of spending more than $250,000 from his campaign funds on such expenses as a trip to Italy, videogames for his son, and a plane ticket for the family's rabbit, Eggburt.[16]

What's the common link in all of these examples? The size of the fraud varies substantially—taking pens from the office supply cabinet obviously isn't equivalent to writing off extravagant family trips as a business expense. But in all of these cases, some people knew what was happening, and they chose to look the other way. Maybe it was the administrative assistant who processed the charges, or the treasurer of the campaign committee who saw the travel receipt for the rabbit, or the auditing firm that verified the company's tax returns. Most of us would make the same choice if we found ourselves in their shoes, because the professional consequences of calling someone out for bad behavior can be substantial, especially if that person is in a powerful position.

It's not just individuals who may benefit from ignoring bad behavior; so may their employers, especially if the individual is highly placed. Matthew Quade and his colleagues at Baylor University collected data from more than three hundred pairs of employees and their supervisors working in a range of different jobs across the country.[17] Supervisors rated their employees' unethical behavior, such as falsifying time or expense reports or misusing confidential information, and their overall job proficiency. Employees then completed measures assessing how much they felt ostracized in the workplace. Ostracism, for the purpose of the study, was rated through statements like, "Others ignored you at work" and "Others at work treated you as if you weren't there."

The survey revealed that the relationship between unethical behavior and ostracism depended on how productive the employee was. For those who were not very productive, engaging in unethical behavior led to ostracism. But for those who were rated by their supervisors as highly productive, there was no association between unethical behavior and ostracism. Poor-performing employees, noted the researchers, may be called out for bad behavior that is ignored when employees are regarded as valuable to an organization. In other words, "high job performance may offset unethical behavior."

This helps explain why 21st Century Fox gave Bill O'Reilly, the top-rated host of Fox News, a contract extension in 2017 and agreed to pay him an estimated $25 million a year—even though the company was aware of multiple claims of sexual harassment against him. O'Reilly was eventually fired, but only after these claims—and the associated settlements—were made public, at which point the financial cost of lost advertising dollars presumably became too much to bear.

Social Costs of Standing Up to Bad Behavior

On March 16, 1968, American soldiers killed an estimated five hundred Vietnamese civilians—elderly men, women, and children—living in the village of My Lai. Dozens were shot after being pushed into an irrigation ditch. As this massacre was unfolding, Warrant Officer Hugh Thompson Jr., a helicopter pilot, saw what was happening. Although he was outranked by the captains and lieutenants who were directing this attack, Thompson landed his helicopter between the soldiers and the civilians, ordered the soldiers to stop, and threatened to use the helicopter's machine guns on anyone who continued to shoot. His actions stopped the massacre.

This is the story of My Lai that many of us know. But it's not the complete story. Following his courageous intervention, Hugh Thompson made an official report of the incident to his commander, and later, after news of the massacre became public, to the House Armed Services Committee. He was heavily criticized both by his fellow soldiers and by members of the public for his actions.[18]

"I'd received death threats over the phone," he told *60 Minutes* in 2004. "Dead animals on your porch, mutilated animals on your porch some mornings when you get up."[19] He was not formally recognized for his heroic actions until March 6, 1998, three decades after the killings, when he was awarded the Soldier's Medal—given for heroism not involving conflict with an enemy.

The costs of standing up to bad behavior in any work environment can be substantial, but perhaps especially so when the culture of the place puts a strong emphasis on loyalty. This is true in particular of the military and the police. In a survey of over 3,700 police officers across the country, nearly 80 percent said a code of silence exists within police culture. A full 46 percent said they had personally seen misconduct by another officer that they didn't report.[20]

What leads so many police officers—otherwise notably courageous people—to fail to report bad behavior? Officers mention several factors, including a belief that their report will be ignored, fear that they will be disciplined or fired, and pressure from other officers to stay silent. But the most common reason cited by far to justify their silence is fear of being ostracized by other officers. As Lorenzo Davis, a former Chicago police officer put it, "The code of silence works a lot like a family situation. You cannot tell on your family members. You just know that. No one has to tell you that. If you have a partner, you're going to back up your partner."[21]

Even in egregious cases, far too many people choose to ignore bad behavior out of loyalty to an organization, even if the behavior in question directly contradicts its values. Nowhere is this disconnect more apparent than in the world of religion.

When the gymnast Rachael Denhollander was a young girl, before she suffered sexual abuse at the hands of Larry Nassar, she had been abused by another man, a member of her family's own church. A college student from their Baptist church started singling her out for attention when she was just seven years old. He bought her gifts, walked with her to and from Sunday School, regularly hugged her, and encouraged her to sit on his lap. The counselor who led the church's sexual abuse support group recognized the behavior as a likely precursor to sexual abuse and warned her parents. But when her parents reached out to friends in their Bible study group, they were strongly discouraged from taking any action. Their friends told them they were overreacting. One family stopped socializing with the Denhollanders, out of concern that they could be accused next. So Rachael's parents decided to do nothing. Two years later, after the student had left the church, Rachael told her parents that he had masturbated while Rachael sat on his lap one evening. But they never told anyone. As her mother said to a *Washington Post* reporter, "We had already tried once and weren't believed. What was the point?"[22]

We have all read the devastating stories of the Roman Catholic Church's decades-long cover-up of sexual abuse committed by priests, but other religious institutions are not immune. Stories of overlooked sexual abuse by leaders have emerged concerning Southern Baptist leaders in Texas, administrators at the evangelical Christian Bob Jones University, and in the Orthodox Jewish community in New York City. One of the reasons that victims are treated like troublemakers within religious—and other—communities, writes Amy Davidson Sorkin in the *New Yorker,* is that "there is the illusion that being community-minded means protecting the strongest, rather than the most vulnerable members of a community."[23]

The Slippery Slope of Bad Behavior

In the fall of 2018, the psychological community was stunned when they heard that current and former students of Dartmouth College's Department of Psychological and Brain Sciences had filed a lawsuit accusing three well-known faculty members of engaging in inappropriate behavior—including sexual harassment and assault—over more than sixteen years. (In August 2019 Dartmouth settled the lawsuit for $14.4 million, although the college did not admit liability.) As Leah Somerville, director of the Affective Neuroscience and Development Laboratory at Harvard University, wrote, describing her own experience as a graduate student at Dartmouth: "If you are steeped in an environment with toxic norms, it is likely that you can't even see it for yourself. For example, while I was there it was common for certain faculty members to joke about details of trainees' sex lives in the lab and public settings. At first, this made me very uncomfortable. But as those types of exchanges happened regularly and became more egregious, they seemed less and less scandalous. Right under my nose, social norms shifted. As a wider array of behaviors are deemed acceptable, other inappropriate conversations and actions risk becoming normalized as well."[24]

Toxic environments often grow gradually, as unethical behavior starts with something small, but then continues and expands. Even when individual members of a group are aware that inappropriate behavior is occurring, they may stay silent because they believe others don't find such behavior problematic. In this way, group norms gradually shift over time.

This process helps explain how so many members of the Republican Party who initially—and sometimes vehemently—opposed

Donald Trump when he was a presidential candidate came to support him after his election. Trump spent much of his campaign mocking and denigrating the Republican Party establishment—often by tweet—and emphasizing his own status as an outsider. So it wasn't surprising that many Republican leaders failed to endorse him during the primaries and voiced serious reservations about key pillars of his platform. Before his election, numerous Republican leaders expressed concern about Trump's offensive language and policies, objecting to his description of Mexicans as rapists, to his proposal of a so-called Muslim ban, and to his bragging about grabbing women "by the pussy."

When he was elected president, I wondered how senators and congresspeople would react. To my disappointment, some of his most vocal critics soon became fervent champions. Before Trump's election, South Carolina senator Lindsay Graham described Trump as a "jackass," "a kook," and a "race-baiting, xenophobic, religious bigot." He even went so far as to say, "You know how you make America great again? Tell Donald Trump to go to hell."[25] Graham proudly tweeted his own decision not to vote for Trump. But after the election, he changed his tune. He began golfing with the president regularly, and pronounced on Fox News, "We have got a president and a national security team that I've been dreaming of for eight years."[26]

This abrupt about-face cannot simply be brushed aside as a matter of opportunism. It sometimes seems as if, with a few notable exceptions, the moral compass of the Republican Party has shifted. As the outspoken conservative David Brooks notes, "Supporting Trump requires daily acts of moral distancing, a process that means that after a few months you are tolerant of any corruption. You are morally numb to everything."[27] Former FBI director James Comey has also grappled with the question of why so many people in the Trump administration have failed to acknowledge or confront his dishonesty. In an opinion piece in the *New York Times,* he noted that "it starts with your sitting silent while he lies, both in public and private, making you complicit by your silence." He continued:

> In meetings with him, his assertions about what "everyone thinks" and what is "obviously true" wash over you, unchallenged, . . . because he's the president and he rarely stops talking. As a result, Mr. Trump pulls all of those present into a silent circle of assent. Next comes Mr. Trump attacking institutions and values you hold dear—things you have always said must be protected and which you criticized past leaders for not supporting strongly enough. Yet you are silent.[28]

The process starts with staying silent, but then gradually transmogrifies into acquiescence, such that by the end, vehement critics find themselves voicing support for policies—and a person—whom they must still recognize on some level to be deeply flawed. In Comey's words, "While the entire world is watching, you do what everyone else around the table does—you talk about how amazing the leader is and what an honor it is to be associated with him. You use his language, praise his leadership, tout his commitment to values. And then you are lost. He has eaten your soul."

This gradual shift by so many leaders in the Republican Party may be puzzling to many, but not to social psychologists. As described in Chapter 1, most participants in the Milgram study fully followed the orders of the authority figure to deliver dangerous shocks to an innocent person, but only because the intensity of the shock escalated gradually over time. Once one heads down the road of giving that first shock—it's tiny, only 15 volts—it becomes very hard psychologically to extricate oneself. This same process helps explain why leaders in the Republican Party who chose to support Candidate Trump despite his offensive comments then found it hard to speak out against President Trump when he made equally or more offensive remarks. Perhaps they believed in the larger vision he was peddling of a proud and secure America with lower taxes, more conservative judges, and fewer immigrants. But perhaps they simply needed to justify their past support by heading further down the same road, for better or worse. As empirical research tells us, once you take a small step in the wrong direction, it becomes hard to change course.

Francesca Gino at the University of North Carolina and Max Bazerman at the Harvard Business School designed a series of studies to test whether people would be less likely to report bad behavior if it built up gradually over time. They asked participants to serve as "auditors" and to accept or reject the estimates other people gave about the number of pennies in a jar.[29] In some cases these estimators gradually inflated their numbers over time—increasing by just forty cents on each round—while in others they made more abrupt changes—jumping by four dollars. Fifty-two percent of the auditors in the gradual change condition approved the estimates, compared with only 24 percent of those in the abrupt change condition. The authors attribute this difference to the "boiling frog effect," a reference to the belief that a frog dropped into boiling water will immediately jump out, whereas one that is dropped into lukewarm water that is slowly brought to a boil will stay put, as it fails to recognize the gradual increase in temperature—until it is too late.

Real-world cases of corporate fraud provide even stronger evidence of the slippery slope of temptation. Interviews with thirteen financial executives indicted for accounting fraud revealed that their behavior in virtually all cases escalated gradually. Here's how one former chief financial officer described it: "Crime starts small, it progresses very slowly. First you work off the books. Some people say it's not a crime, okay, we'll rationalize it and say it's not a crime." And once you start down this path of bad behavior, it's really hard to pull yourself out. "It may seem like it's . . . it's, you know, trivial or benign or whatever the term you want to use, when you first cross the line, " said one former administrative officer, "but all you have to do is put your toe across the line . . . then you're in, and once you're in, you're in."[30]

Changing Workplace Culture

Problematic behavior hurts organizations of all types—from corporations and universities, to military and intelligence agencies, to hospitals and police departments. A report by the Association of Certified Fraud Examiners revealed that unethical behavior by employees costs most organizations about 5 percent of their annual revenue.[31] In extreme cases—think of Bill O'Reilly or the movie producer Harvey Weinstein—the financial costs can be considerably higher.

Eliminating this bad behavior takes more than just identifying a few bad actors—though toxicity at the top does tend to trickle down. It requires changing the workplace culture more broadly. Workplaces need to foster a culture in which ethical behavior involves doing what's right, not protecting the bad behavior of coworkers. In a speech to the Chicago City Council following the death of Laquan McDonald, Mayor Rahm Emanuel talked about the code of silence among Chicago police: "This problem is sometimes referred to as the Thin Blue Line. It is the tendency to ignore, deny or in some cases cover-up the bad actions of a colleague or colleagues. No officer should be allowed to behave as if they are above the law just because they are responsible for upholding the law. We cannot ask citizens in crime-ravaged neighborhoods to break the code of silence if we continue to allow a code of silence to exist within our own police department."[32]

One of the key factors that inhibits many of us from speaking up is our fear of the social consequences. People who report colleagues for engaging in unethical behavior are often described as "rats" or "snitches." But even people labeled by the more neutral term "whistleblower" are often regarded askance. As Jeffrey Wigand, who revealed that his employer, the tobacco company Brown & Williamson, had intentionally added chemicals to its tobacco in order to make cigarettes more addictive, writes in the foreword to *The Corporate Whistleblower's Survival Guide,* "The name whistleblower needs to be replaced. Why? The term is laden with pejorative connotations, such as rat, tattletale, fink and turncoat."[33] His suggestion for a replacement? "Person of conscience."

Hire Ethical Leaders

So what can an organization do to create a culture that truly values ethical behavior, not just in the mission statement, but in everyone's actions? Like so many things, an organization's ethical culture flows down from the top. Jonathan Haidt, a professor of ethical leadership at New York University's Stern School of Business, stresses that "leaders must be willing to hire, fire, and promote based on core values, not just hitting bottom-line targets or advancing the business's growth."[34]

Haidt spearheads a nonprofit company, Ethical Systems, that provides companies with research-based strategies for creating a culture that promotes ethical, honest, and moral decision-making.[35] His first piece of advice is that leaders should model ethical behavior themselves—not just in their words, but in their actions. That can include taking a pay cut if the company hits hard times or walking away from a lucrative deal that will hurt investors. Haidt and others have pointed to James Burke, the former CEO of Johnson & Johnson, as a leader who put customers' health above profits. In 1982, after seven people died from taking Tylenol capsules that had been laced with cyanide, he ordered the recall of over thirty-one million bottles of the pain reliever. Haidt also identifies the commitment of Tony Hsieh, the CEO of Zappos, to demonstrate moral leadership by using the same size cubicle as his employees, reducing hierarchy within the company and prioritizing personal accountability for all employees.

Haidt identifies a few common traits among leaders who are rated by their employees as highly ethical. First, they are conscientious, meaning that they are careful, thoughtful, and detailed-oriented.[36] Leaders with these traits don't take shortcuts or let the ball drop.

Second, they place high importance on their own moral identity, meaning whether they are honest, caring, and compassionate.[37] Ethical leaders also think about moral issues in a complex way, with a focus on principles of fairness, justice, and human rights.[38]

Companies should keep in mind that ethical leadership pays off—and taking ethical shortcuts doesn't. A study summarized in the *Harvard Business Review* found that CEOs whose employees gave them high marks for character—including integrity, responsibility, forgiveness, and compassion—had an average return on assets of 9.35 percent over a two-year period—nearly five times larger than those with low ratings.[39] Leaders with the highest character marks are recognized by their employees as standing up for what's right, expressing concern for the common good, letting go of mistakes (made by themselves and others), and expressing empathy. Those with the lowest ratings show the inverse: they lie, can't be trusted to honor promises, blame others for problems, punish people for mistakes, and show little care for others. Ethical leaders motivate better behavior from their employees, and this leads to better profits.

There are a number of possible reasons why ethical leadership is so effective, many of which are probably correlated.[40] People who work for companies with ethical leaders have higher job satisfaction and commitment, in part because they feel that the leader cares about them and treats them fairly. These companies may, as a result, experience lower rates of turnover. People also model their behavior on the leader, so they are less likely to engage in unethical behavior themselves, which can be costly. Employees who notice wrongdoing in a company that values ethical leadership may be more likely to report that behavior to management, because they trust that their decision to report will be appreciated—not retaliated against—and that fair and appropriate procedures will be followed. This allows problematic behavior to stop at a relatively early point, instead of escalating.

Finding leaders who will model ethical behavior is all the more important given evidence that people in powerful positions are less likely than those in lower-level positions to take the moral high road. Researchers at Northwestern and at Tilburg University in the Netherlands conducted a series of studies in which they assigned participants (Dutch university students) to either high-power or low-power roles.[41] Those in the high-power role were told to imagine that they were the prime minister; those in the low-power role, a civil servant. They were then asked to read and respond to three moral dilemmas: whether it is acceptable to (1) speed when late for an appointment, if there is no traffic on the road; (2) omit money earned from a side job on tax forms; (3) keep a stolen, abandoned bicycle rather than turning it in to the police. Half of the participants were asked whether such behavior was acceptable for people in general. The other half were asked whether they themselves would feel right engaging in the behavior.

Did power influence moral judgment? Absolutely. People in low-power positions generally judged the acts as equally unacceptable whether committed by others or by themselves. In two of the cases, they even judged their own behavior more harshly than that of others. But people in high-power positions consistently rated the same behavior as less acceptable if committed by other people than by themselves.

This study provides some insight into the hypocrisy we often see in leaders of all types. It suggests that people with power hold others to higher standards than they hold themselves—even if this power is exercised on a short-term basis and randomly assigned. One of the authors of the study, Adam Galinsky, noted the relevance of the results to recent scandals: "For instance, we saw some politicians use public funds for private benefits while calling for smaller government, or have extramarital affairs while advocating family values."[42] Additional examples are rife, from pastors who preach their commitment to helping the poor while owning private jets, to high profile members of the Hollywood community who actively promote their pro-woman values while sexually harassing other members of that some community.

What can companies do to make sure they are hiring ethical leaders, who not only talk the talk but walk the walk? Jonathan Haidt recommends choosing leaders who focus not on immediate short-term gains—when unethical actions can pay off—but on the long-term outlook of the company—when such actions can result in serious and lasting consequences. And those leaders should set the same rules for themselves as for others. Having a leader who models ethical behavior won't ensure that all employees follow suit, but it's an essential first step.

Refuse to Tolerate Unethical Behavior

Organizations that want to foster an open and ethical culture have to make their nontolerance of unethical behavior clear at multiple levels. The message needs to come from company leaders and supervisors, but also from coworkers and peers. Ethics training can't be one-size-fits-all, and it shouldn't be limited to an online video that you click through half-heartedly before returning to work. Leaders need training in how to convey their expectation that employees will behave morally in ways both big and small.

Stopping unethical behavior early on is important, since fraudulent acts tend to escalate over time as individuals try to justify their initial missteps. Former *New York Times* reporter Jayson Blair resigned in 2003 after he was found to have fabricated and plagiarized a number of articles. "It's kind of the slippery slope that starts to happen," he explained. "I think once you realize that you can get away with something, once you cross over that line, you somehow have to rationalize how 'I am a good person, and I did this, so somehow this has to be ok, I've got to make this ok.' So then it becomes a lot easier to do it."[43]

Companies can start by establishing rules that restrict tempting but dishonest actions. Some hospitals have banned pharmaceutical companies from gift-giving, for example. It turns out that physicians who receive perks from these companies—from meals to paid speaking engagements to lavish resort trips—write more prescriptions and recommend more expensive drugs.[44] One study published in the *Journal of the American Medical Association* compared the number of prescriptions written by over two thousand physicians at nineteen academic medical centers before and after such gift-restriction policies were implemented.[45] Prescriptions of name-brand drugs decreased by 5 percent. This may sound like a small change, but it amounts to billions of dollars.

Organizations also need to make clear that employees at all levels will be held to the same ethical standards. Far too often company leaders ignore bad behavior by "stars" whom they feel they can't afford to alienate or lose—academics who bring in lots of grant money, hedge fund managers with high-profile clients, Oscar-winning film producers. Employees who see a prominent person getting away with problematic behavior understand that the organization tolerates unethical practices. This knowledge decreases their willingness to report rule violations and may well increase their own likelihood of acting unethically.

Christopher Bauman at the University of California Irvine and colleagues from the University of Southern California and the University of Michigan did a study to examine how willing people were to punish common types of fraud, such as lying on expense reports and stealing office supplies (as described in stories that the study participants read).[46] These are relatively small infractions—and hence employees may see them as no big deal—but over time they add up and are very costly for companies. The researchers found that if the participants had been told that higher-ups in the company were also engaging in fraudulent behavior, they did not recommend punishing the employees. CEOs should take this finding to heart if they want to foster ethical behavior company-wide.

Another strategy for combating corporate fraud is to create strong anti-retaliation policies. Researchers at North Carolina State University and Bucknell found that people are significantly more likely to report fraudulent behavior to the appropriate party within their company when they don't fear retaliation for doing so.[47] This approach can be especially advantageous for publicly traded companies; it allows them to address problems before the Securities and Exchange Commission is notified, at which point the consequences of such behavior are far more serious.

Companies also need to keep in mind that whistleblowing can help avoid future problems. Jaron Wilde at the University of Iowa's Tippie College of Business examined 317 large, publicly traded firms that had received complaints from a whistleblower to the Occupational Safety and Health Administration.[48] He found that firms that had received a complaint engaged in less fraudulent behavior—accounting irregularities and evasive tax filings—in the following two years than did similar companies that had not received a complaint. Wilde believes that reporting led companies to be more cautious in their financial practices, in order to reduce their risk of future legal trouble.

What's the takeaway from all of this research? Refusing to tolerate unethical behavior—at all levels—pays off. Employees who recognize that ethical behavior is expected, even required, will be less tempted to take small steps in the wrong direction. They will also feel comfortable reporting problematic behavior, which helps stop it at an early stage. Creating a culture in which ethical behavior is a priority for all employees may require shifts in company norms, but it ultimately helps the bottom line.

Create Cues and Reminders

One of the simplest approaches to pushing people toward ethical behavior is to create subtle reminders. Many colleges and universities require students to write or sign an honor pledge at the start of an exam, verifying that they neither gave nor received help. This strategy is designed to remind students of the importance of doing honest academic work and to increase students' self-awareness of their own behavior as they start the exam. As described in Chapter 2, greater self-awareness reduces people's tendency to withdraw effort on group tasks, in part because we all like to think of ourselves as good people who do the morally right thing. And even small cues that increase self-awareness—like signing your name—can push people toward more ethical behavior.

Max Bazerman at Harvard Business School and his colleagues designed a clever study to test whether a simple signature in fact reduces unethical behavior.[49] They asked students and employees at universities in the southeastern United States to complete a series of math problems, for which they would receive one dollar for each right answer. After taking the test, the participants were told to score themselves, using an answer key provided by the researcher. Participants were then handed one of three forms to use to report their score and collect their money. One form simply asked for the number of problems they solved correctly. The other two forms also asked for the number of correct solutions, but in addition, participants were required to sign their names immediately below a statement saying that to the best of their knowledge, the information provided on the form was correct and complete. In one case, this signature box was placed at the top of the form, meaning that participants signed before recording the number of problems they had solved correctly. In the other case, the signature box was placed at the bottom of the form, after the number of problems solved correctly had been recorded.

When the researchers collected the forms (along with the answer sheets so they could check whether participants had reported their scores honestly), they found striking results. More than half of those who completed the forms with no signature and with the signature at the bottom of the form had cheated: 64 percent and 79 percent, respectively. But only 37 percent of those who signed at the top inflated their score.

Now, one major limitation of this study is that cheating to get a few extra dollars in a research study may not seem like truly unethical behavior. It's certainly not the same as engaging in dishonest behavior in a real-world setting, in which both the risks and the rewards are substantially greater.

So to test the effects of a signature in a more realistic setting, these same researchers collaborated with an automobile insurance company, again in the southeastern United States. They created two different versions of the standard policy review form used by the company, which asks customers to report the current odometer mileage of the cars they are insuring. (Lower odometer mileage indicates less driving—and thus less risk of accidents—and therefore results in a reduced insurance premium.) Customers were randomly assigned to receive one of two forms that were identical in every respect except for the location of the statement "I promise that the information I am providing is true," which they had to sign. Half of the forms had this statement at the beginning of the form, and half at the end. The researchers then compared the mileage reported by customers on the two types of forms.

Once again, placement of the signature mattered. People who signed at the beginning of the form reported higher mileage—26,098 miles, on average—than those who signed at the end—23,671. This simple shift led to a more than 10 percent increase in the reported odometer reading. These findings provide strong evidence that simply reminding people of their intention to behave honestly before they have a chance to do otherwise can go a long way toward increasing ethical behavior.

When we are reminded of who we are—which signing our name surely does—we are also reminded of our intentions to be a good person who does the right thing. It's precisely why I make all students in my classes sign a pledge at the start of each exam I give.

This type of subtle cue is especially important since unethical choices often don't arise following careful and deliberative thought, but rather accidentally and almost unintentionally. Think about the college student who is feeling anxious during an exam and makes the spontaneous choice to glance at a neighbor's exam to "check" an answer, or a journalist frantically working on deadline who fabricates a quote. These people are engaging in dishonest behavior almost unintentionally. The choice is made quickly, and little—if any—thought is given to the potential consequences.

Another subtle strategy for pushing people toward ethical behavior, then, is to ask people to reflect on a time when they did not behave honorably and which they now regret. To test this strategy, Ayelet Fishbach at the University of Chicago Booth School of Business and Oliver J. Sheldon at Rutgers Business School created a series of experiments to test whether simply thinking about one's own prior behavior could lead people to make more ethical choices.[50] In one study, business school students participated in a simulated negotiation in which they served as brokers representing either the buyer or the seller of a historic New York City brownstone. The buyer's plan was to demolish the brownstone to build a hotel. The seller's goal was to sell only to a buyer who would preserve it. Before starting the negotiation, half of the students were asked to think about a time they had cheated or bent the rules in some way to get ahead; the others were not asked to do so.

The researchers found that asking people to reflect on their own bad behavior in the past did indeed reduce their willingness to do so again. Forty-five percent of the students who had first been asked to recall a time when they had acted unethically lied to close the brownstone deal—but that number shot up to 67 percent for those who weren't asked about prior unethical behavior. Asking someone to recall a time in which they've behaved poorly may not be as effective at eliciting ethical behavior as asking them to affirmatively commit to doing so by signing their name, but it may at least push them to think about the choice they are making.

Other studies by these same researchers revealed that cues that remind people to behave honestly—such as writing about their own values and beliefs, or reflecting on the temptations of unethical behavior—decrease people's intention to falsely call in sick, steal office supplies, or work slowly to avoid additional tasks. Reminding people of how tempting it can be to behave dishonestly seems to improve their ability to resist subsequent pulls toward unethical behavior. Why would that be?

Many of us think of small forms of dishonest behavior as no big deal. We don't think much of speeding, failing to report extra income, adding a personal lunch to our expense account, copying a few sentences from Wikipedia, or slightly fudging data. But if we're asked to stop and think, we generally recognize that these things are wrong. "People often think that bad people do bad things and good people do good things, and that unethical behavior just comes down to character," writes Oliver Sheldon, the lead author on this study. "But most people behave dishonestly sometimes, and frequently, this may have more to do with the situation and how people view their own unethical behavior than character, per se."[51]

These research findings—in both lab-based and real-world settings—illustrate the point I made in Chapter 1 about the myth of monsters. Most people who engage in unethical behavior don't do so intentionally and deliberately. They fall into it by making small, seemingly inconsequential choices. And small tweaks in the environment—signing a form, thinking about past behavior—can encourage people to make better choices.

Even subtle cues can help employees resist temptation. Melissa Bateson and her colleagues at Newcastle University conducted a creative study to examine whether small reminders could lead to more ethical behavior.[52] The coffee station in Bateson's office ran on the honor system: people could help themselves to coffee and tea and were asked to simply leave money in the tray. But since no one monitored who contributed, or how much, the system encouraged people to contribute less than they should. To see whether reminders of honesty would increase contributions, they taped one of two posters right beside the coffee station for ten weeks, alternating which poster was seen each week. One of the posters showed a pair of eyes. The other was a picture of flowers.

The results surprised even the researchers. During the weeks in which the poster with the eyes appeared, contributions were nearly three times as high as in the weeks in which the flower poster appeared.

All of these examples illustrate the power of very small tweaks in the environment—signing your name at the top of a page, thinking about your own prior behavior, looking at a pair of eyes—that can push people toward making better choices. Ethical behavior may not require long and intensive trainings by human resources departments or college deans. Subtle strategies may go a long way toward helping the bottom line.

Create a Culture of Speaking Up

To establish an ethical workplace, it helps to create a culture in which all employees feel comfortable raising concerns about problematic behavior. Employees who identify such behavior are often hesitant to speak up because they fear retaliation and ostracism. This allows the bad behavior to continue and could potentially lead to serious costs down the road.

Workers' reluctance to challenge higher-ups can sometimes have life-threatening consequences. Several airplane crashes in the United States during the 1970s were attributed to crewmembers' failure to challenge bad decision-making by the pilot, including the crash of a United Airlines flight in Portland, Oregon, in which the plane literally ran out of gas. Research that was triggered by these accidents led to a greater understanding of the psychological factors that prompted the crew to defer to the pilot as well as to fundamental changes in training procedures within the aviation industry.[53] Airlines began using a NASA-developed program known as Cockpit Resource Management, which is widely credited with helping make flying safer.

Many organizations have implemented programs designed to create a culture of accountability in which all employees have a responsibility for maintaining a healthy office environment. Employees are given specific instructions to speak up and either directly intervene or file a complaint when they witness problematic behavior.

One of the best examples of how work culture can change—not overnight, but over time—can be found in the New Orleans Police Department. This department was the target of a number of lawsuits over the years, stemming from incidents in which officers were accused of planting evidence, shooting unarmed people, and covering up their actions. Public trust in the police force was very low. In 2014 a new police superintendent, Michael S. Harrison, was brought in to change the culture of the department. He started by introducing a new training program, developed by police officers with the support of outside experts, designed to reduce police misconduct.[54] All of the over one thousand members of the police department are now required to attend the program, known as "Ethical Policing Is Courageous," or EPIC.

EPIC focuses on changing the common norms that undergirded the existing culture of silence—ignoring bad behavior by fellow officers—to one of protecting citizens by preventing unethical behavior from occurring.[55] EPIC works to build the expectation that officers will step up when they see another officer engaging in bad behavior, whether it's lying on a report or planting evidence or assaulting a suspect. But officers can also prevent incidents from occurring in the first place. They are taught how to become active bystanders who intervene if they see fellow officers on the verge of engaging in unnecessary harmful behavior. They're told to step in and to encourage their colleague to walk away to avoid doing something they will later regret. The EPIC program teaches officers that loyalty does not mean joining in on, or ignoring, bad behavior; rather, it means trying to prevent it. "Active bystandership is contagious," says New Orleans deputy chief Paul Noel. "It's hard to resist an outspoken co-worker who is intent on doing the right thing."[56]

How did this impressive program come about? It's largely rooted in long-standing work conducted by Ervin Staub, a psychology professor at the University of Massachusetts Amherst, who has devoted his career to studying the factors that help overcome bystander inaction. Staub's interest in this topic dates back to his childhood in Hungary, when his family, like other Jewish families, was designated to be killed in the Holocaust. They were helped by the Swedish diplomat Raoul Wallenberg, who saved thousands of Hungarian Jews, and by Staub's nanny, a Christian woman who felt a sense of loyalty to the family and decided to put her own life on the line to help them. Staub has worked in school settings to reduce bullying, has developed programs to prevent genocide and other forms of group violence, and, most recently, has created a training program for police departments to tackle the seemingly endemic problem of officers tolerating and even covering for bad behavior by their peers.

His involvement with police departments began following the 1991 Rodney King case. King was severely beaten by several Los Angeles police officers while others stood around and watched. California law enforcement officers asked Staub to develop a program to train police departments in bystander intervention techniques that could help police prevent their fellow officers from harming civilians. Staub concluded that the only way to have an impact was to profoundly transform the culture of the force. His aim was to reduce the perceived cost of intervening by reducing the fear of ostracism or demotion. "If, in the system, you're supposed to support

your fellow officer all the time and you don't, you're often ostracized or outcast by your fellow officers and even superiors, so the
cost of you intervening can be pretty substantial," Staub says. "That's
one of the reasons why it's so important for the entire system, including superiors, to buy into the training, so that the culture really
changes."[57] This program formed the basis of the EPIC program now
used in New Orleans.

EPIC is now supported by all of the New Orleans Police Department's leaders, including the superintendent of police, who proudly
wears the same badge given to all officers after they've completed the
EPIC training. The badge conveys to the team his own commitment
to ethical standards and his willingness to be confronted if his own
behavior is ever inappropriate. Police departments in other cities—
including Albuquerque, Baton Rouge, Honolulu, and St. Paul—are
now taking steps to adopt this program.[58] Harrison, who started the
program while in New Orleans, was appointed police commissioner
in Baltimore in March 2019, where he intends to implement it.

Changing workplace culture—whether a police department, law
firm, or, say, the Senate—is never easy. There's usually pushback initially, at least from some. And if that pushback comes from the top,
it's virtually impossible to shift the culture. Staub writes about an
experience during his training with a police department in California
when he asked participants to practice strategies for intervening and
a police captain refused, saying, "I don't do role plays."[59]

Some people may fear that creating a culture of speaking up leads
to an unpleasant work environment, in which employees are constantly reporting on one another. But that's not the case. Establishing
a culture of ethical behavior from the top down means that most
employees will follow appropriate rules and norms. Those who don't
are generally stopped early on, before problematic behavior has a
chance to escalate. But what if the problem is at the top?

Ethical training is especially important in situations where lower-
power employees fear reporting on higher-power ones, such as in

hospitals, police departments, or the military.[60] As aviation expert John Nance describes in his book *Why Hospitals Should Fly,* the culture in these organizations emphasizes the responsibility of all team members, regardless of their position, to speak up.[61] Nance believes that leaders need to convey this message to colleagues at all levels. "You know, I'm a very good leader, but I'm also a fallible human being," he concedes. "However, if I put a team around me who have no barriers or hesitation to communicate, because I have nurtured their ability to do so and made it clear it's part of their job, I know that any mistake I make is not going to be allowed to metastasize into a negative impact."[62]

Creating a culture in which employees believe that both supervisors and coworkers support honest exchanges rests on two important features. First, employees need to believe that reporting will have an impact, that their concerns will be taken seriously, and that leaders won't look the other way, especially if such behavior is committed by people in powerful positions. Second, they need to feel that their coworkers share their concern about unethical behavior and will respect their decision to report misconduct. Even in cases in which supervisors clearly encourage the reporting of misconduct, those who fear personal retaliation, such as social exclusion by their coworkers or professional marginalization, are likely to stay silent.

David Mayer and his colleagues at the Ross School of Business at the University of Michigan examined whether broad company culture influences whether people report unethical conduct.[63] In the first study, they gave in-depth surveys regarding ethical behavior to approximately two hundred employees at a large corporation. Respondents answered questions about whether their boss held people to high ethical standards ("My supervisor disciplines employees who violate ethical standards") and whether their coworkers engaged in ethical behavior ("My coworkers carefully consider ethical issues when making work-related decision"). They were then asked how likely they would be to report violations of the company's ethical standards. The second study surveyed thirty-four thousand employees at sixteen different companies, again asking about whether their boss and coworkers engaged in ethical behavior. They also asked respondents whether they had ever observed unethical behavior, and if so, how they had responded, and whether fear of retaliation influenced their decision.

Data from both studies revealed consistent findings: people were more willing to report unethical behavior if they believed that others in the workplace—supervisors as well as coworkers—shared their concern. In cases in which either the boss or coworkers—or both—didn't appear to see the conduct as problematic, they tended to stay silent, at least in part because they feared retaliation. Ethical behavior, therefore, thrives in companies in which such behavior is clearly valued by all. It's not enough to have a boss punishing unethical behavior if your coworkers will label you a snitch for going to HR, and it's not enough to have coworkers who support ethical behavior if you know your boss will just look the other way.

These findings are, sadly, not surprising. Why would people go to the trouble of reporting unethical behavior if they would personally face negative consequences for doing so, either from higher-ups or from colleagues? This fear, of course, is what leads most people to stay silent even in cases of extraordinarily bad behavior. It's hard to do the right thing if you know you'll pay a severe personal or professional price. Doing so takes moral courage.

Part III

Learning to Act

9

Understanding Moral Rebels

Shortly after arriving for duty at Abu Ghraib Prison in late 2003, during the US occupation of Iraq, twenty-four-year-old Army Reserve specialist Joe Darby received a CD from a fellow soldier that was filled with photos of Iraqi prisoners. Many of the images showed Iraqis being tortured and humiliated. Joe struggled with what to do. He recognized that what his fellow soldiers were doing to the prisoners was wrong, but he worried about retribution if he reported the abuse. And he felt tremendous loyalty to his friends, some of whom had participated in these acts. Eventually he sent an anonymous letter describing what he had seen—with a copy of the CD—to the US Army Criminal Investigation Command. "I knew I had to do something," he told investigators. "I didn't want to see any more prisoners being abused because I knew it was wrong."[1]

Many people were aware of the ongoing mistreatment of Iraqi prisoners—officers and enlisted soldiers who witnessed this abuse directly, medics who treated the prisoners, members of the intelligence agencies, and those who saw the photos or heard about what was going on. Abusive behavior was so widely tolerated that a picture of naked prisoners stacked in a human pyramid was used as a screensaver on a computer in the interrogation room at the prison. A few people tried to report or stop this abuse, but no one went as far as Joe Darby.

Darby paid a high price for his decision to speak out. Although he was promised anonymity by military investigators and continued to serve in Iraq, his name was revealed a few months later. People called him a "rat" and a traitor. He left the army and was put under protective custody after receiving death threats. Darby's case was particularly high profile, but this type of treatment of whistleblowers is, unfortunately, not unusual.

What explains Darby's willingness to report the abuse, when so many others did not? The earlier chapters in this book outlined the psychological and neurological basis for our natural human tendency to stay silent in the face of bad behavior. Yet despite the strong pull to inaction, some people choose to act. Understanding what enables these people to do so may provide insight into how we can activate more bystanders and create more moral rebels.

Defining Moral Courage

We often hear dramatic stories of people who risk their lives to save someone: jumping into a frozen pond to rescue a drowning child, leaping onto subway tracks to help someone who has fallen, or grabbing a gun from a shooter. Such actions to protect others when there is a risk of substantial harm require tremendous physical courage and extraordinary bravery and are, of course, to be commended. But people who engage in these types of heroic actions are generally praised and celebrated. They have no reason to fear the social consequences of their actions—and are, in fact, likely to receive considerable social rewards. These actions require bravery in the face of great danger, but they do not require overcoming social pressure. In other words, they require physical courage, not moral courage.

Some acts, to be sure, require both physical and moral courage. Examples of people risking their lives to do the right thing include students who stood up to the tanks when the Chinese military massacred demonstrators in Tiananmen Square in 1989, and Muslims who hid their Christian neighbors from Islamist militants intent on killing non-Muslims in the Philippines in 2017. Senator John McCain showed remarkable physical courage during more than five years of torture when he was held as a prisoner of war in North Vietnam, but he also demonstrated moral courage for refusing an offer of early release that he knew would be used for propaganda purposes. Journalists working in war zones often show both moral and physical courage, sometimes paying with their lives.

But moral courage doesn't have to involve life-threatening situations. By itself, moral courage entails a willingness to incur social ostracism for doing the right thing. Telling a bully to cut it out, confronting a colleague who uses a racist slur or abusive language, or calling out a friend for sexual misconduct—all of these are acts of moral courage because they involve confronting bad behavior in situations where social norms push us toward silence. People can and do pay a price for these actions—they may become the bully's target, miss out on a promotion, or lose a friend. But they rarely face substantial physical danger.

Those who display moral courage are what psychologists call "moral rebels"—people who "take a principled stand against the status quo, who refuse to comply, stay silent, or simply go along when this would require they compromise their values."[2] Moral rebels steadfastly defend their principles in the face of potentially negative social consequences such as disapproval, ostracism, and career setbacks.[3] Later in this chapter, and more extensively in Chapter 10, I'll examine what you can do to develop these traits in yourself and to help foster them in others.

What Makes a Moral Rebel

What enables someone to risk serious consequences to act in the face of bad behavior? It turns out that moral rebels tend to have certain traits in common.

First, those who show moral courage generally feel good about themselves.[4] They tend to have high self-esteem and to feel confident about their own judgment, values, and ability. These traits may help them resist social pressure to conform. But moral rebels don't just feel confident that they are right. They also believe that their actions will make a difference.[5] They are able to intervene because they are confident that their intervention will serve a purpose and have an impact.

Confidence in one's judgment and ability to affect the course of events turns out to be associated with moral courage in a wide range of situations, from resisting peer pressure to engage in antisocial behavior to confronting harassment in the workplace. In 2017, researchers in Belgium decided to investigate the factors that predict how people respond to workplace bullying.[6] They asked employees of both public and private organizations of varying sizes to complete a series of personality questionnaires. These included assessments of their belief in a just world ("Do people tend to get what they deserve?") and self-efficacy ("Are you confident you can achieve your goals?"). The participants then read a vignette in which a boss psychologically harassed or bullied his assistant and were asked if they would support the assistant either privately or publicly. Those who reported that they generally felt confident in their own ability to act—agreeing with statements like, "I will be able to achieve most of the goals that I have set for myself" and "When facing difficult tasks, I am certain that I will accomplish them"—were less likely to be afraid of the consequences of intervening. Another study of bullying found similar results: students with high self-efficacy scores were more likely to help defend their peers against bullies.[7]

A high level of confidence is important because believing that their actions can make a difference appears to be one of the crucial ingredients that propels people from meaning well to doing the right thing. Why speak up (and risk the consequences of doing so) if you don't believe it will matter?

High self-esteem and self-confidence are good predictors of moral courage not only in adults but also in adolescents, who face tremendous pressure to fit in with their social group. Adolescents and young adults who are high in self-esteem are more likely to stand up for what they believe is right, even if doing so goes against their peers.[8] They are also better able to resist peer pressure to engage in substance abuse and in antisocial behavior such as writing on school walls or ignoring a "no trespassing" sign.[9]

To better understand the specific personality traits that underpin moral courage, Tammy Sonnentag at Xavier University and Mark Barnett at Kansas State University studied the characteristics of over two hundred seventh and eighth graders.[10] They first asked the students to rate their own willingness to stand up to others and say or do the right thing in the face of social pressure to stay silent and go along with the crowd. Next, they asked all students in each grade, and one teacher, to rate the tendency of each student to adhere to his or her moral beliefs and values in the face of pressures not to do so. This method allowed researchers to assess whether students who self-identified as moral rebels actually did behave in ways that were visible to others, and weren't just imagining themselves to be courageous. Finally, all students completed a series of questionnaires assessing other personality traits, including self-esteem, self-efficacy (confidence), assertiveness, need to belong, and social vigilantism (a tendency to press one's beliefs on others).

The researchers found a high level of agreement between students themselves, their peers, and their teacher as to who was a moral rebel. These students' acts of moral courage, then, must have been obvious enough for others to recognize and remember. Because standing up to defend one's own beliefs is rare among adolescents, it was probably easy for both students and teachers to identify those who did so.

These young moral rebels tended to possess particular personality traits. They generally felt good about themselves, rating themselves highly on statements such as, "I feel I have a number of good qualities" and "I can do things as well as most other people." They were also confident about their ability to accomplish their goals and to stand up to social pressure, agreeing with statements like, "I will be able to successfully overcome many challenges" and "I follow my own ideas even when pressured by a group to change them."

But these students didn't just feel confident and good about themselves. They also believed that their own views were superior to those of others, and thus that they had a social responsibility to share those beliefs.[11] They agreed with statements like, "I feel a social obligation to voice my opinion" and "If everyone saw things the way that I do, the world would be a better place." This belief in the correctness of their views helped them speak up when other students tended to stay quiet.

Perhaps most important, these students were less concerned about fitting in with the crowd. That means that when push comes to shove, and they have to choose between fitting in and doing the right thing, they will probably choose to do what's right.

These results tell us that moral courage isn't a straightforward trait. It's not the same as feeling good about yourself or having confidence in your ability to act. Instead, moral rebels seem to have a distinct combination of characteristics that provide them with the skills and resources they need to take action, even in the face of social pressure to stay silent.

Studies of adults have uncovered a similar set of characteristics in moral rebels. To assess the personality correlates of moral courage, Alexandrina Moisuc and her colleagues at the University of Clermont Auvergne in France conducted a series of studies examining people's likelihood of intervening in different types of situations.[12] They recruited both college students and community members to read and respond to various scenarios. One involved teenagers on a train making jokes about gay and disabled people. Another described a man at the zoo hitting his three-year-old son in the face. In a third, a person threw a tissue on the sidewalk right next to a trash can. They asked participants whether they would express their disapproval in some way.

The researchers found substantial differences between those who indicated that they would do something and those who said they wouldn't. The people who reported that they would likely confront the perpetrators had higher levels of independence—a lack of hesitation to express thoughts, even when they differed from others—and of extraversion—being outgoing, sociable, and energetic. They also had higher scores on scales of altruism and social responsibility, suggesting that they felt compassion for the victim and a moral obligation to help, and they tended to feel accepted by their peers.

One drawback with studies such as this one is that they rely on self-reporting about intentions. What we really want to know is whether certain personality variables actually predict helping behavior in the real world. After all, many of us, maybe even most of us, imagine that we'd step up in an emergency, but as we've seen, we often don't live up to our good intentions.

To get around this problem, researchers at Columbia University looked at the personality traits of a select group of people who helped others in a real-world emergency: the Holocaust.[13] Although acting in this situation clearly required physical courage, it also required moral courage to take action when most others were doing nothing. The researchers compared personality traits among three different groups of adults: those who had rescued at least one Jewish person during the Holocaust, those who had provided no help, and those who left Europe before the start of World War II.

People who risked their own lives to help Jews differed in several ways from those who did not. They scored higher on independence and perceived control, indicating that they were willing to stick with their own beliefs even if others disagreed and that they felt their life outcomes were due to their own efforts and choices. They also scored higher on risk-taking and were comfortable with tasks that involved danger. This combination of attributes appears to have given them the confidence to show courage. But they had other important traits, too, that have to do with concern about others: altruism, empathy, and social responsibility. These traits would have driven them to feel compassion and a need to act, even at great personal risk.

The Holocaust, of course, was quite a different kind of event from the more mundane situations in which most of us find ourselves pondering whether to act.

To investigate this kind of everyday situation, researchers at Hannover Medical School in Germany asked a local hospital for the names of people who had administered first aid to car accident victims.[14] They contacted these people and asked them to complete personality questionnaires. Thirty-four people agreed to do so. The researchers also asked people who had seen the accident but had not provided help to complete the same questionnaire. Those who had provided help scored higher on perceived control, empathy, and social responsibility—exactly the same characteristics as those who had rescued Jews in Nazi Germany.

All of these studies together paint a picture of a moral rebel—someone who is confident, independent, and altruistic, with high self-esteem and a strong sense of social responsibility.

Lack of Social Inhibition

One of the most important characteristics of moral rebels is that they have relatively little concern about fitting in with the crowd and are not afraid to speak up in support of their beliefs and values.

These traits emerged in a study by researchers at Boston College, who examined how students at a New England high school responded to homophobic behavior by their classmates.[15] They asked students how often they had heard or seen some type of homophobic behavior—a slur or joke about gay, lesbian, or bisexual people—over the course of the previous month and whether they had responded in some way, such as trying to get the perpetrator to stop, sticking up for the student who was targeted, or telling an adult. The students also completed self-report ratings of various personality traits, including courage ("I have taken frequent stands in the face of strong opposition," "I can face my fears"), leadership ("I take charge," "I am the first to act"), and altruism ("I am concerned about others," "I make people feel welcome").

Two-thirds of the students reported having witnessed some type of homophobic behavior, but their responses varied considerably. Girls were more likely to respond than boys, as were gay, lesbian, or bisexual students compared with heterosexual students. These findings are in line with prior work showing that girls tend to be more empathic to victims of bullying and that people tend to speak out more for those in their in-group. Students who rated themselves higher in altruism and courage also responded more frequently. These students were probably less concerned about the potential social costs of stepping up and more concerned with the consequences of ignoring harmful behavior. General leadership traits, however, were not associated with higher rates of response. The researchers hypothesized that some high school students might engage in homophobic behavior as a way to gain status, by putting down or ridiculing social inferiors.

Unlike the students in this study who spoke out, people who are self-conscious or embarrass easily tend to remain silent in the face of bad behavior. They are especially concerned with the social consequences of awkward interactions and may go to some lengths to avoid these situations. They have been found to avoid even low-risk social confrontations, like telling someone they have ink on their face or food in their teeth.[16]

Fear of awkward social interactions doesn't just inhibit people from taking action in situations of little consequence, when they can easily justify not doing anything because the consequences are minimal. Psychologists have found that people who are especially concerned with appearing poised—and thus highly intent on avoiding embarrassment by being perceived as overreacting—are less likely to help someone who seems to be choking.[17] Even though the consequences could be much more serious in this situation, there is still enough ambiguity (perhaps the person is just coughing) to allow people who worry about feeling foolish to refrain from offering help.

Individual variation in how much people care about fitting in with the crowd has now been associated with variation in certain brain structures. A team of researchers from New York University, University College London, and Aarhus University in Denmark designed an experiment to look at the link between structural differences in the brain and the willingness to stand up to social pressure.[18] The researchers first measured the volume of gray matter in the brains of twenty-eight people using a technique known as voxel-based morphometry, which uses three-dimensional brain images taken during MRI scans. (Gray matter processes information in the brain, including muscle control, seeing and hearing, memory, emotions, decision-making, and self-control.) They asked study participants to list and rate twenty songs they liked and then gave them ratings of those songs, supposedly from music experts, that disagreed with some of their rankings. Participants were then given a chance to re-rank their song preferences, which let the researchers measure how much they would change their ratings to conform to those of the "experts."

People who changed their ratings the most also showed greater gray matter volume in one particular part of the brain, the lateral orbitofrontal cortex (OFC). We know from other research that the

OFC helps guide us away from things we want to avoid.[19] It's the part of the brain that creates memories of events that led to some type of aversive outcome, such as getting a small electric shock from touching a particular lever. These people were apparently especially concerned with avoiding the unpleasantness of having preferences that deviated from the "correct" ones.

What does this tell us about moral rebels? People clearly vary in how attuned they are to social conflict, and this tendency is reflected in anatomical differences in the brain. In other words, for some people, feeling different feels really bad. For other people, it may not matter as much, which makes it easier for them to stand up to social pressure. But this research doesn't tell us where these differences come from in the first place. Are some people born with more gray matter in the OFC, or does resisting social pressure increase the volume of this region? We don't know. But what we do know is that individual differences in the ability to stand up to social influence can be mapped out in the brain.

More recent research has examined whether these individual differences in susceptibility to social influence are reflected not just in structural differences in the brain, but in neural response patterns. Emily Falk and her colleagues at the University of Pennsylvania brought in teenagers who had just gotten drivers' licenses and measured how their brains responded to social exclusion using Cyberball, the standard experimental procedure in which participants are first included and then excluded from a ball-tossing game.[20] (This procedure was described in Chapter 4.)

One week later, these same teenagers participated in two driving simulations, designed to measure patterns of risk-taking. They completed one alone, and the other with a male teenage passenger (actually an accomplice of the experimenter). In half of the cases, the accomplice/passenger was a nonrisky driver who said, "Sorry I was a little late getting here. I tend to drive slowly, plus I hit every yellow light." In the others he was a risky driver who said, "Sorry I was a little late getting here. Normally I drive way faster, but I hit like every red light." The researchers then examined the participants' driving patterns.

As they had predicted, those who were more bothered by exclusion in the Cyberball game were more influenced by the presence of a peer during the driving simulation. Teenagers who showed the greatest increases in activity in parts of the brain associated with social pain (the anterior insula and anterior cingulate cortex) and mentalizing (the dorsal medial prefrontal cortex, right temporal parietal junction, and posterior cingulate cortex) when excluded engaged in riskier driving when they were with a peer (either the nonrisky or the risky driver) than when they were alone. They were especially likely to drive through a yellow light—the measure of risky driving tested in this study—when they were with the fast-driving peer.

Some adolescents, this study shows, feel worse than others when excluded, and when with a peer, they are more likely to engage in risky behavior. "The kids who are the most sensitive in the brain scanner when they're being excluded," explained lead author Emily Falk, "are then also the kids that go on to take more risks when they are driving with a passenger. They're speeding up to gun it through the yellow light."[21]

Another study by these same researchers provides additional evidence that neural patterns related to social exclusion can predict a teenager's tendency to conformity. Male teenagers completed a two-part study that started with the same social exclusion task—Cyberball—while hooked up to an fMRI scanner, followed by a similar driving simulation, again done both alone and with a male passenger who described himself as either a generally slow or fast driver.[22]

Once again, teenagers with certain patterns of brain activity in response to social exclusion showed higher rates of conformity. In this study, those with greater connectivity between the regions of the brain that respond to social pain and mentalizing were more likely to conform to their peers' approach to driving. So while the earlier study had shown that teens who had higher activity in the parts of the brain that respond to social pain (rejection) and mentalizing (attempting to understand others' thoughts and feelings) conformed more, this one showed that higher connectivity between these two regions also resulted in higher rates of conformity. It demonstrated a direct link between a neurological response to exclusion and a motivation to conform to one's peers as a way to avoid experiencing social pain.

People who feel less need to conform may be willing to take more physical as well as social risks. In his book *On Killing*, the military psychologist Dave Grossman looked for factors that Air Force pilots who shot down the most enemy planes had in common.[23] He found that they had often been in fights when they were children, but they were not the bullies; they were the ones who fought back against the bullies. They "weren't timid about confronting other people," a trait that served them well when they were in battle.[24]

This disregard for what other people think may have been behind Joe Darby's decision to reveal the Iraqi prisoner abuse to military investigators. Robert Ewing, Darby's high school teacher and football coach, described him as independent and not the eager-to-please type. "If Joe believed in something, he had no problems challenging me," Ewing told the *Washington Post*. "When he believed in something, he defended it." In an interview on *CBS News*, he said that Darby "wasn't one that went along with his peers. . . . [He] didn't worry about what people thought."[25]

The Empathy Factor

In 1999, Kathryn Bolkovac, a former police officer, was hired by a private British military contractor called DynCorp to work as a human rights investigator with the United Nations International Police Task Force in Bosnia and Herzegovina. In the course of her work, she discovered that DynCorp officers were engaging in sexual misconduct. They were hiring prostitutes and raping underage girls, and were involved in sex trafficking. When she reported these offenses to higher-ups, she was demoted and then fired. (In 2002, she won her lawsuit for wrongful termination.)

What led her to speak up? For Bolkovac, a mother of three, one factor was the personal connection she felt to the girls who were being abused. As she told National Public Radio, "I'd be lying if I said there certainly weren't moments when the children—my own girls—were going through my mind."[26]

Prosocial behavior—that is, behavior that is intended to help another person—can be motivated by two different pathways, according to Daniel Batson at the University of Kansas.[27] One pathway, the egoistic pathway, is largely self-focused: we provide help if the rewards to us outweigh the costs. This pathway is the one that is operating if we hand a homeless person a dollar to make ourselves feel better: doing so costs us very little—only a dollar—and the reward of doing so—avoiding the guilt we'd feel from simply walking by—is greater. But according to Batson's empathy-altruism hypothesis, there is another pathway, which is other-focused—it's motivated by a genuine desire to help the other person, even if we incur a cost for doing so. Following this pathway, we act altruistically when we feel empathy for a person and can truly imagine a situation from their perspective.[28] This ability to see the world from someone else's perspective can lead us to help, even if there are considerable costs. Bolkovac's ability to imagine her own children undergoing abuse likely provided the empathy that helped push her to report the misconduct.

Empathy may also explain why we are more likely to help a friend than a stranger or an acquaintance. People are more likely to defend a victim of workplace bullying who is a friend rather than simply a coworker.[29] College students also report a greater willingness to intervene in a potential sexual assault situation when the victim is a friend than a stranger.[30]

Researchers at the University of Puget Sound and the University of Texas at Austin examined whether college students would be more willing to defend a victim of cyberbullying when that person was a friend.[31] Some students were asked to think about an example, from the previous six months, of Facebook cyberbullying in which they knew the victim. Others were asked to imagine learning that embarrassing pictures were posted to a friend's Facebook page without their consent. Students in both groups indicated whether and how they would respond. Greater anonymity and group size both reduced the likelihood of intervention. But one factor increased students' willingness to intervene: how close they felt to the victim.

Meghan Meyer and her colleagues at the University of California Los Angeles asked participants to come into the lab with their best friend to test whether they would show different patterns of neural response when witnessing social pain experienced by a friend versus a stranger.[32] Using an fMRI machine, they measured participants' brain response while they watched two Cyberball games during which a person was excluded; in one, the excluded person was their best friend, and in the other, the person was a same-gender stranger (in reality the games were pre-recorded simulations).

When people thought their friend was being ostracized, the regions of the brain that became activated were those that correspond to emotional pain—the dorsal anterior cingulate cortex and insula. (These are the same regions that are activated when we experience emotional pain ourselves.) When they thought they were watching a stranger being ostracized, the activated regions were the ones we use when we are thinking about other people's traits, beliefs, and intentions—the dorsal medial prefrontal cortex, precuneus, and temporal pole. So it appears that watching a friend experience social pain makes us feel as if we are experiencing that pain ourselves—in other words, we feel empathy—but watching a stranger's pain does not.

Although people consistently feel more empathy for a friend or loved one in need than a stranger, individuals show considerable variation in their level of empathy. To measure these differences, researchers typically ask how much others' emotions influence their own.[33] This includes taking pleasure in their joy—"When a friend tells me about his good fortune, I feel genuinely happy for him"— as well as sharing their sorrow—"When someone gets hurt in my presence, I feel sad." Those who score higher on these measures report more willingness to stand up to bad behavior in both lab experiments and real-world situations. Students who feel intense psychological distress when they see someone in need, for example, are more likely to defend peers who are being bullied.[34]

A series of studies by Ruud Hortensius and his colleagues at Maastricht University in the Netherlands explored how people with different degrees of empathy responded in an emergency. They first measured participants' degree of personal discomfort when seeing someone in need—asking how strongly they agreed with statements like, "I tend to lose control during emergencies" and "When I see someone who badly needs help in an emergency, I go to pieces." True empathy was assessed in their response to statements like, "I often have tender, concerned feelings for people less fortunate than me" and "I am often quite touched by things that I see happen."[35] Study participants then watched a video portraying a woman either falling to the floor (the emergency) or getting up off the ground (the nonemergency), with either zero, one, or four bystanders present. Participants were told to watch the video and to press a "go" or "no go" button as quickly as possible after determining if anyone in the video needed help. While participants were watching the video, researchers delivered a pulse to the motor cortex, a part of the brain in charge of muscle activity, using transcranial magnetic stimulation. The participants' "action preparedness" (how prepared they were to respond to the stimulation) was assessed by means of an electrode attached to a muscle located between the wrist and base of the thumb. This procedure is commonly used by neuroscientists to evaluate whether stimulation of a particular part of the brain cues the body to act. In this way, the researchers were able to tell not just how quickly people responded, but how activated their muscles were.

Participants who reported feeling higher levels of distress and empathy responded faster to the emergency than a nonemergency when no bystanders were present. But people who ranked themselves as high in personal distress—indicating that they felt more acutely uncomfortable when they saw someone in need—showed reduced action preparedness in emergencies when more bystanders were present. This suggests that for people who are primarily concerned about feeling bad when seeing someone in need, knowing that other people could help reduces their own likelihood of acting. For those who were high in empathy, no association was found between the number of potential helpers present and the degree of motor response. Highly empathic people showed muscle activation even when other potential helpers were available.

Even when people intervene in an emergency, then, their behavior may be motivated by different factors. For some people, helping is driven by their own desire to stop feeling uncomfortable. If someone else can step up and help, they are perfectly glad to sit back and watch that person act. But for others, helping is driven by concern for the person in need—not for their own personal well-being. For these people, the number of other possible helpers is irrelevant.

In an effort to identify the neurological underpinning of empathy, Abigail Marsh and her colleagues at Georgetown University examined differences in patterns of brain activity in nineteen people who had engaged in a quite extraordinary act of generosity: donating a kidney to a total stranger.[36] The donors' amygdala—a part of the brain that processes emotions—was found to be 8 percent larger than it is in most people, and it also showed greater activity.

We need to be cautious about interpreting this finding, which illustrates correlation, not causation. It's possible that these kidney donors were born with larger and more active amygdalas, which caused them to care more about other people. But it's also possible that engaging in this type of extreme altruism could actively rewire the brain. Regardless of the causal connection, it does appear that extraordinary altruists show distinct patterns of neural activity that are associated with a greater responsiveness to emotion. People who demonstrate this type of selfless giving may experience the costs of helping differently from the rest of us. *Not* helping may actually make them feel worse.

There is also evidence that people who engage in extraordinary acts of altruism show distinct patterns of neurological responses to two types of painful experiences: experiencing pain themselves and watching someone else experience pain. In one study, researchers measured empathy in nearly sixty people, half of whom had donated a kidney to a stranger and half of whom had not.[37] Each participant was then paired with a stranger to complete a series of trials. In one set of trials, participants watched their partner receive painful pressure to the right thumbnail while researchers recorded their brain activity using fMRI imaging. In another set, the participants themselves received the thumbnail pressure, again while their brain activity was assessed. Researchers then compared the two sets of brain activity.

For most of us, experiencing pain ourselves feels far worse than watching a stranger experience pain. But the brains of those who had demonstrated extraordinary altruism responded in almost the same way to their own pain as to that of others, suggesting that they were experiencing someone else's pain as though it were their own. For people who feel others' pain so deeply, the choice to donate a kidney to a stranger may therefore make sense: if they feel pain themselves from knowing that someone else is in pain, helping that person would make them feel better.

Donating a kidney to a stranger may be an example of physical rather than moral courage. Few people will think less of you for the decision, and it does have physical risks. But the discoveries of these studies have implications for moral courage, too, since the ability to feel empathy is an important characteristic of those who are willing to face social consequences for doing the right thing.

Finding Your Inner Moral Rebel

We've seen in this chapter that moral rebels have particular traits that most of us do not. They feel good about themselves, they feel empathy for others, and they don't care much about fitting in. This combination of traits enables some people—like Joe Darby—to stand up for what's right.

But what about the rest of us? Are we doomed to be the silent bystanders who don't dare call out bad behavior? Fortunately, no. For those of us who don't come by this tendency naturally, it is possible to develop the ability to stand up to social pressure.[38] In other words, we can all learn to be moral rebels.

First, we need to see moral courage in action. Social learning theory, developed by Albert Bandura at Stanford University, has shown that people learn how to behave by watching others in their environment, including their parents, teachers, and other role models. Watching people we look up to show moral courage can inspire us to do the same. "Children who grew up watching their parents stick their necks out for others," notes the psychology professor Julie Hupp, "are likely to do the same."[39]

Parental modeling helps explain who undertakes acts of moral courage during times of violence and civic unrest. Many of the civil rights activists who participated in marches and sit-ins in the southern United States in the 1960s had parents who displayed moral courage and civic engagement, as did many of the Germans who rescued Jews during the Holocaust.[40] A study by sociologists Hollie Nyseth Brehm and Nicole Fox found that one of the strongest predictors of whether people chose to help refugees during the 1994 genocidal massacres in Rwanda was having parents who had helped others.[41] More than half of the people they interviewed who had rescued at least one refugee reported that their parents or grandparents had done so during previous episodes of violence in their country. Models of moral courage may therefore go a long way toward helping inspire future courageous actions.

Second, we need skills, and we need to practice them. Even if we want to do the right thing, it's hard to do if we lack the skills needed to resist the crowd. Parents, teachers, and other adults can help cultivate these skills in children by encouraging them both to recognize social pressure and to question authority. Joe Dimow, one of the few people who successfully defied the experimenter in the Milgram study, which urged participants to inflict ever-increasing shocks, credited his decision to the fact that he had grown up in a family that was "steeped in a class-struggle view of society, [which] taught me that authorities would often have a different view of right and wrong than mine."[42]

Developing these skills can help people stand up to social influence, even during the teenage years, when fitting in is such a high priority. Psychologists at the University of Virginia recruited more than 150 families with a child in seventh or eighth grade to participate in a study on the link between social skills, close friendships, parent–teen relationships, and substance abuse.[43] Teenagers completed questionnaires assessing how they would handle difficult situations—including conflicts with peers, parents, and teachers, as well as situations in which they might be tempted to engage in delinquent behaviors, such as shoplifting. They also engaged in two interactions with their mothers: they discussed a contentious family issue (grades, friends, household rules), and they asked for advice or support about a problem they were having. Researchers video-taped these interactions and coded how effectively the teenagers could stand up for what they believed in and how warm and supportive their mothers were. Two and three years later, these same teenagers were asked about their level of substance abuse, including both alcohol and marijuana.

The nature of the teens' interactions with their mothers predicted substance abuse later on much more than you might think. Teenagers who held their own in an argument with their mother—using reasoned arguments instead of whining, pressure, or insults—were the most resistant to peer pressure to use drugs or drink alcohol later on. In contrast, teenagers who easily backed down during arguments, suggesting that they gave in even when they weren't actually persuaded that their position was wrong, were much more likely to later reporting drinking or using marijuana. These teenagers probably showed a similar pattern of initially offering token resistance to pressure from friends, only to then give in. Teenagers who had high levels of support from their mothers were also less likely to report substance abuse. These mothers showed warmth and positivity during the interaction, conveying that they valued and appreciated their child as a person. (Although this study only included mothers, it's quite likely that persuasive argument and support from fathers would produce equivalent benefits.)

The exact mechanism underpinning these links isn't clear. Is it the intimacy of the relationship that matters, or the experience of rationally articulating a point of view? One possibility is that teenagers who have practiced making effective arguments are better able to use these same techniques with peers. They have learned how to express their own opinions and to stick with them under pressure. Teenagers who have warm and supportive relationships with their parents may also be less dependent on their friends' opinions. On some level, they may understand that even if a decision costs them a friend, their mom or dad will always be in their corner.

Third, we need to develop our ability to feel empathy. Spending time with and really getting to know people from different backgrounds—ethnic, religious, political, cultural—is one activity that helps. Nicola Abbott and Lindsey Cameron at the University of Kent demonstrated that white British high school students who had more contact with people from different ethnic groups—in their neighborhood, at school, and on sports teams—had higher levels of empathy and were more open to and interested in people from different cultural backgrounds.[44] They also saw people from different minority groups in more positive ways—identifying them as honest, friendly, and hardworking—and were less likely to suggest that they were stupid, lazy, or dirty. This greater exposure paid off. Students who were higher in empathy and openness, and lower in bias, were more likely to state that if a classmate used an ethnic slur, they would directly challenge that person, support the victim, or tell a teacher. It's certainly possible that some of the students would not carry through these good intentions to intervene in an actual incident, but having such intentions is at least an important first step.

Actively working to foster empathy in others, especially young people, is also crucial. Empathy is decreasing among college students, according to a meta-analysis combining the results of seventy-two studies of American college students over a thirty-year period—1979 to 2009.[45] College students in the 2000s are less likely than those in the 1970s to agree with statements such as, "I sometimes try to understand my friends better by imagining how things look from their perspective" and "I often have tender, concerned feelings for people less fortunate than me."

This decline in empathy has come with a corresponding rise in narcissism—an overly positive view of the self—in college students during this same time period.[46] Other societal factors may also contribute to the loss of empathy, including an increasing focus on individual success instead of relationships with others.[47] The reasons for this transformation aren't clear. Social media? Parenting practices? The high-pressure college admissions process? But the consequences are indisputable. A lower level of empathy produces fewer moral rebels.

There are a few things that parents, teachers, and community members can do to counteract this trend. For starters, they can emphasize that empathy is a skill and not a fixed trait. Although some people appear to have higher innate levels of empathy, we can all develop this ability with practice.[48] Carol Dweck and her colleagues at Stanford University have demonstrated that simply learning that empathy can be developed increases our willingness to try to understand someone else's perspective.[49] People who are told that empathy can be cultivated have been found to be more willing to talk to someone who holds a conflicting view on a social or political issue and to listen to the personal story of a person from a different racial group.

These stories should give us all hope. Empathy is the crucial first step to becoming a moral rebel, and it is a trait that anyone can develop.

10

Becoming a Moral Rebel

Much of this book has focused on the psychological factors that underlie the tendency for most people to remain silent bystanders when they see someone in trouble. But I have also introduced you to many people who have shown admirable moral courage. We can't simply stand by and wait for moral rebels to step up in the face of bad behavior, though. What we really need is for more people to speak up, regardless of their natural inclination. In other words, we need to create more moral rebels.

I've already touched on quite a few strategies we can all use—at home, in school, at work, in our community—to prompt moral courage and create much-needed change. Let's revisit some of these and pull them all together.

Believe in Change

Many of us stay silent in the face of bad behavior because we believe that one person speaking up can't really make a difference. If everyone shares that belief and no one chooses to act, the bad behavior continues. One key step in creating moral rebels is to help people understand the cost of silence and to persuade them that their actions count.

Aneeta Rattan and Carol Dweck at Stanford University examined whether people's beliefs about the effectiveness of calling out prejudice would influence their willingness to do so.[1] They asked black, Latino, and mixed-race students to participate in an online discussion with a partner about how admissions decisions should be made. Each student was paired with the same partner, a white sophomore named Matt—actually a role played by the experimenter. At some point in the exchange, Matt wrote, "I was really worried that I had to be even more overqualified because of the whole diversity admissions thing . . . so many schools reserve admissions for students who don't really qualify the same way so I was pretty freaked out."

The researchers were interested in seeing who would express some type of disapproval of Matt's statement.

First, the bad news: only about 25 percent of students overall challenged Matt. But there's good news, too: those who had indicated in a previously administered survey that they believed that one's personality could change were far more likely to express concern about the comment. Nearly 37 percent of them confronted Matt. The others may have thought there was no point calling out Matt's bad behavior if their intervention wouldn't make any difference.

To test whether an even more blatant expression of bias would result in higher rates of intervention, these same researchers conducted a second study in which students read a scenario describing their hypothetical first day at a summer internship at a prestigious company. In the scenario, as the participant is talking with other interns about first impressions of the company, one of the male interns comments, "I'm really surprised at the types of people who are working here . . . with all of this 'diversity' hiring—women, minorities, foreigners, etc., I wonder how long this company will stay on top?"

Most of the participants rated this statement as highly offensive. They were then asked whether they would confront the person who said it ("I would calmly but firmly communicate my point of view to try to educate him") or would avoid engaging with him ("I would do my best to pretend it didn't happen"). They also indicated how likely they would be to withdraw from future interactions with him.

This time the students were being asked what they *thought* they would do, rather than being observed in action—but as in the first study, their beliefs about the possibility of changing people's minds made a big difference. Those who thought that personality was malleable (which Dweck identifies as central to a "growth mindset") were more likely to report that they would confront the intern who had made the offensive comment. They were also less likely to say they would withdraw from future interactions with him. Those with a "fixed mindset," who believed that personality traits and ability are innate and largely unchangeable, tended to be more passive and avoidant. So if you want to muster the courage to speak up, a good place to start is to believe that it can make a difference.

Learn Skills and Strategies

Simply believing in the power of change isn't enough to make most of us confront bad behavior. We also need specific skills for doing so, preferably ones that don't feel too confrontational. As seen in Chapter 4, people who have some kind of specialized training—such as first aid or CPR—are more likely to intervene in the face of physical danger. Training plays an equally important role in helping people intervene when there is a social cost.

One big fear most of us have about confronting bad behavior is feeling awkward or uncomfortable. We don't want to make a scene or feel embarrassed. Learning simple strategies can foster moral courage, but we need a repertoire of skills. After all, confronting a colleague who you suspect is inflating travel expenses requires a different approach than calling out a sexist remark made by a team-mate. As we saw in Chapter 1, the people who were best able to resist orders in the Milgram experiment were those who did so in more varied ways.[2]

One strategy for speaking up is to find a short and clear way of expressing concern or disapproval. This doesn't get you embroiled in a lengthy "teachable moment" or humiliate the other person. It simply identifies—for the person engaging in the behavior, but also for those observing it—that the comment or action isn't OK.

One study examining responses to homophobic comments in the workplace found that the most effective type of confrontation was calm but direct: "Hey, that's not cool" or "Don't use that word."[3] A similar approach could be used for almost any type of harmful be-havior, from stopping the schoolyard bully to calling out a colleague who treats subordinates poorly. Openly expressing disapproval clearly communicates what isn't acceptable, an essential first step in creating new social norms.

Another option is to make the discomfort about you, not them. This reduces the risk that you will make the person feel bad or de-fensive, but it still indicates that their comment or behavior was wrong. One way of doing this is to reveal a personal connection to explain your reaction. You could say, "I was raised in the Catholic Church, so that comment is hard for me to hear," or "A close friend of mine was sexually assaulted in high school, so jokes about rape make me uncomfortable."

Yet another strategy is to assume that the comment is meant to be humorous (even if it isn't) and to respond as though it were. You could respond to a sexist comment about electing a woman as pres-ident, for example, by saying, "I know you're just trying to be funny, but some people really do think that women are too emotional to be president!" This approach clarifies that you disagree with the comment—both to the person who said it and to others—but it doesn't make the person who made the remark appear stupid or bad.

It shifts them from the out-group to the in-group and brings them to your side.

Practice, Practice, Practice

Learning different techniques for confronting bias or unethical behavior can make a difference, but it's not enough to learn skills and strategies: it's essential to practice using them. Actively playing out different types of responses to offensive remarks or problematic behavior helps reduce inhibitions about speaking up and makes responding feel more normal. It also increases our confidence that we can intervene in a real-world situation.

The most effective programs—in schools, colleges, and the workplace—not only provide training on how to handle difficult situations but also give participants plenty of opportunities to practice with planned activities and roleplays. This is a prominent feature of bystander intervention programs used to prevent sexual assault among high school and college students, as well as the EPIC training program for police officers in New Orleans.

Training plus practice has even been shown to be effective with young children. Researchers at the University of Texas presented a program on how to respond to sexist remarks to children in kindergarten through third grade classes at an elementary school in the southwestern United States.[4] All of the kids received lessons about bullying and gender stereotyping, which gave examples of sexist comments: "Only boys can play this game," "You can't be the doctor, you have to be the nurse," "Boys are better at math than girls." The students were then divided into two groups. Those in the first group were told two stories about other children who had confronted sexist remarks by their peers and were asked to draw a picture illustrating their favorite part of one of the stories. Children in the second group practiced acting out set responses to sexist comments, such as "Give it a rest, no group is best!" or "I disagree! Sexism is silly to me!"

After the training, the researchers deliberately exposed students from both groups to a sexist remark to evaluate their response. They asked each child individually to carry a counter-stereotypic item to the main office so that it could supposedly be returned to a person who had lost it: girls carried a tool belt, boys a purse. On the way to the office, a same-gender child (who was following instructions from the researchers and had been specifically selected by their teachers for their acting ability) made a sexist comment, saying "Purses are for girls!" or "Tool belts are for boys!" A hidden observer recorded exactly how the child responded, which researchers later coded into one of four categories: agreeing ("I know!"), ignoring (just walking past the other child), objecting ("That's mean!"), or challenging ("There is no such thing as something being just for boys.").

The results highlight the benefits of practice. Twenty percent of the children in the group that had practiced responding to sexist comments challenged this remark in some way, compared with only 2 percent in the other group. Learning strategies for how to respond to biased remarks isn't enough, at least for most of us: we also need practice.

Sweat the Small Stuff

Another key strategy for developing moral rebels is to teach people that taking small steps in the right direction—or even refusing to take a single step in the wrong direction—can make a big difference. As we saw in earlier chapters, that's precisely the approach used in the most effective programs designed to prevent bullying in schools, sexual assault in colleges, and problematic behavior in police officers. That's why children—and teachers—are taught to intervene when they see subtle forms of aggression, such as name-calling and ostracism, instead of waiting for bullying to escalate into more severe forms. It's also why businesses need to create subtle reminders that trigger ethical behavior, so that employees aren't tempted to take an initial small step toward problematic behavior.

On a more global level, research shows that teaching people how seemingly small steps can escalate into violence can help defuse dangerous situations and motivate action. The psychologists Ervin Staub and Laurie Pearlman have found that it is possible to increase people's feelings of empathy and reduce their tendency to obey authority figures.[5] In their work on promoting healing and reconciliation in Rwanda, Burundi, and Congo they communicated the serious consequences of inaction in the face of bad behavior through workshops and radio dramas that emphasized such themes as "Passivity facilitates the evolution of harm doing whereas actions by people inhibit it" and "Devaluation increases the likelihood of violence while humanization decreases it." An assessment one year later showed that exposure to messages of this kind increased people's willingness to speak up. Once people understand the consequences of silence, they are more likely to act. Resistance to seemingly small acts, such as using dehumanizing language and physically segregating different groups, may help prevent the outbreak of genocidal behavior.

These findings powerfully demonstrate the importance of prompting people to intervene early. They also show that a person who starts out by simply taking a single step in the right direction can become a moral rebel. Germans who helped Jews were ordinary people who recognized a need to help those who were being persecuted.[6] They often began by performing a very small action, such as buying food or supplies for their Jewish neighbors, who were not able to shop in most stores. After these modest steps, they often moved up to larger and riskier acts, such as hiding a person for a short period of time.

The type of life-risking help provided by rescuers in Nazi Germany is an extreme and, thankfully, unusual example. But the same process is at work in all sorts of more mundane situations, from refusing to let a classmate copy homework, to calling out a racist comment at the office, to reporting hazing on an athletic team. Becoming a moral rebel may start with something as simple as taking a single courageous step.

Foster Empathy

In 2017, Kristina Rapuano, a graduate student in psychology and neuroscience at Dartmouth College, made the difficult decision to report her academic adviser, William Kelley, to college authorities. She told college administrators that, following a night of heavy drinking at a conference two years earlier, Kelley had raped her. Her decision to file a report came only after she learned that he had allegedly continued to engage in sexual misconduct with other female students. As Rapuano told the *New York Times,* "I felt almost protective about wanting to end this pattern that was extending across generations. I realized it was going to continue."[7]

Rapuano's empathy for other women gave her the courage to incur the costs of calling out bad behavior. Empathy is a common trait of moral rebels. Many programs designed to empower people to intervene when witnessing bad behavior, such as bullying or sexual assault, focus on creating empathy for the victim as a way of motivating action. As we saw in Chapter 9, spending time with people who are racially or culturally different from us can increase our ability to feel empathy and our likelihood of stepping up if they need help.

This is simultaneously depressing and encouraging. We live in an increasingly polarized society, with people divided into "us" and "them"—in the United States this comes in the form of red states versus blue states, viewers of MSNBC versus Fox News, coastal elites versus the "real Americans" living in the heartland. These divisions make it harder to feel empathy for those who are different from us because we do not spend much time with them. It may also help explain why the level of empathy in America appears to be decreasing.

But keep in mind that empathy is not an inborn trait; it is one that can be developed. Some people may naturally and easily be able to see the world through someone else's eyes, but the rest of us can become more empathic—and thus more morally courageous—by deliberately expending the time and energy to do so.

Widen the In-Group

Most of us are far more willing to help a friend than a stranger. We defend friends who are victims of workplace bullying and intervene to protect friends from sexual assault.[8] We are even more likely to help some strangers than others—those with whom we believe we have something in common, such as being fans of the same team.

A relatively easy way to increase our willingness to step up is to broaden our in-group by focusing on what we have in common with others instead of how we differ. Perhaps you remember the study in Chapter 2 showing that fans of the Manchester United soccer team were much more likely to help a stranger in need if he was wearing a Man U jersey than if he wore the jersey of an opposing team.[9] In a follow-up study, these researchers again recruited Manchester United fans and exposed them to the same emergency—a person falling and appearing to be in pain. In some cases this person wore a Manchester United jersey, in others a Liverpool jersey, and in still others, a plain T-shirt.

But in this version of the study, before participants witnessed the accident, they wrote a short essay about how much they had in common with other soccer fans. They also answered a series of questions about how important being a soccer fan was to them and how connected they felt to other fans. The goal of these exercises was to create a sense of shared broad identity—soccer fans—instead of a narrower identity—fans of a particular team.

Eighty percent of the participants stopped to offer help to the person wearing the Manchester United jersey, and only 22 percent stopped to help the person in a plain T-shirt. But unlike the earlier study—where few people helped the person wearing a rival jersey—this time a full 70 percent stopped to help the person wearing the Liverpool jersey.

Broadening how we think about ourselves and our connections to others—as college students instead of as fraternity brothers, as American or British rather than as members of a particular race or religion, or even, ultimately, simply as fellow human beings—can help us overcome the firmly ingrained human tendency toward inaction.

Look for Ethical Leaders

My son Robert was in a lacrosse team locker room one spring morning when team members started talking about their weekend plans. After a boy on the team mentioned that he was going to a dance that night with a date, another boy jokingly said, "What's his name?" As other kids on the team laughed, the coach quickly intervened, saying, "His date might be a boy, his date might be a girl, it doesn't matter."

When Robert shared that story with me, I was struck by how profoundly grateful I was that his coach had conveyed that message in a locker room. Role models who are in a leadership or authority role—like coaches, teachers, and political leaders—are particularly important when it comes to inspiring moral courage. Their words and actions send a clear message of what is and is not acceptable behavior.

Early on in my career at Amherst, I was teaching a class of about twenty-five that included five students who were on the football team. These students attended regularly but never participated in class discussions, and it set a pretty bad example for other students.

They were highly visible—in part because they were all substantially larger than the other students in the class—and they were also part of a high-status campus group. Trying to facilitate class discussions became like pulling teeth. After a few weeks of feeling demoralized, I tried something new. I emailed the head football coach, EJ Mills, explained what was happening, and asked for his help.

EJ responded with a clever solution. He asked for the players' names and then emailed all of them, copying me. His email was short: "Anyone who doesn't talk in Professor Sanderson's class next week doesn't play on Saturday." The problem, as you can probably imagine, was immediately solved.

This type of strong message from someone in a leadership position can go a long way toward establishing social norms of all types. A study of three thousand college football players examined whether the expectations that their coaches communicated about appropriate off-field conduct were correlated with the likelihood that the athletes would intervene when witnessing problematic behavior.[10] Players were asked whether their coach or a member of the athletic department had ever spoken to them or to the team about three topics: appropriate treatment of members of the opposite sex, relationship violence, and speaking up if they saw something happening around them that was not right. They were also asked if their coach would strongly discipline players for poor off-field behavior. The players were then asked to rate how likely they would be to "intervene in a situation that could lead to inappropriate sexual behavior."

Coaches' words mattered. Players who had heard—from coaches or another member of the athletic department—about the importance of good behavior and who had been encouraged to speak up if they witnessed problematic behavior were more likely to say that they would intervene to prevent inappropriate sexual behavior. Players whose coaches emphasized that violations of off-field conduct would be punished were also more likely to report that they would intervene to stop such behavior. This study doesn't tell us whether these players would in fact follow through on their intentions. But it does indicate that coaches at least play a role in creating such intentions.

Remember that leaders come in many forms. Some leaders are formally defined—a coach, the CEO, the police commissioner, a college president. But many people can serve in informal leadership roles. Older students in high schools and colleges often model behavior for their younger peers. New hires look to more senior employees to learn organizational norms. The presence of just one ethical leader in an organization can motivate others to follow, leading to a ripple effect of moral courage.

Find a Friend

Throughout this book I've described many acts of moral courage in which friends prompt each other to do the right thing, from the two high school seniors who stood up for a bullied freshman by creating a "sea of pink" to the two Swedish graduate students who reported a sexual assault at Stanford. In an example from the corporate world, two employees—Erika Cheung and Tyler Shultz—revealed what they knew about fraud going on in the blood-testing company Theranos, even though they knew they would face severe personal and professional repercussions. One key to moral courage is to find a friend who shares your outrage and is willing to stand by your side.

Doug McAdam, a sociologist at Stanford University, found that the best predictor of who will challenge prevailing social norms is having company, so you don't have to do it alone.[11] The four black college students who started a sit-in at the Woolworth's lunch counter in Greensboro, North Carolina, in 1960 were good friends and roommates. Three of them had attended the same high school. Their friendship helped them overcome the challenges they faced, from taunts to racist slurs to threats of violence.

These examples match up with research showing that resisting social pressure is far easier if you are not alone. In Solomon Asch's
study of judging line lengths, the single biggest predictor of participants' ability not to conform to an incorrect answer given by the
group was the presence of one other person who also defied the
group. Similarly, in the Milgram study, where participants were ordered to give shocks, most stopped doing so if another supposed participant refused first.[12] For those of us who aren't naturally moral
rebels, finding a like-minded friend to stand by our side can be an
essential step toward giving us the ability to show moral courage.

Shift Social Norms

Earlier chapters emphasized how very difficult it is for most of us to
defy what we believe to be the norms of our group, whether that
group is our friends, fraternity brothers, or colleagues. But two strategies can help move people from being silent bystanders to active
helpers: shifting the norms, and making people aware that their perception of the norms may actually be wrong.

People coming into a new environment, such as a new school, college, or job, are not aware of existing norms. This creates an opportunity to shape these newcomers' beliefs in ways that encourage
speaking up. Peer leaders in a high school or college could express
the value of bystander action, and workplace leaders could make a
point of emphasizing a workplace culture focused on intervention
instead of inaction. "You need to shift the mindset, so [police] officers realize that if they remain passive as bystanders they are responsible for what their fellow officers do," says Ervin Staub, whose research forms the basis for the EPIC program now used by the New
Orleans police department. "You have to do it in a way that does
not undermine their loyalty to each other, but changes what loyalty
means—stopping excess violence rather than hiding it behind a code
of silence."[13]

Shifting norms can actually work to change behavior. In one creative study, researchers compared different types of messages given to hotel guests to encourage reusing their towels—something that helps conserve energy.[14] In one case, hotel guests received the standard pro-environmental message: "Help Save the Environment: You can show your respect for nature and help save the environment by reusing your towels during your stay." Other guests received a similar message, but with a twist: "Join Your Fellow Guests In Helping To Save the Environment: Almost 75 percent of guests who are asked to participate in our new resource savings program do help by using their towels more than once. You can join your fellow guests to help save the environment by reusing your towels during your stay."

The second message was more effective. Around 38 percent of those who received the first message reused their towels. But that number increased to 48 percent for those who received the second message, indicating that learning about what others are doing can help to change people's behavior. If we think that most members of our group (in this case hotel guests) are engaging in a certain behavior, then many of us will think that we should be too.

Simply informing people about the actual norms within their social group can also push people to change their behavior. Research by Alan Gerber and his colleagues at Yale University demonstrated that informing people about social norms for voting led to a sizeable increase in voter turnout—far more than simply telling people that voting is a civic duty.[15] In one study, eighty thousand households in Michigan were sent one of four mailings encouraging them to vote. One mailing reminded them that voting was a civic duty, another told them their voting participation was being studied by researchers using public records, a third listed voter participation within their household, and a fourth listed voter participation within both their household and their neighborhood. The fourth message was by far the most effective: it increased voter turnout 8.1 percent over those who received no mailing. In contrast, the least effective message—voting as a civic duty—increased turnout by only 1.8 percent. Low level social pressure—in this case, merely educating people about actual voter rates in their neighborhood—is an effective way to increase civic engagement.

Informing people about existing social norms is especially important when people's perceptions of them are actually wrong. As we saw in Chapter 3, people often misperceive others' thoughts and feelings because they rely on what people express in public, which may not be in line with their private beliefs. This can lead to a situation in which each individual is privately bothered by what's going on, but no one speaks up because they (wrongly) believe others don't share their concerns. Correcting these misperceptions, and understanding the psychological forces that create and maintain them, can go a long way toward changing people's behavior. Correcting misperceived norms can help people stand up to bullies, drink less, intervene in cases of sexual assault, and call out offensive language in the workplace.

Change the Culture

If just enough of us choose to become moral rebels, we can change the culture to one of courage and action instead of silence and inaction.

Recent research by Damon Centola at the University of Pennsylvania suggests that large-scale social change doesn't require the support of the majority.[16] In fact, if only about 25 percent of people in a group take a stand, that is enough to create a tipping point that can relatively quickly lead to the establishment of a new norm. A small but vocal minority can change what's seen as socially expected, whether it's recycling a bottle instead of tossing it in the trash or voting instead of staying home.

One of the most vivid examples of rapid norm change is that of the acceptance of gay marriage. My daughter Caroline was born in 2004, the same year that Massachusetts became the first state to legalize gay marriage. In 2015, the US Supreme Court ruled that same-sex couples had a fundamental right to marriage. I remember remarking to Caroline how unbelievable a transition this was: from gay marriage being illegal in every state to being legal nationwide, in just eleven years. Her response? "What took so long?" Yet never in my wildest dreams would I have imagined, when I was her age, that same-sex couples would someday be able to get married, or that a gay man would be a viable candidate for president of the United States. Maybe it wouldn't take as much as we think to create a culture in which the expectation is that we will act when we hear offensive language, witness sexual misconduct, or see workplace fraud. In *How Change Happens,* the legal scholar Cass Sunstein discusses how social norms that push us toward silence and inaction can and do sometimes collapse, leading to much-needed social change.[17] Sometimes just a single voice can be enough, when that one person gives others the courage to speak up.

It's tempting to make the easy choice—to look the other way and assume someone else will act. But we have to live with the consequences of making that choice, of knowing we could have made a difference but chose not to. As John Steinbeck wrote in *East of Eden,* "Humans are caught—in their lives, in their thoughts, in their hungers and ambitions, in their avarice and cruelty, and in their kindness and generosity too—in a net of good and evil. . . . A man, after he has brushed off the dust and chips of his life, will have left only the hard clean questions: Was it good or was it evil? Have I done well—or ill?"[18]

My hope is that you will be able to use the strategies you have learned about in these pages in your own life so that when it comes time to ask those questions, you will take pride in the answers.

Notes

1. The Myth of Monsters

1. Quoted in S. L. Plous and P. G. Zimbardo, "How social science can reduce terrorism," *Chronicle of Higher Education,* September 10, 2004.
2. S. Klebold, *A Mother's Reckoning: Living in the Aftermath of Tragedy* (New York: Crown, 2016).
3. P. G. Zimbardo, "The human choice: Individuation, reason, and order vs. deindividuation, impulse, and chaos," in *Nebraska Symposium on Motivation,* ed. W. J. Arnold and D. Levine, 237–307 (Lincoln: University of Nebraska Press, 1969).
4. A. Silke, "Deindividuation, anonymity, and violence: Findings from Northern Ireland," *Journal of Social Psychology* 143 (2003): 493–499.
5. E. Diener, R. Lusk, D. DeFour, and R. Flax, "Deindividuation: Effects of group size, density, number of observers, and group member similarity on self-consciousness and disinhibited behavior," *Journal of Personality and Social Psychology* 39 (1980): 449–459.
6. A. J. Ritchey and R. B. Ruback, "Predicting lynching atrocity: The situational norms of lynchings in Georgia," *Personality and Social Psychology Bulletin* 44, no. 5 (2018): 619–637.
7. Some neuroscience researchers have been criticized for making a particular statistical error, the nonindependence error, when testing their predictions. This error occurs when researchers first use one statistical

test to select which data to analyze and then use a second (nonindependent) statistical test to analyze the data. Some of these statistical concerns are detailed in, for example, American Psychological Association, "*P*-values under question," *Psychological Science Agenda,* March 2016, https://www.apa.org/science/about/psa/2016/03/p-values; A. Abbot, "Brain imaging studies under fire," *Nature* News, January 13, 2009, https://www.nature.com/news/2009/090113/full/457245a.html.

8. Massachusetts Institute of Technology, "When good people do bad things," *ScienceDaily,* June 12, 2014, https://www.sciencedaily.com /releases/2014/06/140612104950.htm.

9. M. Cikara, A. C. Jenkins, N. Dufour, and R. Saxe, "Reduced self-referential neural response during intergroup competition predicts competitor harm," *NeuroImage* 96 (2014): 36–43.

10. A. C. Jenkins and J. P. Mitchell, "Medial prefrontal cortex subserves diverse forms of self-reflection," *Social Neuroscience* 6, no. 3 (2011): 211–218; W. M. Kelley, C. N. Macrae, C. L. Wyland, S. Caglar, S. Inati, and T. F. Heatherton, "Finding the self? An event-related fMRI study," *Journal of Cognitive Neuroscience* 14 (2002): 785–794; C. N. Macrae, J. M. Moran, T. F. Heatherton, J. F. Banfield, and W. M. Kelley, "Medial prefrontal activity predicts memory for self," *Cerebral Cortex* 14, no. 6 (2004): 647–654.

11. Quoted in A. Trafton, "Group mentality," MIT Technology Review website, posted August 5, 2014, https://www.technologyreview.com/s /529791/group-mentality/.

12. S. Milgram, "Behavioral study of obedience," *Journal of Abnormal and Social Psychology* 67, no. 4 (1963): 371–378.

13. J. M. Burger, "Replicating Milgram: Would people still obey today?" *American Psychologist* 64 (2009): 1–11; D. Doliński, T. Grzyb, M. Folwarczny, P. Grzybała, K. Krzyszycha, K. Martynowska, and J. Trojanowski, "Would you deliver an electric shock in 2015? Obedience in the experimental paradigm developed by Stanley Milgram in the 50 years following the original studies," *Social Psychological and Personality Science* 8, no. 8 (2017): 927–933.

14. W. H. Meeus and Q. A. Raaijmakers, "Administrative obedience: Carrying out orders to use psychological–administrative violence," *European Journal of Social Psychology* 16 (1986): 311–324.

15. T. Blass, "Attribution of responsibility and trust in the Milgram obedience experiment," *Journal of Applied Social Psychology* 26 (1996): 1529–1535.

16. A. Bandura, "Moral disengagement in the perpetration of inhumanities," *Personality and Social Psychology Review* 3, no. 3 (1999): 193–209.

17. H. A. Tilker, "Socially responsible behavior as a function of observer responsibility and victim feedback," *Journal of Personality and Social Psychology* 14, no. 2 (1970): 95–100.

18. J. M. Burger, Z. M. Girgis, and C. C. Manning, "In their own words: Explaining obedience to authority through an examination of participants' comments," *Social Psychological and Personality Science* 2 (2011): 460–466. Two-thirds of those whose comments during the study suggested that they felt personally responsible for harming the learner stopped before giving the maximum shock, while only 12 percent of those who kept giving shocks up to the highest level ever expressed any feelings of personal responsibility.

19. E. A. Caspar, J. F. Christensen, A. Cleeremans, and P. Haggard, "Coercion changes the sense of agency in the human brain," *Current Biology* 26, no. 5 (2016): 585–592.

20. E. Filevich, S. Kühn, and P. Haggard, "There is no free won't: antecedent brain activity predicts decisions to inhibit," *PloS One* 8, no. 2 (2013): e53053.

21. S. D. Reicher, S. A. Haslam, and J. R. Smith, "Working toward the experimenter: reconceptualizing obedience within the Milgram paradigm as identification-based followership," *Perspectives on Psychological Science* 7, no. 4 (2012): 315–324.

22. L. Ross and R. E. Nisbett, *The Person and the Situation: Perspectives of Social Psychology* (London: Pinter and Martin, 2011).

23. Milgram, "Behavioral study of obedience."

24. M. M. Hollander, "The repertoire of resistance: Non-compliance with directives in Milgram's 'obedience' experiments," *British Journal of Social Psychology* 54 (2015): 425–444.

25. F. Gino, L. D. Ordóñez, and D. Welsh, "How unethical behavior becomes habit," *Harvard Business Review* blogpost, September 4, 2014, https://hbr.org/2014/09/how-unethical-behavior-becomes-habit.

26. D. T. Welsh, L. D. Ordóñez, D. G. Snyder, and M. S. Christian, "The slippery slope: How small ethical transgressions pave the way for larger future transgressions," *Journal of Applied Psychology* 100, no. 1 (2015): 114–127.

27. I. Suh, J. T. Sweeney, K. Linke, and J. M. Wall, "Boiling the frog slowly: The immersion of C-suite financial executives into fraud," *Journal of Business Ethics* (July 2018): 1–29.

28. B. T. Denny, J. Fan, X. Liu, S. Guerreri, S. J. Mayson, L. Rimsky, et al., "Insula-amygdala functional connectivity is correlated with habituation to repeated negative images," *Social Cognitive and Affective Neuroscience* 9 no. 11 (2014): 1660–1667.

29. N. Garrett, S. C. Lazzaro, D. Ariely, and T. Sharot, "The brain adapts to dishonesty," *Nature Neuroscience* 19 (2016): 1727–1732.

30. B. Gholipour, "How telling small lies can make you stop caring about big ones," *HuffPost,* October 24, 2016, https://www.huffpost.com/entry/brain-dishonesty_n_580e4b26e4b0a03911edfff9.

31. S. J. Gilbert, "Another look at the Milgram obedience studies: The role of the gradated series of shocks," *Personality and Social Psychology Bulletin* 7, no. 4 (1981): 690–695.

32. A. Modigliani and F. Rochat, "The role of interaction sequences and the timing of resistance in shaping obedience and defiance to authority," *Journal of Social Issues* 51, no. 3 (1995): 107–123.

33. D. J. Packer, "Identifying systematic disobedience in Milgram's obedience experiments: A meta-analytic review," *Perspectives on Psychological Science* 3, no. 4 (2008): 301–304.

34. S. A. Ifill, *On the Courthouse Lawn: Confronting the Legacy of Lynching in the Twenty-First Century* (Boston: Beacon Press, 2007).

35. M. L. King, "Address at the Fourth Annual Institute on Nonviolence and Social Change at Bethel Baptist Church," Montgomery, AL, December 3, 1959, https://kinginstitute.stanford.edu/king-papers/documents/address-fourth-annual-institute-nonviolence-and-social-change-bethel-baptist-0.

2. Who Is Responsible?

1. M. Gansberg, "37 who saw murder didn't call the police: Apathy at stabbing of Queens woman shocks inspector," *New York Times,* March 27, 1964. The original story claimed that there were thirty-eight witnesses and that only one called the police, after Kitty was already dead.

2. S. M. Kassin, "The killing of Kitty Genovese: What else does this case tell us?" *Perspectives on Psychological Science* 12, no. 3 (2017): 374–381.

3. J. M. Darley and B. Latané, "Bystander intervention in emergencies: Diffusion of responsibility," *Journal of Personality and Social Psychology* 8 (1968): 377–383.

4. T. Theisen, "Florida teens heard on video mocking, laughing at man as he drowns in pond, authorities say," *Orlando Sentinel,* July 20, 2017, https://www.orlandosentinel.com/news/os-cocoa-drowning-20170720 -story.html.

5. E. Levensen, "Fraternity pledge died 'alone in a room full of people' at party," *CNN,* December 21, 2017, https://www.cnn.com/2017/12/20/us /fsu-fraternity-pledge-death-grand-jury/index.html.

6. D. Boyle, "Muslim women's hijab grabbed by man who tried to pull off headscarf in London's Oxford Street," *Telegraph,* October 18, 2016, https://www.telegraph.co.uk/news/2016/10/18/muslim-womans-hijab -grabbed-by-man-who-tried-to-pull-off-headsca/.

7. "Chinese toddler left for dead in hit-and-run crash dies," *BBC,* October 21, 2011, https://www.bbc.com/news/world-asia-pacific-15398332.

8. G. Pandey, "India rape: Bystanders ignored Vishakhapatnam attack," *BBC,* October 24, 2017, https://www.bbc.com/news/world-asia-india -41736039.

9. M. Plötner, H. Over, M. Carpenter, and M. Tomasello, "Young children show the bystander effect in helping situations," *Psychological Science* 26, no. 4 (2015): 499–506.

10. Association for Psychological Science, "Children less likely to come to the rescue when others are available," *ScienceDaily,* March 24, 2015, https://www.sciencedaily.com/releases/2015/03/150324132259.htm.

11. S. J. Karau and K. D. Williams, "Social loafing: A meta-analytic review and theoretical integration," *Journal of Personality and Social Psychology* 65 (1993): 681–706.

12. S. Freeman, M. R. Walker, R. Borden, and B. Latané, "Diffusion of re-sponsibility and restaurant tipping: Cheaper by the bunch," *Personality and Social Psychology Bulletin* 1, no. 4 (1975): 584–587.

13. K. D. Williams, S. A. Nida, L. D. Baca, and B. Latané, "Social loafing and swimming: Effects of identifiability on individual and relay perfor-mance of intercollegiate swimmers," *Basic and Applied Social Psychology* 10 (1989): 73–81.

14. B. Latané, K. Williams, and S. Harkins, "Many hands make light the work: The causes and consequences of social loafing," *Journal of Personality and Social Psychology* 37, no. 6 (1979): 822–832.

15. S. M. Garcia, K. Weaver, G. B. Moskowitz, and J. M. Darley, "Crowded minds: The implicit bystander effect," *Journal of Personality and Social Psychology* 83 (2002): 843–853.

16. D. H. Cymek, "Redundant automation monitoring: Four eyes don't see more than two, if everyone turns a blind eye," *Human Factors* 7 (2018): 902–921.

17. F. Beyer, N. Sidarus, S. Bonicalzi, and P. Haggard, "Beyond self-serving bias: Diffusion of responsibility reduces sense of agency and outcome monitoring," *Social Cognitive and Affective Neuroscience* 12 (2017): 138–145.

18. When people played a dice-throwing game with two partners, the FRN amplitude was smaller if the participant got to toss three dice than if they tossed one die and the partners tossed the other two. P. Li, S. Jia, T. Feng, Q. Liu, T. Suo, and H. Li, "The influence of the diffusion of responsibility effect on outcome evaluations: Electrophysiological evidence from an ERP study," *NeuroImage* 52, no. 4 (2010): 1727–1733.

19. M. van Bommel, J.-W. van Prooijen, H. Elffers, and P. A. M. Van Lange, "Be aware to care: Public self-awareness leads to a reversal of the bystander effect," *Journal of Experimental Social Psychology* 48, no. 4 (2012): 926–930.

20. M. Levine and S. Crowther, "The responsive bystander: How social group membership and group size can encourage as well as inhibit bystander intervention," *Journal of Personality and Social Psychology* 95 (2008): 1429–1439.

21. N. L. Kerr and S. E. Bruun, "Dispensability of member effort and group motivation losses: Free-rider effects," *Journal of Personality and Social Psychology* 44, no. 1 (1983): 78–94.

22. A. S. Ross, "Effect of increased responsibility on bystander intervention: The presence of children," *Journal of Personality and Social Psychology* 19, no. 3 (1971): 306–310.

23. R. E. Cramer, M. R. McMaster, P. A. Bartell, and M. Dragna, "Subject competence and minimization of the bystander effect," *Journal of Applied Social Psychology* 18 (1988): 1133–1148.

24. R. F. Baumeister, S. P. Chesner, P. S. Senders, and D. M. Tice, "Who's in charge here? Group leaders do lend help in emergencies," *Personality and Social Psychology Bulletin* 14 (1988): 17–22.

25. J. C. Turner, M. A. Hogg, P. J. Oakes, S. D. Reicher, and M. S. Wetherell, *Rediscovering the Social Group: A Self-Categorization Theory* (Oxford: Basil Blackwell, 1987).

26. M. Levine, A. Prosser, D. Evans, and S. Reicher, "Identity and emergency intervention: How social group membership and inclusiveness of group

boundaries shape helping behavior," *Personality and Social Psychology Bulletin* 31 (2005): 443–453.

27. M. Levine and R. Manning, "Social identity, group processes, and helping in emergencies," *European Review of Social Psychology* 24 (2013): 225–251.

28. M. Slater, A. Rovira, R. Southern, D. Swapp, J. J. Zhang, C. Campbell, and M. Levine, "Bystander responses to a violent incident in an immersive virtual environment," *PLOS One* 8, no. 1 (2013): e52766.

29. A. Dobrin, "The real story of the murder where 'no one cared,'" *Psychology Today* blog, posted March 8, 2014, https://www.psychologytoday .com/us/blog/am-i-right/201403/the-real-story-the-murder-where-no -one-cared; H. Takooshian, D. Bedrosian, J. J. Cecero, L. Chancer, A. Karmen, J. Rasenberger, et al., "Remembering Catherine 'Kitty' Genovese 40 years later: A public forum," *Journal of Social Distress and the Homeless* 5 (2013): 63–77.

3. The Perils of Ambiguity

1. R. L. Shotland and M. K. Straw, "Bystander response to an assault: When a man attacks a woman," *Journal of Personality and Social Psychology* 34 (1976): 990–999.

2. E. Staub, "A child in distress: The influence of age and number of witnesses on children's attempts to help," *Journal of Personality and Social Psychology* 14, no. 2 (1970): 130–140. These results may differ from those discussed in Chapter 2, where children were less likely to help the experimenter when in a group, because of different experimental conditions—in Staub's study, the children knew each other, and the distress situation was more dangerous.

3. R. D. Clark and L. E. Word, "Where is the apathetic bystander? Situational characteristics of the emergency," *Journal of Personality and Social Psychology* 29 (1974): 279–287.

4. R. D. Clark and L. E. Word, "Why don't bystanders help? Because of ambiguity?" *Journal of Personality and Social Psychology* 24 (1972): 392–400.

5. J. Drury, C. Cocking, and S. Reicher, "The nature of collective 'resilience': Survivor reactions to the 2005 London bombings," *International Journal of Mass Emergencies and Disasters* 27, no. 1 (2009): 66–95.

6. C. Cocking, J. Drury, and S. Reicher, "Bystander intervention during the 7/7 London bombings: An account of survivor's [sic] experiences,"

PowerPoint presentation, n.d., www.sussex.ac.uk/affiliates/panic/BPS%
20london%20bystanders%202007.ppt.

7. P. Fischer, T. Greitemeyer, F. Pollozek, and D. Frey, "The unresponsive
bystander: Are bystanders more responsive in dangerous emergencies?"
European Journal of Social Psychology 36, no. 2 (2006): 267–278.

8. R. Philpot, L. S. Liebst, M. Levine, W. Bernasco, and M. R. Lindegaard,
"Would I be helped? Cross-national CCTV footage shows that intervention is the norm in public conflicts," *American Psychologist* (2019),
advance online publication, doi: 10.1037/amp0000469.

9. P. Fischer, J. I. Krueger, T. Greitemeyer, C. Vogrincic, A. Kastenmüller,
D. Frey, et al., "The bystander-effect: A meta-analytic review on by-
stander intervention in dangerous and non-dangerous emergencies,"
Psychological Bulletin 137, no. 4 (2011): 517–537.

10. L. Ashburn-Nardo, K. A. Morris, and S. A. Goodwin, "The Confronting
Prejudiced Responses (CPR) model: Applying CPR in the workplace," *Academy of Management Learning and Education* 7 (2008):
332–342.

11. B. Latané and J. M. Darley, "Group inhibition of bystander intervention in emergencies," *Journal of Personality and Social Psychology* 10
(1968): 308–324.

12. J. A. Harrison and R. B. Wells, "Bystander effects on male helping behavior: Social comparison and diffusion of responsibility," *Representa-
tive Research in Social Psychology* 19, no. 1 (1991): 53–63.

13. E. Staub, "Helping a distressed person: Social, personality, and stimulus
determinants," in *Advances in Experimental Social Psychology,* vol. 7,
ed. L. Berkowitz, 293–341 (New York: Academic Press, 1974).

14. C. Kilmartin, T. Smith, A. Green, H. Heinzen, M. Kuchler, and D. Kolar,
"A real time social norms intervention to reduce male sexism," *Sex Roles*
59, no. 3–4 (2008): 264–273.

15. J. R. B. Halbesleben, "The role of pluralistic ignorance in the reporting
of sexual harassment," *Basic and Applied Social Psychology* 31, no. 3
(2009): 210–217.

16. D. T. Miller and C. McFarland, "Pluralistic ignorance: When similarity
is interpreted as dissimilarity," *Journal of Personality and Social Psychology* 53, no. 2 (1987): 298–305.

17. J. D. Vorauer and R. K. Ratner, "Who's going to make the first move?
Pluralistic ignorance as an impediment to relationship formation,"
Journal of Social and Personal Relationships 13 (1996): 483–506.

18. J. N. Shelton and J. A. Richeson, "Intergroup contact and pluralistic ignorance," *Journal of Personality and Social Psychology* 88, no. 1 (2005): 91–107.

19. M. van Bommel, J.-W. van Prooijen, H. Elffers, and P. A. M. Van Lange, "Booze, bars, and bystander behavior: People who consumed alcohol help faster in the presence of others," *Frontiers in Psychology* 7 (2016), article 128.

20. S. D. Preston and F. B. de Waal, "Empathy: Its ultimate and proximate bases," *Behavioral and Brain Sciences* 25 (2002): 1–20.

21. N. H. Frijda, *The Emotions* (Cambridge: Cambridge University Press, 2006); P. J. Lang, "The motivational organization of emotion: Affect reflex connections," in *The Emotions: Essays on Emotion Theory*, ed. S. van Goozen, N. E. van de Poll, and J. A. Sergeant, 61–96 (Hillsdale, NJ: Erlbaum, 1993).

22. R. Hortensius and B. de Gelder, "The neural basis of the bystander effect: The influence of group size on neural activity when witnessing an emergency," *Neuroimage* 93, pt. 1 (2014): 53–58.

23. J. Lipman-Blumen, *The Allure of Toxic Leaders: Why We Follow Destructive Bosses and Corrupt Politicians—And How We Can Survive Them* (New York: Oxford University Press, 2006).

24. B. Latané and J. Rodin, "A lady in distress: Inhibiting effects of friends and strangers on bystander intervention," *Journal of Experimental Social Psychology* 5, no. 2 (1969): 189–202.

25. "Couples recognized suspect from TV reports," *CNN,* March 13, 2003, http://www.cnn.com/2003/US/West/03/13/smart.witnesses/index.html.

26. Although the name of the pilot has never been determined, the announcement does appear to be authentic. See L. Zuckerman, "Name of pilot who roused passengers still a mystery," *New York Times,* October 1, 2001; D. Mikkelson, "Pilot's Advice," Snopes, https://www.snopes.com/fact-check/blanket-advice/.

4. The Considerable Costs of Helping

1. J. M. Darley and C. D. Batson, "'From Jerusalem to Jericho': A study of situational and dispositional variables in helping behavior," *Journal of Personality and Social Psychology* 27 (1973): 100–108.

2. J. F. Dovidio, J. A. Piliavin, S. L. Gaertner, D. A. Schroeder, and R. D. Clark, "The arousal: cost-reward model and the process of intervention:

A review of the evidence," *Review of Personality and Social Psychology* 12 (1991): 83–118.

3. J. A. Piliavin and I. M. Piliavin, "Effect of blood on reactions to a victim," *Journal of Personality and Social Psychology* 23 (1972): 353–361.

4. C. Sasson, D. J. Magid, P. Chan, E. D. Root, B. F. McNally, A. L. Kellermann, and J. S. Haukoos, "Association of neighborhood characteristics with bystander-initiated CPR," *New England Journal of Medicine* 367, no. 17 (2012): 1607–1615.

5. C. Sasson, C. C. Keirns, D. Smith, M. Sayre, M. Macy, W. Meurer, et al., "Small area variations in out-of-hospital cardiac arrest: Does the neighborhood matter?" *Annals of Internal Medicine* 153, no. 1 (2010): 19–22.

6. E. Y. Cornwell and A. Currit, "Racial and social disparities in bystander support during medical emergencies on US streets," *American Journal of Public Health* 106, no. 6 (2016): 1049–1051.

7. C. E. Ross, J. Mirowsky, and S. Pribesh, "Powerlessness and the amplification of threat: Neighborhood disadvantage, disorder, and mistrust," *American Sociological Review* 66, no. 4 (2001): 568–591.

8. N. M. Steblay, "Helping behavior in rural and urban environments: A meta-analysis," *Psychological Bulletin* 102, no. 3 (1987): 346–356.

9. J. K. Swim and L. L. Hyers, "Excuse me—what did you just say?!: Women's public and private responses to sexist remarks," *Journal of Experimental Social Psychology* 35 (1999): 68–88.

10. E. H. Dodd, T. A. Giuliano, J. M. Boutell, and B. E. Moran, "Respected or rejected: Perceptions of women who confront sexist remarks," *Sex Roles* 45, no. 7–8 (2001): 567–577.

11. K. Kawakami, E. Dunn, F. Karmali, and J. F. Dovidio, "Mispredicting affective and behavioral responses to racism," *Science* 323, no. 5911 (2009): 276–278.

12. J. Steenhuysen, "Whites may be more racist than they think: study," Reuters, January 8, 2009, https://www.reuters.com/article/us-racism/whites-may-be-more-racist-than-they-think-study-idUSTRE5076YX20090108.

13. N. I. Eisenberger, "The neural bases of social pain: Evidence for shared representations with physical pain," *Psychosomatic Medicine* 74, no. 2 (2012): 126–135.

14. N. I. Eisenberger, M. D. Lieberman, and K. D. Williams, "Does rejection hurt? An fMRI study of social exclusion," *Science* 302, no. 5643 (2003): 290–292.

15. C. N. DeWall, G. MacDonald, G. D. Webster, C. L. Masten, R. F. Baumeister, C. Powell, et al., "Acetaminophen reduces social pain: Behavioral and neural evidence," *Psychological Science* 21, no. 7 (2010): 931–937.

16. D. Mischkowski, J. Crocker, and B. M. Way, "From painkiller to empathy killer: Acetaminophen (paracetamol) reduces empathy for pain," *Social Cognitive and Affective Neuroscience* 11, no. 9 (2016): 1345–1353.

17. "When you take acetaminophen, you don't feel others' pain as much," *Ohio State News,* May 9, 2016, https://news.osu.edu/when-you-take -acetaminophen-you-dont-feel-others-pain-as-much/.

18. T. L. Huston, M. Ruggiero, R. Conner, and G. Geis, "Bystander intervention into crime: A study based on naturally-occurring episodes," *Social Psychology Quarterly* 44, no. 1 (1981): 14–23.

19. A. Fantz, "Cub Scout leader, ex-teacher confronted London terrorist," *CNN,* May 24, 2013, https://www.cnn.com/2013/05/23/world/europe /uk-woman-terrorists/index.html.

20. E. D. Murphy, "Bystander performs CPR at gym, saves man's life," © *Portland Press Herald* [Maine], posted on *EMS1.com,* April 6, 2017, https://www.ems1.com/ems-products/cpr-resuscitation/articles /227897048-Bystander-performs-CPR-at-gym-saves-mans-life/.

5. The Power of Social Groups

1. S. E. Asch, "Effects of group pressure upon the modification and distortion of judgment," in *Groups, Leadership and Men,* ed. H. Guetzkow, 177–190 (Pittsburgh: Carnegie Press, 1951).

2. M. J. Salganik, P. S. Dodds, and D. J. Watts, "Experimental study of inequality and unpredictability in an artificial cultural market," *Science* 311, no. 5762 (2006): 854–856.

3. E. Robinson and S. Higgs, "Liking food less: The impact of social influence on food liking evaluations in female students," *PloS One* 7, no. 11 (2012): e48858.

4. R. B. Cialdini, R. R. Reno, and C. A. Kallgren, "A focus theory of normative conduct: Recycling the concept of norms to reduce littering in public places," *Journal of Personality and Social Psychology* 58, no. 6 (1990): 1015–1026; A. W. Kruglanski and D. M. Webster, "Group members' reactions to opinion deviates and conformists at varying degrees

of proximity to decision deadline and of environmental noise," *Journal of Personality and Social Psychology* 61, no. 2 (1991): 212–225; S. Schachter, "Deviation, rejection, and communication," *Journal of Abnormal and Social Psychology* 46, no. 2 (1951): 190–207.

5. L. M. Janes and J. M. Olson, "Jeer pressures: The behavioral effects of observing ridicule of others," *Personality and Social Psychology Bulletin* 26, no. 4 (2000): 474–485.

6. D. K. Campbell-Meiklejohn, D. R. Bach, A. Roepstorff, R. J. Dolan, and C. D. Frith, "How the opinion of others affects our valuation of objects," *Current Biology* 20, no. 13 (2010): 1165–1170.

7. A. Shestakova, J. Rieskamp, S. Tugin, A. Ossadtchi, J. Krutitskaya, and V. Klucharev, "Electrophysiological precursors of social conformity," *Social Cognitive and Affective Neuroscience* 8, no. 7 (2013): 756–763.

8. V. Klucharev, K. Hytönen, M. Rijpkema, A. Smidts, and G. Fernández, "Reinforcement learning signal predicts social conformity," *Neuron* 61, no. 1 (2009): 140–151.

9. Cell Press, "Brain mechanisms of social conformity," *ScienceDaily* website, January 16, 2009, https://www.sciencedaily.com/releases/2009/01/090114124109.htm.

10. P. Shaw, N. Kabani, J. P. Lerch, K. Eckstrand, R. Lenroot, N. Gotay, et al., "Neurodevelopmental trajectories of the human cerebral cortex," *Journal of Neuroscience* 28 (2008): 3586–3594.

11. A. E. Guyer, V. R. Choate, D. S. Pine, and E. E. Nelson, "Neural circuitry underlying affective responses to peer feedback in adolescence," *Social Cognitive and Affective Neuroscience* 7 (2012): 82–91; C. Sebastian, E. Viding, K. D. Williams, and S. J. Blakemore, "Social brain development and the affective consequences of ostracism in adolescence," *Brain and Cognition* 72 (2010): 134–135; L. H. Somerville, "The teenage brain: Sensitivity to social evaluation," *Current Directions in Psychological Science* 22, no. 2 (2013): 121–127.

12. L. J. Knoll, L. Magis-Weinberg, M. Speekenbrink, and S. J. Blakemore, "Social influence on risk perception during adolescence," *Psychological Science* 26 (2015): 583–592.

13. M. Gardner and L. Steinberg, "Peer influence on risk taking, risk preference, and risky decision making in adolescence and adulthood: An experimental study," *Developmental Psychology* 41, no. 4 (2005): 625–635.

14. A. E. Curry, J. H. Mirman, M. J. Kallan, F. K. Winston, and D. R. Durbin, "Peer passengers: How do they affect teen crashes?" *Journal of Adolescent Health* 50 (2012): 588–594.

15. B. Simons-Morton, N. Lerner, and J. Singer, "The observed effects of teenage passengers on the risky driving behavior of teenage drivers," *Accident Analysis and Prevention* 37 (2005): 973–982.

16. E. E. Nelson, E. Leibenluft, E. B. McClure, and D. S. Pine, "The social re-orientation of adolescence: A neuroscience perspective on the process and its relation to psychopathology," *Psychological Medicine* 35 (2005): 163–174.

17. L. E. Sherman, A. A. Payton, L. M. Hernandez, P. M. Greenfield, and M. Dapretto, "The power of the like in adolescence: Effects of peer influence on neural and behavioral responses to social media," *Psychological Science* 27, no. 7 (2016): 1027–1035.

18. E. B. McClure, "A meta-analytic review of sex differences in facial expression processing and their development in infants, children, and adolescents," *Psychological Bulletin* 126, no. 3 (2000): 424–453; A. J. Rose and K. D. Rudolph, "A review of sex differences in peer relationship processes: Potential trade-offs for the emotional and behavioral development of girls and boys," *Psychological Bulletin* 132, no. 1 (2006): 98–131.

19. S. Nolen-Hoeksema and S. J. Girgus, "The emergence of gender differences in depression during adolescence," *Psychological Bulletin* 115, no. 3 (1994): 424–443.

20. A. E. Guyer, E. B. McClure-Tone, N. D. Shiffrin, D. S. Pine, and E. E. Nelson, "Probing the neural correlates of anticipated peer evaluation in adolescence," *Child Development* 80, no. 4 (2009): 1000–1015.

21. D. A. Prentice and D. T. Miller, "Pluralistic ignorance and alcohol use on campus: Some consequences of misperceiving the social norm," *Journal of Personality and Social Psychology* 64, no. 2 (1993): 243–256.

22. C. A. Sanderson, J. M. Darley, and C. S. Messinger, "'I'm not as thin as you think I am': The development and consequences of feeling discrepant from the thinness norm," *Personality and Social Psychology Bulletin* 28, no. 2 (2002): 172–183.

23. C. A. Sanderson, J. M. Wallier, J. E. Stockdale, and D. J. A. Yopyk, "Who feels discrepant and how does feeling discrepant matter? Examining the presence and consequences of feeling discrepant from personal and

social norms related to thinness in America and British high school girls," *Journal of Social and Clinical Psychology* 27 (2008): 995–1020.

24. Sanderson, Darley, and Messinger, "I'm not as thin as you think I am."

25. Prentice and Miller, "Pluralistic ignorance and alcohol use."

26. G. Bohner, F. Siebler, and J. Schmelcher, "Social norms and the likelihood of raping: Perceived rape myth acceptance of others affects men's rape proclivity," *Personality and Social Psychology Bulletin* 32, no. 3 (2006): 286–297.

27. H. W. Perkins and D. W. Craig, "A successful social norms campaign to reduce alcohol misuse among college student-athletes," *Journal of Studies on Alcohol* 67 (2006): 880–889.

28. C. M. Schroeder and D. A. Prentice, "Exposing pluralistic ignorance to reduce alcohol use among college students," *Journal of Applied Social Psychology* 28, no. 23 (1998): 2150–2180.

29. J. A. Mutterperl and C. A. Sanderson, "Mind over matter: Internalization of the thinness norm as a moderator of responsiveness to norm misperception education in college women," *Health Psychology* 21, no. 5 (2002): 519–523.

30. K. M. Turetsky and C. A. Sanderson, "Comparing educational interventions: Correcting misperceived norms improves college students' mental health attitudes," *Journal of Applied Social Psychology* 48 (2018): 46–55.

31. *Report I of the 40th Statewide Investigating Grand Jury,* redacted by order of PA Supreme Court, Office of the Attorney General, Commonwealth of Pennsylvania, July 27, 2018, pp. 7, 1, https://www .attorneygeneral.gov/report/.

32. R. Denhollander, "The price I paid for taking on Larry Nassar," op-ed, *New York Times,* January 26, 2018.

33. ABC News, *Nightline,* May 9, 2017, https://abcnews.go.com/Nightline /video/details-emerge-horrific-penn-state-fraternity-house-party -47290537.

6. At School

1. I use the phrase "died by suicide" intentionally instead of the more commonly used phrase "committed suicide," based on current recommendations from the psychology community. S. Beaton, P. Forster, and M. Maple, "Suicide and language: Why we shouldn't use the 'C' word,"

InPsych, Australian Psychological Association, February 2013, https://www.psychology.org.au/publications/inpsych/2013/february /beaton; J. Ravitz, "The words to say—and not to say—about suicide," *CNN*, June 11, 2018, https://www.cnn.com/2018/06/09/health/suicide -language-words-matter/index.html.

2. N. Alavi, T. Reshetukha, E. Prost, K. Antoniak, C. Patel, S. Sajid, and D. Groll, "Relationship between bullying and suicidal behaviour in youth presenting to the emergency department," *Journal of the Canadian Academy of Child and Adolescent Psychiatry* 26, no. 2 (2017): 70–77.

3. S. M. Swearer and S. Hymel, "Understanding the psychology of bullying: Moving toward a social-ecological diathesis–stress model," *American Psychologist* 70, no. 4 (2015): 344–353.

4. P. O'Connell, D. Pepler, and W. Craig, "Peer involvement in bullying: Insights and challenges for intervention," *Journal of Adolescence* 22 (1999): 437–452.

5. K. Rigby and P. T. Slee, "Bullying among Australian school children: Reported behavior and attitudes toward victims," *Journal of Social Psychology* 131, no. 5 (1991): 615–627; L. Jenkins and A. B. Nickerson, "Bystander intervention in bullying: Role of social skills and gender," *Journal of Early Adolescence* 39, no. 2 (2019): 141–166.

6. Quoted in S. Wolpert, "'Cool' kids in middle school bully more, UCLA psychologists report," UCLA Newsroom, January 24, 2013, http:// newsroom.ucla.edu/releases/cool-middle-school-kids-bully-242868.

7. M. Sandstrom, H. Makover, and M. Bartini, "Social context of bullying: Do misperceptions of group norms influence children's responses to witnessed episodes?" *Social Influence* 8, no. 2–3 (2013): 196–215.

8. T. Pozzoli and G. Gini, "Why do bystanders of bullying help or not? A multidimensional model," *Journal of Early Adolescence* 33 (2013): 315–340; T. Pozzoli, G. Gini, and A. Vieno, "The role of individual correlates and class norms in defending and passive bystanding behavior in bullying: A multilevel analysis," *Child Development* 83 (2012): 1917–1931.

9. L. R. Barhight, J. A. Hubbard, S. N. Grassetti, and M. T. Morrow, "Relations between actual group norms, perceived peer behavior, and bystander children's intervention to bullying," *Journal of Clinical Child and Adolescent Psychology* 46, no. 3 (2017): 394–400; Pozzoli, Gini, and Vieno, "The role of individual correlates and class norms."

10. V. Kubiszewski, L. Auzoult, C. Potard, and F. Lheureux, "Witnessing school bullying: To react or not to react? An insight into perceived social

norms regulating self-predicted defending and passive behaviours," *Educational Psychology* 39, no. 9 (2019): 1174–1193.

11. I. Peritz, "Students give world a lesson in courage," *Globe and Mail,* April 26, 2018.

12. C. Salmivalli, K. Lagerspetz, K. Björkqvist, K. Österman, and A. Kauki-ainen, "Bullying as a group process: Participant roles and their relations to social status within the group," *Aggressive Behavior* 22 (1996): 1–15.

13. R. Faris and D. Felmlee, "Casualties of social combat: School networks of peer victimization and their consequences," *American Sociological Review* 79, no. 2 (2014): 228–257.

14. "For most adolescents, popularity increases the risk of getting bullied," Press release, American Sociological Association, April 1, 2014, https://www.asanet.org/press-center/press-releases/most-adolescents -popularity-increases-risk-getting-bullied.

15. Quoted in T. Pearce, "Popular kids more likely to be bullies, study finds," *Globe and Mail,* February 8, 2011.

16. G. Gini, P. Albiero, B. Benelli, and G. Altoè, "Determinants of adoles-cents' active defending and passive bystanding behavior in bullying," *Journal of Adolescence* 31, no. 1 (2008): 93–105.

17. L. N. Jenkins and S. S. Fredrick, "Social capital and bystander behavior in bullying: Internalizing problems as a barrier to prosocial interven-tion," *Journal of Youth and Adolescence* 46, no. 4 (2017): 757–771.

18. J. R. Polanin, D. L. Espelage, and T. D. Pigott, "A meta-analysis of school-based bullying prevention programs' effects on bystander intervention behavior," *School Psychology Review* 41 (2012): 47–65.

19. J. Pfetsch, G. Steffgen, M. Gollwitzer, and A. Ittel, "Prevention of ag-gression in schools through a bystander intervention training," *Interna-tional Journal of Developmental Science* 5, no. 1–2 (2011): 139–149.

20. S. Low, K. S. Frey, and C. J. Brockman, "Gossip on the playground: Changes associated with universal intervention, retaliation beliefs, and supportive friends," *School Psychology Review* 39, no. 4 (2010): 536–551.

21. H. W. Perkins, D. W. Craig, and J. M. Perkins, "Using social norms to reduce bullying: A research intervention among adolescents in five middle schools," *Group Processes and Intergroup Relations* 14, no. 5 (2011): 703–722.

22. E. L. Paluck, H. Shepherd, and P. M. Aronow, "Changing climates of conflict: A social network experiment in 56 schools," *Proceedings of*

the National Academy of Sciences of the United States of America 113, no. 3 (2016): 566–571.

23. E. L. Paluck, "Changing climates of conflict: A social network experiment in 56 schools," Research brief, Woodrow Wilson School of Public and International Affairs, Princeton University, January 2016, https://wws.princeton.edu/faculty-research/research/item/changing -climates-conflict-social-network-experiment-56-schools.

24. J. A. Kelly, D. A. Murphy, K. J. Sikkema, R. L. McAuliffe, R. A. Roffman, L. J. Solomon, et al., "Randomised, controlled, community-level HIV-prevention intervention for sexual-risk behaviour among homosexual men in US cities. Community HIV Prevention Research Collaborative," *Lancet* 350, no. 9090 (1997): 1500–1505; E. L. Paluck, "Peer pressure against prejudice: A high school field experiment examining social network change," *Journal of Experimental Social Psychology* 47, no. 2 (2011): 350–358.

25. M. M. Ttofi and D. P. Farrington, "Effectiveness of school-based programs to reduce bullying: A systematic and meta-analytic review," *Journal of Experimental Criminology* 7 (2011): 27–56.

26. J. Juvonen, H. L. Schacter, M. Sainio, and C. Salmivalli, "Can a school-wide bullying prevention program improve the plight of victims? Evidence for risk × intervention effects," *Journal of Consulting and Clinical Psychology* 84, no. 4 (2016): 334–344.

27. Quoted in S. Wolpert, "Anti-bullying program focused on bystanders helps the students who need it the most," UCLA Newsroom, February 1, 2016, http://newsroom.ucla.edu/releases/anti-bullying-program-focused -on-bystanders-helps-the-students-who-need-it-the-most.

28. Kubiszewski, Auzoult, Potard, and Lheureux, "Witnessing school bullying."

29. T. Jungert, B. Piroddi, and R. Thornberg, "Early adolescents' motivations to defend victims in school bullying and their perceptions of student-teacher relationships: A self-determination theory approach," *Journal of Adolescence* 53 (2016): 75–90.

30. E. Staub, "The roots of evil: Personality, social conditions, culture and basic human needs," *Personality and Social Psychology Review* 3 (1999): 179–192.

31. J. M. Hektner and C. A. Swenson, "Links from teacher beliefs to peer victimization and bystander intervention: Tests of mediating processes," *Journal of Early Adolescence* 32, no. 4 (2012): 516–536.

32. K. L. Mulvey, S. Gönültaş, E. Goff, G. Irdam, R. Carlson, C. DiStefano, and M. J. Irvin, "School and family factors predicting adolescent cognition regarding bystander intervention in response to bullying and victim retaliation," *Journal of Youth and Adolescence* 48 (2019): 581–596.

33. E. Ahmed, "'Stop it, that's enough': Bystander intervention and its relationship to school connectedness and shame management," *Vulnerable Children and Youth Studies* 3, no. 3 (2008): 203–213.

34. Quoted in M. Shipman, "Family, school support makes kids more likely to stand up to bullying," *NC State News*, November 12, 2018, https:// news.ncsu.edu/2018/11/support-bullying-intervention/.

7. In College

1. J. Cui and B. O'Daly, "DKE case raises questions about fraternity bans," *Yale Daily News,* October 27, 2016.

2. D. Lisak and P. M. Miller, "Repeat rape and multiple offending among undetected rapists," *Violence and Victims* 17 (2002): 73–84.

3. P. R. Sanday, *Fraternity Gang Rape: Sex, Brotherhood, and Privilege on Campus* (New York: New York University Press, 1990).

4. S. B. Boeringer, "Influences of fraternity membership, athletics, and male living arrangements on sexual aggression," *Violence against Women* 2 (1996): 134–147; L. Lackie and A. F. de Man, "Correlates of sexual aggression among male university students," *Sex Roles* 37 (1997): 451–457; P. Y. Martin, "The rape prone culture of academic contexts: Fraternities and athletics," *Gender and Society* 30, no. 1 (2016): 30–43; S. McMahon, "Rape myth beliefs and bystander attitudes among incoming college students," *Journal of American College Health* 59, no. 1 (2010): 3–11; S. K. Murnen and M. H. Kohlman, "Athletic participation, fraternity membership, and sexual aggression among college men: A meta-analytic review," *Sex Roles* 57 (2007): 145–157.

5. T. Crosset, J. Benedict, and M. MacDonald, "Male student athletes reported for sexual assault: A survey of campus police departments and judicial affairs offices," *Journal of Sport & Social Issues* 19 (1995): 126–140.

6. B.-R. Young, S. L. Desmarais, J. A. Baldwin, and R. Chandler, "Sexual coercion practices among undergraduate male recreational athletes, intercollegiate athletes, and non-athletes," *Violence against Women* 23, no. 7 (2017): 795–812.

7. E. T. Bleecker and S. K. Murnen, "Fraternity membership, the display of degrading sexual images of women, and rape myth acceptance," *Sex Roles* 53, no. 7–8 (2005): 487–493.

8. S. Houseworth, K. Peplow, and J. Thirer, "Influence of sport participation upon sex role orientation of Caucasian males and their attitudes toward women," *Sex Roles* 20, no. 5–6 (1989): 317–325.

9. J. B. Kingree and M. P. Thompson, "Fraternity membership and sexual aggression: An examination of mediators of the association," *Journal of American College Health* 61 (2013): 213–221.

10. Murnen and Kohlman, "Athletic participation, fraternity membership, and sexual aggression."

11. J. R. Mahalik, B. D. Locke, L. H. Ludlow, M. A. Diemer, R. P. Scott, M. Gottfried, and G. Freitas, "Development of the Conformity to Masculine Norms Inventory," *Psychology of Men and Masculinity* 4 (2003): 3–25.

12. C. A. Franklin, L. A. Bouffard, and T. C. Pratt, "Sexual assault on the college campus: Fraternity affiliation, male peer support, and low self-control," *Criminal Justice and Behavior* 39 (2012): 1457–1480; D. K. Iwamoto, W. Corbin, C. Lejuez, and L. MacPherson, "College men and alcohol use: Positive alcohol expectancies as a mediator between distinct masculine norms and alcohol use," *Psychology of Men and Masculinity* 15 (2014): 29–39.

13. S. Boeringer, C. Shehan, R. Akers, "Social contexts and social learning in sexual coercion and aggression: Assessing the contribution of fraternity membership," *Family Relations* 40, no. 1 (1991): 58–64.

14. R. C. Seabrook, L. M. Ward, and S. Giaccardi, "Why is fraternity membership associated with sexual assault? Exploring the roles of conformity to masculine norms, pressure to uphold masculinity, and objectification of women," *Psychology of Men and Masculinity* 19, no. 1 (2018): 3–13.

15. A. Abbey, "Alcohol's role in sexual violence perpetration: Theoretical explanations, existing evidence, and future directions," *Drug and Alcohol Review* 30 (2011): 481–489.

16. B. D. Locke and J. R. Mahalik, "Examining masculinity norms, problem drinking, and athletic involvement as predictors of sexual aggression in college men," *Journal of Counseling Psychology* 52, no. 3 (2005): 279–283.

17. G. B. Forbes, L. E. Adams-Curtis, A. H. Pakalka, and K. B. White, "Dating aggression, sexual coercion, and aggression-supporting

attitudes among college men as a function of participation in aggressive high school sports," *Violence against Women* 12 (2006): 441–455.

18. K. Parker, "Women in majority-male workplaces report higher rates of gender discrimination," Pew Research Center, *FactTank,* March 7, 2018, https://www.pewresearch.org/fact-tank/2018/03/07/women-in -majority-male-workplaces-report-higher-rates-of-gender -discrimination/.

19. C. F. Karpowitz and T. Mendelberg, *The Silent Sex: Gender, Deliberation, and Institutions* (Princeton, NJ: Princeton University Press, 2014).

20. C. Karpowitz and T. Mendelberg, "Is an old boys' club always sexist?" *Washington Post,* October 23, 2014.

21. C. Newlands and M. Marriage, "Women in asset management: Battling a culture of 'subtle sexism,'" *Financial Times,* November 29, 2014.

22. E. Chang, *Brotopia: Breaking Up the Boys' Club of Silicon Valley* (New York: Portfolio, 2018).

23. S. Chira, "We asked women in blue-color workplaces about harassment. Here are their stories," *New York Times,* December 29, 2017.

24. C. Kilmartin, T. Smith, A. Green, H. Heinzen, M. Kuchler, and D. Kolar, "A real time social norms intervention to reduce male sexism," *Sex Roles* 59 (2008): 264–273; C. Loh, C. A. Gidycz, T. R. Lobo, and R. Luthra, "A prospective analysis of sexual assault perpetration: Risk factors related to perpetrator characteristics," *Journal of Interpersonal Violence* 20 (2005): 1325–1348.

25. M. Carlson, "I'd rather go along and be considered a man: Masculinity and bystander intervention," *Journal of Men's Studies* 16 (2008): 3–17.

26. C. M. Dardis, M. J. Murphy, A. C. Bill, and C. A. Gidycz, "An investigation of the tenets of social norms theory as they relate to sexually aggressive attitudes and sexual assault perpetration: A comparison of men and their friends," *Psychology of Violence* 6, no. 1 (2016): 163–171.

27. Dardis, Murphy, Bill, and Gidycz, "An investigation of the tenets of social norms theory."

28. M. P. Thompson, K. M. Swartout, and M. P. Koss, "Trajectories and predictors of sexually aggressive behaviors during emerging adulthood," *Psychology of Violence* 3 (2013): 247–259.

29. P. M. Fabiano, H. W. Perkins, A. Berkowitz, J. Linkenbach, and C. Stark, "Engaging men as social justice allies in ending violence against women: Evidence for a social norms approach," *Journal of American College Health* 52, no. 3 (2003): 105–112.

30. A. L. Brown and T. L. Messman-Moore, "Personal and perceived peer attitudes supporting sexual aggression as predictors of male college students' willingness to intervene against sexual aggression," *Journal of Interpersonal Violence* 25 (2010): 503–517.

31. R. M. Leone and D. J. Parrott, "Misogynistic peers, masculinity, and bystander intervention for sexual aggression: Is it really just 'locker-room talk'?" *Aggressive Behavior* 45 (2019): 55–64.

32. R. M. Leone, D. J. Parrott, and K. M. Swartout, "When is it 'manly' to intervene? Examining the effects of a misogynistic peer norm on bystander intervention for sexual aggression," *Psychology of Violence* 7 (2017): 286–295.

33. "Remarks by the President and Vice President at an event for the Council on Women and Girls," White House, press release, January 22, 2014, https://obamawhitehouse.archives.gov/the-press-office/2014/01/22/remarks-president-and-vice-president-event-council-women-and-girls.

34. T. Rosenbert, "The destructive influence of imaginary peers," *New York Times Opinionator* blog, March 27, 2013, https://opinionator.blogs.nytimes.com/2013/03/27/the-destructive-influence-of-imaginary-peers/.

35. C. Kilmartin, T. Smith, A. Green, H. Heinzen, M. Kuchler, and D. Kolar, "A real time social norms intervention to reduce male sexism," *Sex Roles* 59 (2008): 264–273.

36. C. A. Gidycz, L. M. Orchowski, and A. D. Berkowitz, "Preventing sexual aggression among college men: An evaluation of a social norms and bystander intervention program," *Violence against Women* 17, no. 6 (2011): 720–742.

37. J. A. Mutterperl and C. A. Sanderson, "Mind over matter: Internalization of the thinness norm as a moderator of responsiveness to norm misperception education in college women," *Health Psychology* 21, no. 5 (2002): 519–523; K. M. Turetsky and C. A. Sanderson, "Comparing educational interventions: Correcting misperceived norms improves college students' mental health attitudes," *Journal of Applied Social Psychology* 48 (2018): 46–55.

38. V. L. Banyard, E. G. Plante, and M. M. Moynihan, "Bystander education: Bringing a broader community perspective to sexual violence prevention," *Journal of Community Psychology* 32 (2004): 61–79.

39. S. J. Potter, M. M. Moynihan, and J. G. Stapleton, "Using social self-identification in social marketing materials aimed at reducing violence

against women on campus," *Journal of Interpersonal Violence* 26 (2011): 971–990.

40. L. Salazar, A. Vivolo-Kantor, J. Hardin, and A. Berkowitz, "A web-based sexual violence bystander intervention for male college students: Randomized controlled trial," *Journal of Medical Internet Research* 16, no. 9 (2014): e203; C. Y. Senn and A. Forrest, "'And then one night when I went to class': The impact of sexual assault bystander intervention workshops incorporated in academic courses," *Psychology of Violence* 6, no. 4 (2016): 607–618.

41. S. J. Potter, M. Flanagan, M. Seidman, H. Hodges, and J. G. Stapleton, "Developing and piloting videogames to increase college and university students' awareness and efficacy of the bystander role in incidents of sexual violence," *Games for Health Journal* 8, no. 1 (2019): 24–34.

42. V. L. Banyard, M. M. Moynihan, and E. G. Plante, "Sexual violence prevention through bystander education: An experimental evaluation," *Journal of Community Psychology* 35 (2007): 463–481; A. L. Coker, P. G. Cook-Craig, C. M. Williams, B. S. Fisher, E. R. Clear, L. S. Garcia, and L. M. Hegge, "Evaluation of Green Dot: An active bystander intervention to reduce sexual violence on college campuses," *Violence against Women* 17, no. 6 (2011): 777–796; J. Langhinrichsen-Rohling, J. D. Foubert, H. M. Brasfield, B. Hill, and S. Shelley-Tremblay, "The Men's Program: Does it impact college men's self-reported bystander efficacy and willingness to intervene?" *Violence against Women* 17 no. 6 (2011): 743–759; S. J. Potter and M. M. Moynihan, "Bringing in the bystander in-person prevention program to a U.S. military installation: Results from a pilot study," *Military Medicine* 176, no. 8 (2011): 870–875.

43. J. Katz and J. Moore, "Bystander education training for campus sexual assault prevention: An initial meta-analysis," *Violence and Victims* 28 (2013): 1054–1067; H. H. Kettrey and R. A. Marx, "The effects of bystander programs on the prevention of sexual assault across the college years: A systematic review and meta-analysis," *Journal of Youth and Adolescence* 48 (2019): 212–227.

44. A. L. Coker, B. S. Fisher, H. M. Bush, S. C. Swan, C. M. Williams, E. R. Clear, and S. DeGue, "Evaluation of the Green Dot bystander intervention to reduce interpersonal violence among college students across three campuses," *Violence against Women* 21, no. 12 (2015): 1507–1527.

45. E. N. Jouriles, R. McDonald, D. Rosenfield, N. Levy, K. Sargent, C. Caiozzo, and J. H. Grych, "TakeCARE, a video bystander program to

help prevent sexual violence on college campuses: Results of two randomized, controlled trials," *Psychology of Violence* 6, no. 3 (2015): 410–420; A. Kleinsasser, E. N. Jouriles, R. McDonald, and D. Rosenfield, "An online bystander intervention program for the prevention of sexual violence," *Psychology of Violence* 5, no. 3 (2014): 227–235.

46. E. N. Jouriles, R. McDonald, D. Rosenfield, and K. S. Sargent, "Increasing bystander behavior to prevent adolescent relationship violence: A randomized controlled trial," *Journal of Consulting and Clinical Psychology* 87, no. 1 (2019): 3–15; K. S. Sargent, E. N. Jouriles, D. Rosenfield, and R. McDonald, "A high school-based evaluation of Take-CARE, a video bystander program to prevent adolescent relationship violence," *Journal of Youth and Adolescence* 46, no. 3 (2016): 633–643.

47. V. L. Banyard and M. M. Moynihan, "Variation in bystander behavior related to sexual and intimate partner violence prevention: Correlates in a sample of college students," *Psychology of Violence* 1, no. 4 (2011): 287–301; K. M. Lukacena, T. Reynolds-Tylus, and B. L. Quick, "An application of the reasoned action approach to bystander intervention for sexual assault," *Health Communication* 34, no. 1 (2019): 46–53; S. McMahon, "Rape myth beliefs and bystander attitudes among incoming college students," *Journal of American College Health* 59, no. 1 (2010): 3–11; S. McMahon, P. Treitler, N. A. Peterson, and J. O'Connor, "Bystander intentions to intervene and previous sexual violence education: A latent class analysis," *Psychology of Violence* 9, no. 1 (2019): 117–126.

48. M. Planty, "Third party involvement in violent crime, 1993–99,"NCJ 189100, Bureau of Justice Statistics, Special Report, U.S. Department of Justice, July 2002, https://www.bjs.gov/content/pub/pdf/tpivc99.pdf.

49. P. Y. Martin and R. A. Hummer, "Fraternities and rape on campus," *Gender and Society* 3 (1989): 457–473.

50. M. Winerip, "Stepping up to stop sexual assault," *New York Times,* February 7, 2014.

51. S. E. Humphrey and A. S. Kahn, "Fraternities, athletic teams, and rape: Importance of identification with a risky group," *Journal of Interpersonal Violence* 15, no. 12 (2000): 1313–1322.

52. G. B. Forbes, L. E. Adams-Curtis, A. H. Pakalka, and K. B. White, "Dating aggression, sexual coercion, and aggression-supporting attitudes among college men as a function of participation in aggressive high school sports," *Violence against Women* 12 (2006): 441–455.

53. E. Anderson, "Inclusive masculinity in a fraternal setting," *Men and Masculinities* 10, no. 5 (2008): 604–620.

54. A. A. Boswell and J. Z. Spade, "Fraternities and collegiate rape culture: Why are some fraternities more dangerous places for women?" *Gender and Society* 10, no. 2 (1996): 133–147.

8. At Work

1. J. A. Woodzicka and M. LaFrance, "Real versus imagined gender harassment," *Journal of Social Issues* 57, no. 1 (2001): 15–30.

2. L. F. Fitzgerald, S. Swan, and K. Fischer, "Why didn't she just report him? The psychological and legal implications of women's responses to sexual harassment," *Journal of Social Issues* 51, no. 1 (1995): 117–138.

3. L. M. Cortina and J. L. Berdahl, "Sexual harassment in organizations: A decade of research in review," in *Handbook of Organizational Behavior: Micro Perspectives,* ed. C. Cooper and J. Barling, 469–497 (Thousand Oaks, CA: Sage, 2008).

4. C. C. Miller, "It's not just Fox: Why women don't report sexual harassment," *New York Times,* April 11, 2017, B2.

5. A. Fredin, "The unexpected cost of staying silent," *Strategic Finance* 93 (2012): 53–59.

6. UMass Amherst News Office, "Badgett coauthors report examining harassment complaints," University of Massachusetts Amherst, School of Public Policy, December 13, 2018, https://www.umass.edu/spp/news /badgett-coauthors-report-examining-sexual-harassment-complaints.

7. L. M. Cortina and V. J. Magley, "Raising voice, risking retaliation: Events following interpersonal mistreatment in the workplace," *Journal of Occupational Health Psychology* 8, no. 4 (2003): 247–265.

8. L. Ashburn-Nardo, J. C. Blanchar, J. Petersson, K. A. Morris, and S. A. Goodwin, "Do you say something when it's your boss? The role of perpetrator power in prejudice confrontation," *Journal of Social Issues* 70, no. 4 (2014): 615–636.

9. W. Martinez, S. K. Bell, J. M. Etchegaray, and L. S. Lehmann, "Measuring moral courage for interns and residents: Scale development and initial psychometrics," *Academic Medicine* 91, no. 10 (2016): 1431–1438.

10. C. V. Caldicott and K. Faber-Langendoen, "Deception, discrimination, and fear of reprisal: Lessons in ethics from third-year medical students," *Academic Medicine* 80, no. 9 (2005): 866–873.

11. C. K. Hofling, E. Brotzman, S. Dalrymple, N. Graves, and C. Bierce, "An experimental study of nurse-physician relations," *Journal of Nervous and Mental Disease* 143 (1966): 171–180.

12. D. Maxfield, J. Grenny, R. Lavandero, and L. Groah, "The silent treatment: Why safety tools and checklists aren't enough to save lives," September 2011, https://faculty.medicine.umich.edu/sites/default/files/resources/silent_treatment.pdf.

13. T. Couch, "Skimming and scamming: Detecting and preventing expense reimbursement fraud," *Accounting Today,* June 15, 2018, https://www.accountingtoday.com/opinion/skimming-and-scamming-detecting-and-preventing-expense-reimbursement-fraud.

14. This practice, and the tendency of other colleagues to ignore it, bothered me enough that I wrote a letter to the *Ethicist* column in the *New York Times.* See K. A. Appiah, "How can I make my colleague stop stealing?" *New York Times Magazine,* May 8, 2018.

15. J. F. Burns, "In Britain, scandal flows from modest request," *New York Times,* May 19, 2009.

16. K. Stone, "Rep. Duncan Hunter's wife implicates congressman in vast misuse of campaign funds," *Times of San Diego,* June 13, 2019.

17. M. J. Quade, R. L. Greenbaum, and O. V. Petrenko, "'I don't want to be near you, unless . . .': The interactive effect of unethical behavior and performance onto relationship conflict and workplace ostracism," *Personnel Psychology* 70 (2016): 675–709.

18. R. Goldstein, "Hugh Thompson, 62, who saved civilians at My Lai, dies," *New York Times,* January 7, 2006, C14.

19. R. Leung, "An American hero: Vietnam veteran speaks out about My Lai," *60 Minutes, CBS News,* May 6, 2004.

20. N. Trautman, "Police code of silence facts revealed," International Association of Chiefs of Police, Legal Officers Section, Annual Conference, 2000, https://www.aele.org/loscode2000.html.

21. M. Davey, "Police 'code of silence' is on trial after murder by Chicago officer," *New York Times,* December 3, 2018.

22. J. Pease, "The sin of silence," *Washington Post,* May 31, 2018.

23. A. D. Sorkin, "Isolated victims, from Williamsburg to Notre Dame," *New Yorker,* January 23, 2013.

24. L. H. Somerville, "What can we learn from Dartmouth?" Letter to Young Scientists, *Science,* November 20, 2018, https://www.sciencemag.org/careers/2018/11/what-can-we-learn-dartmouth.

25. T. Kopan, "Lindsey Graham: 'Tell Donald Trump to go to hell,'" *CNN,* December 8, 2015, https://www.cnn.com/2015/12/08/politics/lindsey -graham-donald-trump-go-to-hell-ted-cruz/index.html.

26. K. Sutton, "Lindsay Graham heaps praise on Trump: 'I am all in.'" *Politico,* April 19, 2017.

27. D. Brooks, "Morality and Michael Cohen," op-ed, *New York Times,* March 1, 2019, A23.

28. J. Comey, "How Trump co-opts leaders like Bill Barr," op-ed, *New York Times,* May 2, 2019, A27.

29. F. Gino and M. H. Bazerman, "When misconduct goes unnoticed: The acceptability of gradual erosion in others' unethical behavior," *Journal of Experimental Social Psychology* 45 (2009): 708–719.

30. I. Suh, J. T. Sweeney, K. Linke, and J. Wall, "Boiling the frog slowly: The immersion of C-suite financial executives into fraud," *Journal of Business Ethics* (July 2018): 1–29.

31. Association of Certified Fraud Examiners, "2012 Report to the nations," Key Findings and Highlights, ACFE, Austin, TX, 2012, https://www.acfe .com/rttn-highlights.aspx.

32. P. Schutz, "Department of Justice meets with Chicago police union," WTTW News, December 11, 2015, https://news.wttw.com/2015/12/11 /department-justice-meets-chicago-police-union.

33. T. Devine and T. F. Maassarani, *The Corporate Whistleblower's Survival Guide: A Handbook for Committing the Truth* (Oakland, CA: Berrett-Koehler Publishers, 2011).

34. A. Graham, "The thought leader interview: Jonathan Haidt," *Strategy + Business* newsletter 82, February 1, 2016, https://www.strategy-business .com/article/The-Thought-Leader-Interview-Jonathan-Haidt?gko=ddc37.

35. W. Yakowicz, "A new website that helps CEOs lead more ethically," *Inc.* website, January 22, 2014, https://www.inc.com/will-yakowicz/nonprofit -aims-to-help-ceos-lead-more-ethically.html.

36. F. O. Walumbwa and J. Schaubroeck, "Leader personality traits and employee voice behavior: Mediating roles of ethical leadership and work group psychological safety," *Journal of Applied Psychology* 94, no. 5 (2009): 1275–1286.

37. D. M. Mayer, K. Aquino, R. S. Greenbaum, and M. Kuenzi, "Who displays ethical leadership and why does it matter? An examination of antecedents and consequences of ethical leadership," *Academy of Management Journal* 55, no. 1 (2012): 151–171.

38. J. Jordan, M. E. Brown, L. K. Treviño, and S. Finkelstein, "Someone to look up to: Executive–follower ethical reasoning and perceptions of ethical leadership," *Journal of Management* 39, no. 3 (2013): 660–683.

39. Summary of F. Kiel, "Measuring the return on character," *Harvard Business Review,* April 2015, 20–21, *HBR* website, https://hbr.org/2015/04/measuring-the-return-on-character.

40. "Leadership," Ethicalsystems.org, 2018, https://www.ethicalsystems.org/content/leadership.

41. J. Lammers, D. A. Stapel, and A. D. Galinsky, "Power increases hypocrisy: Moralizing in reasoning, immorality in behavior," *Psychological Science* 21, no. 5 (2010): 737–744.

42. Association for Psychological Science, "Why powerful people—many of whom take a moral high ground—don't practice what they preach," *ScienceDaily,* December 30, 2009, https://www.sciencedaily.com/releases/2009/12/091229105906.htm.

43. Quoted in D. T. Welsh, L. D. Ordóñez, D. G. Snyder, and M. S. Christian, "The slippery slope: How small ethical transgressions pave the way for larger future transgressions," *Journal of Applied Psychology* 100, no. 1 (2015): 114–127.

44. H. Brody, "The company we keep: Why physicians should refuse to see pharmaceutical representatives," *Annals of Family Medicine* 3, no. 1 (2005): 82–85; C. Ornstein, M. Tigas, and R. G. Jones, "Now there's proof: Docs who get company cash tend to prescribe more brand-name meds," *ProPublica,* March 17, 2016, https://www.propublica.org/article/doctors-who-take-company-cash-tend-to-prescribe-more-brand-name-drugs.

45. I. Larkin, D. Ang, J. Steinhart, M. Chao, M. Patterson, S. Sah, et al., "Association between academic medical center pharmaceutical detailing policies and physician prescribing," *Journal of the American Medical Association* 317, no. 17 (2017): 1785–1795.

46. C. W. Bauman, L. P. Tost, and M. Ong, "Blame the shepherd not the sheep: Imitating higher-ranking transgressors mitigates punishment for unethical behavior," *Organizational Behavior and Human Decision Processes* 137 (2016): 123–141.

47. C. P. Guthrie and E. Z. Taylor, "Whistleblowing on fraud for pay: Can I trust you?" *Journal of Forensic Accounting Research* 2, no. 1 (2017): A1–A19.

48. J. H. Wilde, "The deterrent effect of employee whistleblowing on firms' financial misreporting and tax aggressiveness," *Accounting Review* 92, no. 5 (2017): 247–280.

49. L. L. Shu, N. Mazar, F. Gino, D. Ariely, and M. H. Bazerman, "Signing at the beginning makes ethics salient and decreases dishonest self-reports in comparison to signing at the end," *Proceedings of the National Academy of Sciences of the United States of America* 109, no. 38 (2012): 15197–15200.

50. O. J. Sheldon and A. Fishbach, "Anticipating and resisting the temptation to behave unethically," *Personality and Social Psychology Bulletin* 41, no. 7 (2015): 962–975.

51. Society for Personality and Social Psychology, "Anticipating temptation may reduce unethical behavior, research finds," *Science Daily,* May 22, 2015, https://www.sciencedaily.com/releases/2015/05/150522083509.htm.

52. M. Bateson, D. Nettle, and G. Roberts, "Cues of being watched enhance cooperation in a real-world setting," *Biology Letters* 2, no. 3 (2006): 412–414.

53. R. L. Helmreich, A. Merritt, and J. Wilhelm, "The evolution of crew resource management training in commercial aviation," *International Journal of Aviation Psychology* 9, no. 1 (1999): 19–32.

54. E. Staub, "Promoting healing and reconciliation in Rwanda, and generating active bystandership by police to stop unnecessary harm by fellow officers," *Perspectives on Psychological Science* 14, no. 1 (2019): 60–64.

55. J. Aronie and C. E. Lopez, "Keeping each other safe: An assessment of the use of peer intervention programs to prevent police officer mistakes and misconduct, using New Orleans' EPIC program as a potential national model," *Police Quarterly* 20 (2017): 295–321.

56. Quoted in T. Jackman, "New Orleans police pioneer new way to stop misconduct, remove 'blue wall of silence,'" *Washington Post,* January 24, 2019.

57. A. Novotney, "Preventing police misconduct," *Monitor on Psychology* 48, no. 9 (2017): 30.

58. Jackman, "New Orleans police pioneer new way to stop misconduct."

59. Staub, "Promoting healing and reconciliation in Rwanda."

60. D. Maxfield, "How a culture of silence eats away at your company," *Harvard Business Review,* December 7, 2016; W. Martinez, S. K. Bell, J. M. Etchegaray, and L. S. Lehmann, "Measuring moral courage for

interns and residents: Scale development and initial psychometrics," *Academic Medicine* 91, no. 10 (2016): 1431–1438.

61. J. Nance, *Why Hospitals Should Fly: The Ultimate Flight Plan to Patient Safety and Quality Care* (Bozeman, MT: Second River Healthcare, 2008).

62. "Why hospitals should fly: Learning valuable lessons from the aviation industry," Winnipeg Regional Health Authority, press release, April 25, 2015, https://www.wrha.mb.ca/quality/files/JohnNance.pdf.

63. D. M. Mayer, S. Nurmohamed, L. K. Treviño, D. L. Shapiro, and M. Schminke, "Encouraging employees to report unethical conduct internally: It takes a village," *Organizational Behavior and Human Decision Processes* 121 (2013): 89–103.

9. Understanding Moral Rebels

1. K. Zernike, "The reach of war: the witnesses; only a few spoke up on abuse as many soldiers stayed silent," *New York Times,* May 22, 2004.

2. B. Monin, P. J. Sawyer, and M. J. Marquez, "The rejection of moral rebels: Resenting those who do the right thing," *Journal of Personality and Social Psychology* 95, no. 1 (2008): 76–93.

3. W. I. Miller, *The Mystery of Courage* (Cambridge, MA: Harvard University Press, 2000); E. Staub, "The roots of goodness: The fulfillment of basic human needs and the development of caring, helping and non-aggression, inclusive caring, moral courage, active bystandership, and altruism born of suffering," in *Nebraska Symposium on Motivation,* vol. 51: *Moral Motivation through the Life Span,* ed. G. Carlo and C. P. Edwards, 33–72 (Lincoln: University of Nebraska Press, 2005); E. Staub, *The Roots of Goodness and Resistance to Evil: Inclusive Caring, Moral Courage, Altruism Born of Suffering, Active Bystandership and Heroism* (New York: Oxford University Press, 2015).

4. T. L. Sonnentag and M. A. Barnett, "An exploration of moral rebelliousness with adolescents and young adults," *Ethics and Behavior* 23 (2013): 214–236; T. L. Sonnentag and M. A. Barnett, "Role of moral identity and moral courage characteristics in adolescents' tendencies to be a moral rebel," *Ethics and Behavior* 26, no. 4 (2016): 277–299.

5. E. Midlarsky, "Aiding under stress: The effects of competence, dependency, visibility, and fatalism," *Journal of Personality* 39, no. 1 (1971):

132–149; E. Staub, *Personality: Basic Aspects and Current Research* (Englewood Cliffs, NJ; Prentice-Hall, 1980).

6. C. Hellemans, D. Dal Cason, and A. Casini, "Bystander helping behavior in response to workplace bullying," *Swiss Journal of Psychology* 76, no. 4 (2017): 135–144.

7. G. Gini, P. Albiero, B. Benelli, and G. Altoè, "Determinants of adolescents' active defending and passive bystanding behavior in bullying," *Journal of Adolescence* 31, no. 1 (2008): 93–105.

8. Sonnentag and Barnett, "An exploration of moral rebelliousness."

9. M. Y. Bamaca and A. Umana-Taylor, "Testing a model of resistance to peer pressure among Mexican-origin adolescents," *Journal of Youth and Adolescence* 35 (2006): 631–645; T. E. Dielman, P. C. Campanelli, J. T. Shope, and A. T. Butchart, "Susceptibility to peer pressure, self-esteem, and health locus of control as correlates of adolescent substance abuse," *Health Education Quarterly* 14 (1987): 207–221.

10. Sonnentag and Barnett, "Role of moral identity and moral courage characteristics."

11. D. A. Saucier and R. J. Webster, "Social vigilantism: Measuring individual differences in belief superiority and resistance to persuasion," *Personality and Social Psychology Bulletin* 36 (2010): 19–32.

12. A. Moisuc, M. Brauer, A. Fonseca, N. Chaurand, and T. Greitemeyer, "Individual differences in social control: Who 'speaks up' when witnessing uncivil, discriminatory, and immoral behaviours?" *British Journal of Social Psychology* 57 (2018): 524–546.

13. E. Midlarsky, S. F. Jones, and R. P. Corley, "Personality correlates of heroic rescue during the Holocaust," *Journal of Personality* 73, no. 4 (2005): 907–934.

14. H. W. Bierhoff, R. Klein, and P. Kramp, "Evidence for the altruistic personality from data on accident research," *Journal of Personality* 59 (1991): 263–280.

15. V. P. Poteat and O. Vecho, "Who intervenes against homophobic behavior? Attributes that distinguish active bystanders," *Journal of School Psychology* 54 (2016): 17–28.

16. P. M. Zoccola, M. C. Green, E. Karoutsos, S. M. Katona, and J. Sabini, "The embarrassed bystander: Embarrassability and the inhibition of helping," *Personality and Individual Differences* 51, no. 8 (2011): 925–929.

17. D. M. Tice and R. F. Baumeister, "Masculinity inhibits helping in emergencies: Personality does predict the bystander effect," *Journal of Personality and Social Psychology* 49 (1985): 420–428.

18. D. K. Campbell-Meiklejohn, R. Kanai, B. Bahrami, D. R. Bach, R. J. Dolan, A. Roepstorff, and C. D. Frith, "Structure of orbitofrontal cortex predicts social influence," *Current Biology* 22, no. 4 (2012): R123–R124.

19. P. Jean-Richard-dit-Bressel and G. P. McNally, "Lateral, not medial, prefrontal cortex contributes to punishment and aversive instrumental learning," *Learning and Memory* 23, no. 11 (2016): 607–617.

20. E. B. Falk, C. N. Cascio, M. B. O'Donnell, J. Carp, F. J. Tinney, C. R. Bingham, et al., "Neural responses to exclusion predict susceptibility to social influence," *Journal of Adolescent Health* 54, no. 5 suppl. (2014): S22–S31; B. G. Simons-Morton, A. K. Pradhan, C. Raymond Bingham, E. B. Falk, K. Li, M. C. Ouimet, et al., "Experimental effects of injunctive norms on simulated risky driving among teenage males," *Health Psychology* 33, no. 7 (2014): 616–627.

21. Quoted in M. Laris, "Teen drivers' brains may hold the secret to combating road deaths," *Washington Post,* July 2, 2016.

22. N. Wasylyshyn, B. Hemenway Falk, J. O. Garcia, C. N. Cascio, M. B. O'Donnell, C. R. Bingham, et al., "Global brain dynamics during social exclusion predict subsequent behavioral conformity," *Social Cognitive and Affective Neuroscience* 13, no. 2 (2018): 182–191.

23. D. Grossman, *On Killing: The Psychological Cost of Learning to Kill in War and Society* (Boston: Little, Brown, 1995).

24. H. Rosin, "When Joseph comes marching home," *Washington Post,* May 17, 2004.

25. Rosin, "When Joseph comes marching home"; "Praise for Iraq whistleblower," CBS News, May 10, 2004.

26. "A 'whistleblower' made into a Hollywood heroine," *Weekend Edition Saturday,* NPR, June 30, 2011, https://www.npr.org/2011/07/30/138826591/a-whistleblower-made-into-a-hollywood-heroine.

27. C. D. Batson, B. D. Duncan, P. Ackerman, T. Buckley, and K. Birch, "Is empathic emotion a source of altruistic motivation?" *Journal of Personality and Social Psychology* 40, no. 2 (1981): 290–302.

28. N. Eisenberg and R. A. Fabes, "Prosocial development," in *Handbook of Child Psychology,* ed. W. Damon, vol. 3: *Social, Emotional, and Personality Development,* ed. N. Eisenberg, 5th ed., 701–778 (New York:

Wiley, 1998); E. Staub, *Positive Social Behavior and Morality,* vol. 2: *Socialization and Development* (San Diego: Academic Press, 1979).

29. I. Coyne, A.-M. Gopaul, M. Campbell, A. Pankász, R. Garland, and F. Cousans, "Bystander responses to bullying at work: The role of mode, type and relationship to target," *Journal of Business Ethics* 157, no. 3 (2017): 813–827.

30. J. Katz, R. Pazienza, R. Olin, and H. Rich, "That's what friends are for: Bystander responses to friends or strangers at risk for party rape victimization," *Journal of Interpersonal Violence* 30, no. 16 (2015): 2775–2792.

31. N. Brody and A. L. Vangelisti, "Bystander intervention in cyberbullying," *Communication Monographs* 83, no. 1 (2016): 94–119.

32. R. L. Meyer, C. L. Masten, Y. Ma, C. Wang, Z. Shi, N. I. Eisenberger, and S. Han, "Empathy for the social suffering of friends and strangers recruits distinct patterns of brain activation," *Social Cognitive and Affective Neuroscience* 8 (2013): 446–454.

33. M. H. Davis, "Measuring individual differences in empathy: Evidence for a multidimensional approach," *Journal of Personality and Social Psychology* 44 (1983): 113–126.

34. G. Gini, R. Thornberg, and T. Pozzoli, "Individual moral disengagement and bystander behavior in bullying: The role of moral distress and collective moral disengagement," *Psychology of Violence* (in press), doi: 10.1037/vi00000223.

35. R. Hortensius, D. J. L. G. Schutter, and B. Gelder, "Personal distress and the influence of bystanders on responding to an emergency," *Cognitive, Affective and Behavioral Neuroscience* 16, no. 4 (2016): 672–688.

36. A. A. Marsh, S. A. Stoycos, K. M. Brethel-Haurwitz, P. Robinson, J. W. VanMeter, and E. M. Cardinale, "Neural and cognitive characteristics of extraordinary altruists," *Proceedings of the National Academy of Sciences of the United States of America* 111, no. 42 (2014): 15036–15041.

37. K. M. Brethel-Haurwitz, E. M. Cardinale, K. M. Vekaria, E. L. Robertson, B. Walitt, J. W. VanMeter, and A. A. Marsh, "Extraordinary altruists exhibit enhanced self–other overlap in neural responses to distress," *Psychological Science* 29, no. 10 (2018): 1631–1641.

38. E. Staub, "Building a peaceful society: Origins, prevention, and reconciliation after genocide and other group violence," *American Psychologist* 68, no. 7 (2013): 576–589.

39. Quoted in S. Shellenbarger, "Are you a hero or a bystander?" *Wall Street Journal,* August 22, 2012.

40. Staub, "The roots of goodness," 2005.

41. N. Fox and H. N. Brehm, "'I decided to save them': Factors that shaped participation in rescue efforts during genocide in Rwanda," *Social Forces* 96, no. 4 (2018): 1625–1648.

42. Quoted in S. Begley, "Saints and sinners: The science of good and evil," *Newsweek,* April 24, 2009.

43. J. P. Allen, J. Chango, D. Szwedo, M. Schad, and E. Marston, "Predictors of susceptibility to peer influence regarding substance use in adolescence," *Child Development* 83, no. 1 (2012): 337–350.

44. N. Abbott and L. Cameron, "What makes a young assertive bystander? The effect of intergroup contact, empathy, cultural openness, and ingroup bias on assertive bystander intervention intentions," *Journal of Social Issues* 70, no. 1 (2014): 167–182.

45. S. H. Konrath, E. H. O'Brien, and C. Hsing, "Changes in dispositional empathy in American college students over time: A meta-analysis," *Personality and Social Psychology Review* 15, no. 2 (2011): 180–198.

46. J. M. Twenge and J. D. Foster, "Birth cohort increases in narcissistic personality traits among American college students, 1982–2009," *Social Psychological and Personality Science* 1, no. 1 (2010): 99–106.

47. J. M. Twenge, *Generation Me* (New York: Free Press, 2006).

48. J. Zaki, *The War for Kindness: Building Empathy in a Fractured World* (New York: Crown, 2019).

49. K. Schumann, J. Zaki, and C. S. Dweck, "Addressing the empathy deficit: Beliefs about the malleability of empathy predict effortful responses when empathy is challenging," *Journal of Personality and Social Psychology* 107, no. 3 (2014): 475–493.

10. Becoming a Moral Rebel

1. A. Rattan and C. S. Dweck, "Who confronts prejudice? The role of implicit theories in the motivation to confront prejudice," *Psychological Science* 21, no. 7 (2010): 952–959.

2. M. M. Hollander, "The repertoire of resistance: Non-compliance with directives in Milgram's 'obedience' experiments," *British Journal of Social Psychology* 54 (2015): 425–444.

3. L. R. Martinez, M. R. Hebl, N. A. Smith, and I. E. Sabat, "Standing up and speaking out against prejudice toward gay men in the workplace," *Journal of Vocational Behavior* 103, pt. A (2017): 71–85.

4. L. M. Lamb, R. S. Bigler, L. Liben, and V. A. Green, "Teaching children to confront peers' sexist remarks: Implications for theories of gender development and educational practice," *Sex Roles* 61, no. 5–6 (2009): 361–382.

5. E. Staub, "Promoting healing and reconciliation in Rwanda, and generating active bystandership by police to stop unnecessary harm by fellow officers," *Perspectives on Psychological Science* 14, no. 1 (2019): 60–64; E. Staub, "Preventing violence and promoting active bystandership and peace: My life in research and applications," *Peace and Conflict: Journal of Peace Psychology* 24, no. 1 (2019): 95–111.

6. S. P. Oliner and P. M. Oliner, *The Altruistic Personality: Rescuers of Jews in Nazi Europe* (New York: Free Press, 1988).

7. A. Hartocollis, "Dartmouth professors are accused of sexual abuse by 7 women in lawsuit," *New York Times,* November 15, 2018.

8. I. Coyne, A.-M. Gopaul, M. Campbell, A. Pankász, R. Garland, and F. Cousans, "Bystander responses to bullying at work: The role of mode, type and relationship to target," *Journal of Business Ethics* 157, no. 3 (2019): 813–827; J. Katz, R. Pazienza, R. Olin, and H. Rich, "That's what friends are for: Bystander responses to friends or strangers at risk for party rape victimization," *Journal of Interpersonal Violence* 30, no. 16 (2015): 2775–2792.

9. M. Levine, A. Prosser, D. Evans, and S. Reicher, "Identity and emergency intervention: How social group membership and inclusiveness of group boundaries shape helping behavior," *Personality and Social Psychology Bulletin* 31, no. 4 (2005): 443–453.

10. E. Kroshus, T. Paskus, and L. Bell, "Coach expectations about off-field conduct and bystander intervention by U.S. college football players to prevent inappropriate sexual behavior," *Journal of Interpersonal Violence* 33, no. 2 (2018): 293–315.

11. M. Gladwell, "Small change," *New Yorker,* October 4, 2010; D. McAdam, "Recruitment to High-Risk Activism: The Case of Freedom Summer," *American Journal of Sociology* 92, no. 1 (1986): 64–90.

12. V. L. Allen and J. M. Levine, "Consensus and conformity," *Journal of Experimental Social Psychology* 5 (1969): 389–399; V. L. Allen and J. M. Levine, "Social support and conformity: The role of independent

assessment of reality," *Journal of Experimental Social Psychology* 7, no. 1 (1971): 48–58; C. Nemeth and C. Chiles, "Modelling courage: The role of dissent in fostering independence," *European Journal of Social Psychology* 18, no. 3 (1988): 275–280; F. Rochat and A. Modigliani, "The ordinary quality of resistance: From Milgram's laboratory to the village of Le Chambon," *Journal of Social Issues* 51 (1995): 195–210.

13. Quoted in D. Goleman, "Studying the pivotal role of bystanders," *New York Times,* June 22, 1993, C1.

14. N. J. Goldstein, R. B. Cialdini, and V. Griskevicius, "A room with a viewpoint: Using social norms to motivate environmental conservation in hotels," *Journal of Consumer Research* 35 (2008): 472–482.

15. A. Gerber, D. Green, and C. Larimer, "Social pressure and voter turnout: Evidence from a large-scale field experiment," *American Political Science Review* 102, no. 1 (2008): 33–48.

16. D. Centola, J. Becker, D. Brackbill, and A. Baronchelli, "Experimental evidence for tipping points in social convention," *Science* 360, no. 6393 (June 8, 2018): 1116–1119.

17. C. R. Sunstein, *How Change Happens* (Cambridge, MA: MIT Press, 2019).

18. J. Steinbeck, *East of Eden* (New York: Penguin Books, 1992).

Acknowledgments

First, I want to thank my agent, Zoë Pagnamenta, for her initial enthusiasm for my idea and considerable efforts in guiding my proposal. I spent an afternoon sending out query letters to a few agents and received her response expressing interest a few hours later, shortly after midnight. I told my husband the next morning that any agent who would read and respond to an email so late at night was exactly the type of agent I wanted, and that initial instinct was right on target. I am grateful to Zoë's entire team, including Alison Lewis, for support of all kinds; Sara Vitale and Jess Hoare, who helped with translation rights and payments; and Kirsten Wolf.

I am also very thankful for the considerable efforts of my editor, Joy de Menil, in shaping the direction of this book in many ways. During our very first conversation, I told Joy that I had "no idea what I was doing" in terms of writing a book for a general audience. I'm grateful that she didn't believe me, and I appreciate all the time she spent providing thoughtful feedback on multiple drafts, pushing me to share my own interpretations and ideas, and helping me to drop the academic jargon. I also very much appreciate the work of others who have been helpful at Harvard University Press, including Joy Deng, Sonya Bonczek, Graciela Galup, who designed the cover, and Louise Robbins, who painstakingly copyedited the manuscript. I am equally delighted to have worked with the numerous people at HarperCollins UK, including Olivia Marsden (marketing), Jack Smyth (cover design), Helen Upton (public relations), and Jo Thompson (general support and enthusiasm).

Thanks especially to Arabella Pike for her excitement about this project at all stages and careful consideration of the UK market.

Many people contributed to making the book a reality. Thanks to Austin Sarat for organizing—and the office of the dean of the faculty at Amherst College for funding—a book proposal workshop that led to my initial work on the book, and to Cecelia Cancellaro, who was the first person to tell me that yes, this could be a book, and was extremely helpful in shaping my initial thoughts. I thank my colleagues Matt Schulkind and Sarah Turgeon (Amherst College) and Rose Cowell (University of Massachusetts Amherst), who answered questions about neuroscience techniques and neural anatomy, and especially Steve Tompson (University of Pennsylvania), who gave detailed feedback on an early draft of the manuscript. I am particularly appreciative of the thorough and thoughtful comments provided by Ervin Staub (University of Massachusetts Amherst), who brings both personal experience and professional expertise to understanding the bystander effect. I also want to thank the many friends, colleagues, and students who listened to me talk on and on about these ideas—at dinner parties, over lunch, during office hours—and sent along helpful suggestions of research and real-world examples on numerous occasions. Finally, I want to thank my husband, Bart Hollander, for believing in this project throughout its (many) highs and lows, knowing when not to ask "How's it going?" and accepting that our "vacations" often included sitting with me in a coffee shop as I frantically wrote.

Index

Page numbers followed by n indicate notes.

OVERMATTER

'Much of what enables evil people to do evil things is that we stand idly by and let them. In this powerful, well-written book, Catherine Sanderson explains what psychology has taught us about why good people so often do nothing and offers wise suggestions that will enable more of us to step up and be 'moral rebels' when the situation calls for it. If you have ever regretted being silent (and who hasn't?) this is the book for you'

BARRY SCHWARTZ, author of *The Paradox of Choice*

'As unwilling witnesses to injustice, many of us have asked ourselves, "Why doesn't someone *do* something?" Catherine Sanderson answers this question of conscience in her powerfully persuasive book. This brilliant work stands at the intersection of social justice and social psychology. Using insights from academia, the torture chambers of Abu Ghraib, and crime scenes of police brutality, Sanderson analyzes the powerful forces that drive human beings to act against cruelty, injustice and human suffering. The unrelenting rigor of her analysis, sweeping breadth of research and evocative lucidity empower us to act – and also give us hope. This book comes not a moral moment too soon'

CORNELL WILLIAM BROOKS, Harvard Kennedy School
and former President of the NAACP

'I tend to assume that all that can be said about human nature was said by Aristotle. Catherine Sanderson has challenged my prejudice with this lively and engaging book full of interesting observations about human beings and their actions. Or has she "merely" updated Aristotle through the lens of modern social psychology? If so, that's a worthy achievement'

WILLIAM KRISTOL, Director of Defending Democracy Together

'Why do so many people stand silent when someone does something bad? If you find yourself increasingly asking that question these days, you're not alone – and Catherine Sanderson has written the book for you. *The Bystander Effect* reviews the social psychological literature – from Milgram's shocking findings onward – to explain why people who know better sometimes give wrongdoing a pass, and applies the field's findings to everyday life, like bullying in schools, fraud and harassment in the workplace, and to our current political life. A clear and engaging writer, Sanderson offers sound advice on how we can become better at doing what we know is right'   GEORGE CONWAY, co-founder of the Lincoln Project

'Catherine Sanderson, like no other psychologist, invades our minds. Her riveting storytelling challenges us to rethink why we avert our eyes to evil, tolerate bullying, and excuse unforgivable workplace behavior. She plumbs the depths of social norms that too often prevent good people from being good and points to steps all of us can take to become "moral rebels" whose voices can change society for the better'

WALTER V. ROBINSON, former editor of
the *Boston Globe*'s Spotlight team

'This is a rich, powerful, and wide-ranging exploration of moral courage, of inaction and action. It shows what stops people from helping – and what leads them to help others. These are tremendously important issues. The focus on training, and how to influence bystanders to act, is especially valuable'

ERVIN STAUB, author of *The Roots of Goodness and
Resistance to Evil*

'Our world is filled with evidence of cowardice and corruption. Catherine Sanderson explains why, drawing on decades of groundbreaking research ... Offers powerful advice about how each of us can protect our integrity and improve our institutions. This is an urgent and compelling book with a clear agenda for concerned citizens'   JEREMI SURI, author of *The Impossible Presidency*

'In this deeply researched, compulsively readable account, Sanderson offers a thoroughly persuasive analysis of why most people remain silent in situations where they – and we – know full well that their actions could prevent harm. More importantly, she provides a highly practical toolkit for cultivating empathy and learning to be a "moral rebel". A profound and timely contribution to the psychology of compassionate moral action in a heartless world'
R. MARIE GRIFFITH, Director of the
John C. Danforth Center on Religion and Politics,
Washington University in St Louis